Education Is Translation

Education Is Translation

A Metaphor for Change in Learning
and Teaching

Alison Cook-Sather

PENN

University of Pennsylvania Press

Philadelphia

KH

10   9   8   7   6   5   4   3   2   1

Published by
University of Pennsylvania Press
Philadelphia, Pennsylvania 19104-4011

Library of Congress Cataloging-in-Publication Data

Cook-Sather, Alison
    Education is translation : a metaphor for change in learning and teaching /
Alison Cook-Sather.
    p.   cm.
    Includes bibliographical references (p.) and index.
    ISBN-13: 978-0-8122-3889-1
    ISBN-10: 0-8122-3889-3 (cloth : alk. paper)

1. Communication in education. 2. Reflective teaching. I. Title.

LB1033.5 .C68 2005
                                                              2005048452

9/19/06

Contents

Preface

Only connect . . .
—E. M. Forster, *Howards End*

The call to connect assumes and acknowledges that there are spaces, gaps, distances between. The spaces between words and how we negotiate them, the gaps in understanding and how we bridge them, the distances between people and how we span them—these are among the most basic concerns of human beings in general and of educators in particular. Underlying the prevailing social arrangements and established educational practices in the United States is the belief that connections can be established and then permanently fixed—between a word and an idea, within a mind or a heart, in a role or a relationship, through a formal process or an institution. It is this belief that I challenge in this book. Over the past decade I have worked to develop a new metaphor to guide my educational practice, the way I engage in and facilitate the making of meaning in relationship with other people, and the way I understand and support the changing selves of the learners with whom I work: *education is translation*. With this metaphor I argue that instead of trying to fix the connections we make, we need to re-imagine education as an unending process of change in which we strive to connect, temporarily succeed or fail, and then seek to establish new connections.

I write as a former high school and current college teacher, as a researcher of educational theories and practices, as an ongoing learner, and as a person living complex human relationships. I write also as someone born in the United States and a native speaker of English. Drawing on all these aspects of my experience and identity, I use the metaphor of translation to analyze my experience as a learner and researcher and to analyze the educational experiences of several different groups of learners with whom I have worked. Through engaging in this analysis I have learned what Forster may well have meant by his seemingly simple "only": that while connection is not easy, and *complete* connection is perhaps not possible, it is only through the process of trying to connect—trying to find points of intersection when what seems most obvious are divergences, trying to bridge worlds and ways of being when they seem irreconcilably different—that we learn. The forms of reading and interpretation, the forms of revision of words and ways of being, the forms of carrying meaning from one "place" to another in which human beings engage when they strive to connect are the processes upon which I focus in this book. I have come to understand these efforts not as one-time instances of fixing meanings or forms but rather as ongoing processes of translation—as the carrying of meaning from one form or realm to another.

By bringing something very familiar to me—education—into juxtaposition with something much less familiar—translation—I aim to redefine and extend my own understanding of both, to explore ways that such a double redefinition might benefit the formal world of education and, more broadly, to inform the ways that we as human beings interact with the world and with one another. I return to this juxtaposition of seemingly unlike things, and I repeat particularly powerful ways of understanding these unlike things, across the chapters of this book. Everyone has a different set of reasons for undertaking a formal educational experience; every person has her own reasons for wanting to translate herself—that is, to transform herself into a new version of that self that is at once the same and not the same for the transformation. Each chapter of the book evokes a different world within which the metaphor *education is translation* serves as the interpretive frame. I discuss education in terms of the challenges and possibilities it presents when people strive to forge connections between words and worlds, ideas and actions, identities and interactions. I explore students' generative struggles as they attempt to bridge seemingly unlike ideas, discourses, and practices. Through examples drawn from my own experiences and from my observations of others, I explore the ways in which all meaning making—both the deepening or complicating of previous understandings and the generating of new insights—is a process of discerning differences and trying to make connections.

I begin, in Chapter 1, with my own most recent experience as an adult student engaged in a process of learning a new language in a new context. In starting with my educational story, I ground within my lived experience the theories I have been developing over the past several years. In Chapter 2, I provide a detailed explanation of *education is translation*, and to locate this new metaphor within a larger conceptual framework,

I explore some of the dominant and some of the less familiar metaphors that have been evoked to characterize educational institutions, roles, and processes. In Chapters 3, 4, and 5, I provide analyses of learners in three formal educational contexts engaged in processes of translation: college sophomores enrolled in a reading and writing course, college professors from a variety of academic disciplines who worked with students, librarians, and instructional technologists in a professional development workshop, and college seniors enrolled in a teacher preparation program, all affiliated with liberal arts colleges in the northeastern United States.

Each of these groups, and each of the individuals within them, is positioned differently as student, but all of them attempt to engage on two levels in the process I am calling translation. The first is translation on a literal level: a translation of language used in communication. The second is on a metaphorical and reflexive level: a translation of self. These two levels are inextricably entwined and continually inform one another. In Chapter 6, I look across the different educational contexts and students, offer some reflections on what all of this means for educators, and return to my own educational experience to bring the arc of this book to a full circle.

The analytical framework that *education is translation* provides was not one that I discussed with students in the contexts I explore here; rather, it is an interpretive structure through which I strive to re-see my own and others' educational experiences. With translation as a guiding metaphor, I respond to the call to connect in a number of ways. In both how I write and in what I write about, I re-connect the personal and the academic, the division of which I see as one of the most damaging dichotomies imposed at any level of education. In the theoretical foundation I build to support my analysis of education as translation, I connect theoretical perspectives and lived experiences drawn from different fields—anthropology, literary theory, psychology, translation studies, and educational theory—that have not been brought together in just this way before. In analyzing several different kinds of formal educational experience, I re-connect what are generally separated realms of education; these moments in the educational lifespan are typically designated as discrete but are actually related points on a continuum.

Like metaphor itself, which juxtaposes seemingly unlike entities from disparate realms and asks that we understand one in terms of another, this book brings together seemingly different terms and different students from different domains. My hope is that in working to make a connection between two other seemingly unlike things—the process of a certain kind of education and the process of a certain kind of translation—I illustrate the complex, continuous, collaborative, and essential processes of making meaning that I advocate.

A story told from a particular point in my life and my work, this is one of many possible versions that I, or others involved in the educational contexts I explore, could have composed. It is one teacher-student's attempt to illuminate the educational process and the human interactions that animate it in a way that makes sense for her right now. It embraces and advocates the paradox of the "only" in Forster's call to connect by recognizing the difficulty of making connections yet nevertheless continuing to try to make them. It is also a narrative intended to leave openings for others. I have written this book for teachers, students, and administrators at all levels of schooling; for politicians, policymakers, and parents in every public and private arena; for researchers, theorists, and activists in every academic discipline and social context—for everyone who cares about education in its most general and inclusive sense and for everyone who cares about changing education so that it supports every student's life and growth. It is my hope that readers will connect with the argument I make and that it will serve as an inspiration to explore or generate other ways of responding to the call to connect.

Chapter 1
Living Translation

"A language," he said. "It is a world. . . ."
"How would you learn, though. That there are other worlds."
"By same means as you perceive what poems say . . . by metaphor.
By seeing that two things, all unconnected, are connected."
—John Crowley, *The Translator*

In October of 2001, embarking on a year-long junior faculty leave from Bryn Mawr College, I traveled to Göttingen, Germany, with two goals for my time abroad: to learn to speak German and to write a book. I wanted to learn German so that I could speak with Moritz and Lisa, my twin, two-year-old *Patenkinder* (godchildren),[1] who were learning German as their first language at home in the United States.[2] (Their parents, my good friends and colleagues, were also on leave, and together we spent three months in Göttingen.) I wanted as well to create for myself a learning experience that would help me deepen my analysis of formal education and the new metaphor I had developed for understanding it: *education is translation*. I planned to use the time abroad to begin the process of learning German and also to start to pull together chapters of what would become this book. Before I left the United States, I had a vague notion that I would take an intensive language course for a couple of weeks and then dive into working on my book, continuing to learn German from daily interactions with those around me. When I arrived in Germany, however, I chose instead to spend three months enrolled as a full-time student at the Goethe Institute in Göttingen. I did not open a single one of the books that I had lugged across the Atlantic and from which I had planned to draw the theoretical underpinnings of this, my own book. Instead, I concentrated on living the metaphor that I intended to write about.

It is important that I make clear from the outset that although I focus in this opening chapter on my experience of learning a language, the fact that it was a language I learned as opposed to something else is not the premise of the metaphor for education that I have developed and that I explore in this book. As a student of English and a lover of literature, as a former high school English teacher and a current instructor of reading and writing as well as education, and as a researcher of language and literacy in their most all-encompassing senses, I am particularly compelled by questions of language—of relationships between and among words and between and among people. My close relationship with a family who speaks a language other than English intersected for me with this academic interest, and it is for these reasons, and not to privilege language learning as the quintessential example of education as translation, that I focus in this chapter on my experience of learning German.

During my time in Göttingen, I wrote and rewrote a poem to try to capture the complex, exciting, and at times confusing experience I was having. To be living in a new place, to be building a relationship with two young children and their parents that is somewhat out of the ordinary, and to be learning something profoundly new were unsettling in the best of ways.[3] In each of these realms I both pushed the limits of my own understanding—of the importance of context, of the nature of relationships, and of the essence of learning—and I constantly risked not being understood: one of the most disturbing, even if frequent, experiences we have as human beings. I tried to capture all of these qualities of experience in a poem, which was both the first I had written in quite a while and the first I had ever written in German. It started slowly, before I understood exactly what I wanted to express and before I knew much of the language in which I was trying to express it. Soon the poem became a kind of journal, however, a written record to which I turned and returned to document and interpret my experience. As I wrote drafts, I shared them with my friends and teachers, and they both corrected the German and talked through with me the experience I was striving to capture in the poem. Talking about and through the poem with other people was as important as trying to find the words to compose it on my own. I learned intricacies of the German language as I strove to articulate the intricacies of my U.S. American/German experience, and I deepened relationships—with language and with people—as I deepened my understanding.

The original poem appears on the left facing. When I decided to use and analyze it as a way of introducing the themes of this book, I wrote the translation that appears on the right. I place the German and English versions side by side on the page and throughout this chapter in my explication. My goal in doing so is not only to re-render my own experience but also to foreground and to some extent to re-create for readers the challenges of translation that any genuine educational endeavor entails.

Meine sich verändernde Stimme

Meine ursprüngliche Stimme ist klar,
voll mit dem Ton und mit dem Sinn.

Beide *remembered* und immer neu,

sie *resonates* in starke und schöne
strains.
Mit diesem *sound* bin ich immer
Stimmhaft,
wie jedes gutgewebte Lied.

Meine neue Stimme ist dünn und
spärlich,
eine Lautverwickelung,
schlechtgestimmt.
Wenn ich mit dieser Stimme spreche,
I cannot braid the many-threaded chords.

Mit dieser Aussprache bin ich fast
Stimmlos.
Ungewiss, mache ich a *tangled
translation.*

Wenn ich weiter in meiner neuen
Sprache gehe,
sind ab und zu die deutschen Wörter
transparent
und die englischen Wörter plötzlich
fast unbekannt.
Manchmal erkenne ich nur den Sinn:

wenn ich nicht weiß, welche Sprache
sprach oder hörte ich.

Am besten überlege ich meine
Stimme
in jedem bestimmten Zusammenhang.

Denn der Sinn des Gesagten und des
Ungesagten
wird zwischen den Sprechern
fortwährend gemacht.
In this exchange I become newly self-aware.

Ich entdecke nicht nur ein neues
Verständnis:
Sicher und offen, sprech' und hör'
ich zu von neuem.
*Certain and open, I speak and listen
anew.*

My Changing Voice

My original voice is confident and
clear;
it is full of well-tuned sounds and
sense.
Both drawn from memory and
always new,
it resonates in strong and striking
strains.
Through this sound I am consonant,
voiced,
like the notes of every well-woven
song.

My newer voice is thin and scanty,

a tangle of sounds, it sounds badly
tuned.
When I try to speak with this voice,
I cannot braid the many-threaded
chords.
Uttering these sounds I am almost
voiceless.
Uncertain, I produce a tangled
translation.

As I make my way further into my
new language,
the German words become at times
transparent
and the English words suddenly
almost unknown.
Now and then I perceive only
meaning:
I am unsure of which language
I have spoken or heard.

At best I deliberate over my voice

within each unique and particular
context.
Then the meaning of the spoken and
the unspoken
is perpetually made between the
speakers.
In this exchange I become newly
self-aware.

I discover not only a new
understanding:
Certain and open, I speak and listen
anew.
Certain and open, I speak and listen
anew.

I pondered and revised this poem, alone and with friends and teachers, in the halls of the Goethe Institute, as I wandered the busy streets of Göttingen's *Fußgängerzone* (pedestrian zone), and as I traveled throughout different parts of Germany. This reflection and revision were both content and method; struggling with, writing, and reflecting on the poem was one manifestation and embodiment of my educational process. To evoke in greater detail the contexts within which the story of the poem unfolded, I describe the places and people that shaped the educational experience it strives to capture.

I spent the majority of my days at the Goethe Institute.[4] The heart of this institution is a majestic old mansion, whose center tower dates from the end of the nineteenth century. Attached to either side of the original structure are modern buildings that house offices, media resources, and dorm rooms, and behind the mansion is a large garden. The Goethe Institute sits on a wealthy edge of Göttingen beside the Schillerwiesen, a park with open grassy fields and a small stream that threads its way through old beech and oak trees. One can climb to the top of the institute's central tower and look in one direction across the park and up toward Hainberg, the mountain just behind the Schillerwiesen, and to the Harz Mountains beyond, and in the other direction one has a panoramic view of the town of Göttingen. The old part of the building houses a large, wood-paneled central hall with a fireplace flanked by gargoyles of carved stone. Around this fireplace, students often gathered after class to read and discuss literature and poetry or to prepare for one of the many *Ausflüge*—outings, literally "flights out"—within and beyond the town. Wide wood doors off of the central hall open into the mansion rooms that have been converted into classrooms. These rooms are a combination of old and new: nineteenth-century fireplaces, intricate plaster work, and tall wood-framed windows with modern desks, dry-erase boards, and overhead projectors.

I first arrived at this striking intersection of the past and the present early on a Monday morning. I waited in the central hall with other prospective students, and we were each interviewed to assess which course level was most appropriate for us. The interview, like all instruction at the Goethe Institute, was conducted in German, and one of the questions I discerned, with some difficulty, was "Why do you want to learn German?" I knew a few words of the language, but my German was not yet good enough to explain any of my several reasons. Although the explanation that I was a teacher studying education or that I was writing a book using the metaphor of translation or that, for both those reasons, I wanted to create an intensive learning experience for myself might have been more understandable, I explained instead the other reason: that I wanted to learn German so that I could speak with Moritz and Lisa in their mother tongue. What was behind my answer, although I couldn't articulate it yet, was not only that I wanted to learn the ways of speaking and being that would make the relationship I was already developing with the twins an integral part of the world in which their parents wanted them to grow up. I also knew but could not say that I wanted to experience firsthand a formal education about which I had theorized but that I had not lived myself. I wanted to translate myself through this experience into a different version of myself as *Patentante* (godparent), learner, and teacher.

Placed in a *Grundstufe* (basic level course), I spent Mondays through Fridays from 8:15 A.M. until 1:00 P.M. in language classes. In the first course in which I enrolled, I was the only person from the United States. My classmates issued from Brazil, China, England, Egypt, France, India, Japan, Spain, Switzerland, and Thailand. In my second course, a *Mittelstufe* (intermediate level course), I was one of two people from the United States; the other students came from Australia, Brazil, China, Japan, the Ukraine, the Soviet Union, Sweden, and Thailand. Because we originated from so many countries, the only common language we had was the one we were trying to learn. We ranged in age from eighteen to thirty-seven, and we were learning German for a wide variety of reasons—to communicate with friends or significant others, in anticipation of enrolling in German universities, as a result of job-related assignments, or in preparation for careers that would require fluency in German. On occasion some of us knew fragments of one another's native languages, and we would try to conjure these during breaks or after class. But mostly we worked together using what little German we knew to go over our *Hausaufgaben* (homework), to work through the *Übungen* (exercises) in our books, and to help one another try to build our vocabularies.

Our diverse experiences and perspectives informed every aspect of our education at the Goethe Institute, whether those experiences and perspectives were an explicit topic of discussion—such as in lessons focused on typical foods or customs in our homelands or on our beliefs about fairy tales—or whether they were not. Because we all interpreted the texts we read, and one another, through our cultural as well as individual perspectives, we had to be conscious not only of others' but also of our own assumptions and expectations. The most memorable moment for me in which our different histories and perspectives were thrown into stark relief was during a discussion in my basic level course of the history of Germany. We had been divided into groups, and each group was responsible for reading a portion of text, making an outline of the main points, and presenting it to the rest of the class. When one group presented on the Third Reich, a student from Egypt asked why everyone hated Hitler. There was a silence, a sense of disbelief articulated by a few short laughs and a widening of eyes, and then a feeling of earnestness and deep rethinking. It felt as though every person in the room was revisiting his own country's relation to Nazi Germany. Suddenly, the angles from which we came to our study of German became palpable, if not articulated. After this brief silence our teacher stepped in to explain how many people had been killed or oppressed during Hitler's rule. She explained not only the events but also how this specter still looms over the German people today. My sense was that many if not all of us continued to process this moment long after it passed. Although not always thrown into such stark and awkward relief, difference was the norm in these courses; it was ever present and it greatly enriched our education in alternately serious, funny, and surprising ways. We each started in a different place and intended to end up in a different place, and to get there we did our best to learn and to help one another learn.

The small town of Göttingen constituted another context in which my education unfolded. Located in the middle of Germany, this university town has a population of 130,000, 30,000 of whom are students. Approximately 8,500 of the town's inhabitants live within the original section of the town, which is partially surrounded by the old city wall. The oldest church in the town dates from 953, and among the first artisans to populate Göttingen were shoemakers, who established their businesses in the marketplace as early as 1251. Göttingen rose as a university center relatively late—it wasn't until 1732 that the Georg-August-Universität Göttingen was founded—due largely to two factors: the reign of King George II, in whose vast domain Göttingen could be found, and the desire to move the city out of decades, if not centuries, of stagnation.[5]

I often saw my classmates in the afternoons in the town center, at the open-air market in front of the Rathaus (city hall), which dates in its oldest parts from the 1200s. Out of the context of our classroom and pulled from whatever reverie in which we were wandering, we struck up conversations in our nascent German about our shopping exploits, what we thought of the day's lessons at the Goethe Institute, what we planned for the weekend. We walked together or parted ways in the web of cobblestone streets that fan out from the city hall, lined with *Fachwerkhäuser* (half-timbered houses) from the sixteenth and seventeenth centuries. At street level in the center of town almost every one of these buildings is a specialty shop—fresh fruit and vegetables, wine, bread, flowers, clothes, books, watches. The preferred approach to shopping in Göttingen—and one I happily adopted—is to go from shop to shop, enveloped in each by different displays, smells, and clientele, and to slowly gather bread, meat, cheese, vegetables, flowers.

If, as one moves from shop to shop, one looks up at the painted sides of the old buildings in which the shops are housed, one sees studding the pale blues and yellows and greens and grays of the walls modest marble plaques that name the well-known people who lived in the houses and when. Innumerable such markers are scattered about the city commemorating the lives of Johann Wolfgang von Goethe, Arthur Schopenhauer, Otto von Bismarck, Johannes Brahms, Max Planck, and many others. Heinrich Heine, one of Germany's most renowned and widely read poets, lived on the main street just around the corner from the city hall in 1825. Near the oldest church in Göttingen, a plaque commemorating the book burning on May 10, 1933, on the steps of the church records Heine's words: "*Wo man Bücher verbrennt, verbrennt man auch am Ende Menschen*" (Where one burns books, one ultimately burns people, too).[6] Other well-known and not-so-well-known people dwelt in the city: Henry Wadsworth Longfellow lived in the oldest building in the town in 1829. Emmy Noether, then the world's leading female mathematician and the first woman on the faculty at the University of Göttingen, was forced to leave by the Nazis in 1933 and taught at Bryn Mawr College for two years until her death in 1935 at age fifty-three. Walking the winding streets, I not only read the words but also felt the presence of the many lives lived in or simply touched by this town.

The context that encompassed all of these was the country of Germany itself. I spent many afternoons and weekends with Moritz and Lisa and their parents visiting towns such as Goslar and Wernigerode, which lie in the nearby Harz Mountains, or cities somewhat farther away, including Berlin and Hamburg. I reconsidered one branch of my own personal history as I wandered in the Harz Mountains, out of which some of my ancestors migrated to Pennsylvania in the 1720s. To see the landscape out of which they came, to walk the streets of towns in which they might have lived, and to hear and to learn a version of the language they must have spoken awoke in me a sense of history and amplified in me this aspect of my identity. I reconsidered as well some of the country's history and culture as I walked along the famous Unter den Linden, through the former East Berlin, peered into Goethe's office and library in his house in Weimar, or visited the Sababurg, which the Brothers Grimm claim and the local tourist industry promotes as the castle of Sleeping Beauty.

Under the almost always lowering German skies, I saw the contexts in which the language and culture(s) I was learning had developed, and I thought about how historical understandings, misunderstandings, and choices based on both had shaped not only German but also world events. I could drive across what had been the border between East Germany and West Germany and, as a visitor, see no signs of the former differences, and I could walk down a street in Göttingen and see a handmade sign reading "*nie wieder Krieg*" (never again war). A country divided by a war and a city divided by a wall had always seemed incomprehensible to me, partly because it was so outside of my own lived experience. I had felt chilled in 1987 when I had visited East Berlin before anyone knew the Wall would come down in 1989. Now I had just flown to Germany from a country that had mounted the so-called "War against Evil" in response to the destruction of the World Trade Center, damage to the Pentagon, and the loss of many lives in New York, Washington, and Pennsylvania on September 11, 2001. It was a strange time, echoing other clashes of worldviews throughout history, reminding us of the ways in which the world has gotten smaller as it has grown, waking some to increased patriotism, some to increased horror and shame.

As two-year-olds, Moritz and Lisa were unaware of these educational, local, and global contexts; they moved unimpeded through the town and their days, and they learned German as easily as breathing air. They were my teachers as well as my fellow learners as we explored together with equal enthusiasm new German phrases and new *Spielplätze* (playgrounds). Every day I heard new words and constructions in the flow of their speech, and I spoke to them entirely in German, correcting myself as I spoke. Learning within the very personal relationship I had with Moritz and Lisa, learning every day in the town as well as classroom, I was engaged in a kind of saturation experience that we cannot simulate in most formal school settings. Many of the lessons I learned about learning, however, can be applied to any classroom setting. In the chapters that follow I analyze the education of particular groups of college undergraduates and the continuing education of adults re-embracing the role of student. The metaphor for education that I have developed is relevant to other levels and kinds of education, but my focus in this book is on the educational contexts in which I myself have participated most recently— as a student, as a teacher, as a facilitator.

The poem with which I open this chapter narrates my experience of engaging in a formal process of learning as I lived it, and my subsequent analysis illuminates a variety of aspects or qualities of that experience that are also relevant across educational levels. Thus my discussion of the poem introduces and offers an initial explanation of the threads I will trace throughout this book. When I first started writing the poem, I called it "*Meine zwei Stimmen*" (My Two Voices), because I was inspired to write it by what seemed at first to be the experience of trying to add a voice to my existing voice. As I worked on the poem, I changed the title to "*Meine sich verändernde Stimme*" (My Changing Voice) because I wanted to capture the sense that what I was taking on was not just an adding of new words but was and would remain an integrated and ongoing process of change, growth, and development: although my voice was changing, it was still my voice, not an entirely new one.

The changes I was experiencing in my voice embodied the changes I was experiencing in my self. Literary theorist Jonathan Culler writes about this process as manifestations of tensions between the given and the made and between the individual and the social. He asks: Is the self something inner and unique, prior to the acts it performs? Is the self determined by its social attributes? Does the self become what it is through particular acts? Or does the self become what it is through the various subject positions it occupies?[7] Culler also discusses how the process of forming a sense of self "not only foregrounds some differences and neglects others; it takes an internal difference and division and projects it as a difference between individuals or groups."[8] It works in this sense as metaphor works: by bringing together different realms and prompting interaction between them that is transforming.

I became distinctly aware of my "self" as an entity during my time in Göttingen precisely because that self was challenged to evolve in dramatic and new ways—through time, through context, through relationship, through language.[9] In writing the poem and in living each day, I was engaged in "authoring a coherent self-narrative"[10]—consciously and deliberately composing a unique and distinct entity. This entity was, at the same time, "crafted through linguistic exchanges with others."[11] Finding a way to integrate the individual and the social, the conscious and the unconscious, the given and the made, I had to develop what anthropologist Dorinne Kondo calls a sense of self as "inextricable from context" and to speak of "selves in the plural."[12] Faced with a powerful new set of circumstances and challenges that demand new ways of speaking, being, and behaving, I had to, like a child when she initially develops a sense of identity, establish "a sense of a continuing self that extends over time but that also changes over time and that is different in significant ways from others' selves."[13]

This process of learning to speak in new ways as a new self in a new context such that I retained but also reconstituted that self characterizes not only this particular educational experience but also education in general. When one undertakes an educational process one learns new ways of thinking, speaking, reading, and writing, and one is changed, but one does not become an entirely new person. One becomes a new version of oneself: a version with all the old iterations contained within the new that will need to be revised again and again. That is the most basic premise of this book, and it is the story I tell in this chapter of my own experience.

From the beginning I could discern more sense than I could make in German. Alice Kaplan writes that as a young woman she could understand German just by paying attention: "Just by lying there with my ear and listening."[14] This was true for me as well. But perceiving meaning is not the same as producing it. Meaning "refers to connections made in experience as well as to the definition of certain terms."[15] I found producing meaning a far greater challenge than perceiving it. Nevertheless, I wrote the poem primarily in German because I was living in Germany, trying to learn the German language, surrounded by German sound and sense. To write it in English would have felt to me like staying in a former state and trying to write about a new one. But the choice certainly didn't make the composition easy. When I first began writing the poem, I was frustrated by my lack of fluency in the German ways of thinking, speaking, and being. As an adult who had not tried to learn a new language for more than twenty years, I felt suddenly at sea in a medium I had come to take for granted. Like many students, I felt initially overwhelmed by the task ahead of me. During my first weeks of class at the Goethe Institute and struggling to speak the few words of German I knew, I thought to myself about how, at first, a new medium of expression seems completely incomprehensible and unreproducable. The most basic vocabulary, structures, and assumptions seem utterly foreign and inaccessible. My mouth literally could not form the shapes it needed to for me to speak this new language. The linguistic structures in my head prompted me to order words differently from the way they are ordered in German. The requirement when speaking German to be absolutely explicit and clear challenged my tendency to think, speak, and write in more poetic, allusive ways.

These challenges were also possibilities. Although I had many moments of feeling utterly overwhelmed and as though I could not possibly make any headway, for the most part I "felt a pull toward learning."[16] Every day in class or in conversation with people my mind was flooded with a language in which I could sometimes discern or produce meaning and sometimes not. My classmates, teachers, or one or the other of the twins might utter a phrase or ask a question that I could not as yet fully understand. The uncertainty, the disturbance, which John Dewey claims lies at the root of the impulse to learn, drove me forward. Dewey writes of "an *un*settlement" in one's thoughts or understanding, and how the mind strives to overcome that disturbance.[17] The discrepancy between my fluency in English and my inability to fully perceive meaning or to express myself in German—the discrepancy between the known and the new— was the impetus for me to embrace the educational process required to learn German as well as the impetus for writing the poem to capture and record my experience. This discrepancy threw into relief my desire to understand and be understood by people who live a different language, starting with Moritz and Lisa, and my desire to undertake the education that developing such capacities requires. These impulses felt to me like expressions of the very basic human desires we are born with and, if we work at it, can sustain throughout our lives: the desires to communicate, to learn, and to grow.

Looking for ways to connect the known and the new meant for me striving for a balance between "proximity and separateness, intimacy and alterity,"[18] and the poem I was writing provided one realm within which to do that. Although the majority of the poem is written in German, there are words and phrases that I felt compelled to write and to keep in English—such as "resonates" and "strains." These are words for which I could find no satisfactory translations —satisfactory to me in that early stage of my learning—English words for which German words either did not exist (such as "resonates") or did not capture my meaning or the sound that, for me, carried part of the meaning (such as the word "sound" itself). This strong sense of the depths of meaning in a word reminded me that sensibility is profoundly interwoven with language. The vestiges of *"meine ursprüngliche Stimme"* (my original voice) that stud the poem stand in sharp contrast to but also blend in my ear with the German words and sounds that surround them. They embody the sounds and meanings that are so much a part of my identity that I chose to retain them in their original form. They sing for me in English in the same way that the final line of the first stanza, *"wie jedes gutgewebte Lied"* (like every well-woven song), sounds better to me in German than in English. Of Sandra Cisnero's *House on Mango Street*, Azade Seyhan writes: "The transportation of Spanish words and phrases into English and their seamless integration into the text allow her 'to say things in English that have never been said before.'"[19] I left visible my own complicated and polyvocal struggle to find meaning, and the ultimate mix of languages upon which I settled, because at the time that I composed the poem, they felt and sounded right to me—"The letters speak to one another 'without a pause in different voices' [*ohne Pause mit verschiedenen Stimmen*]"[20]—that is, they captured the sounds and senses I strove to articulate from within the in-between-languages place I lived at that point.

I see now that this choice reflects two essential qualities of the educational process. The first is the drive to integrate the known and the new as well as the persisting discrepancies between them. How to be open to, reconcile, and build on the intersection of the familiar and the strange challenges anyone who embarks upon a formal educational project. What is retained, what is lost, and what is gained in the translation process that is education result both from decisions one makes and from the ways that the learning self integrates the changes required and wrought by the educational experience. The second quality reflects what Dewey asserted repeatedly: that the educational process should have no end beyond itself—it is its own end—and it is a process of continual reorganizing, restructuring, and transforming.[21]

At first, the discrepancies between the known and the new dominated my experience and my thinking. Writing in German about my English voice threw into relief how much I felt the latter to be *"klar, voll mit dem*

Ton und mit dem Sinn" (confident and clear, full of well-tuned sounds and sense). These lines capture my perception of my English voice in the only way that I could see it in early October of 2001: in contrast to my nascent German voice, which sounded to me like a "*Lautverwickelung, schlechtgestimmt*" (a tangle of sounds, badly tuned) and with which I would often feel *stimmlos* (voiceless). Ronald Martinez points to "the sheer physical fatigue" of learning a new language, "of trying to fit weird, unfamiliar consonant clusters and vowel sounds to lips and palates long accustomed to the marshmallowy, half-articulated sounds we know as American English."[22] Alice Kaplan writes of her experience of learning how to pronounce the French "r": "In September my 'r' is clunky, the one I've brought with me from Minnesota. It is like cement overshoes, like wearing wooden clogs in a cathedral. It is like any number of large objects in the world—all of them heavy, all of them out of place, all of them obstacles."[23] But one must continue to try to lift and wield these objects, to make the voice stronger and suppler so that it can carry them. Young children do this without thinking and without self-consciousness—they practice and play until they learn. Adults must be more deliberate not only because they are more self-conscious but also because there is more known with which the new must be reconciled and integrated.

The German words with which I was playing—"*Stimme*" (voice), *stimmhaft* (voiced), *schlechtgestimmt* (badly tuned), *stimmlos* (voiceless), *bestimmt* (decided, determined, definite)—were intriguing and important words for me. They all have the root "*Stimme*" or "voice," which in German carries far more and far more various meanings than are immediately obvious in English. Words I do not use but which also build on the same root include "*Stimmung*" (mood), "*stimmberechtigt*" (entitled to vote), and "*stimmungsvoll*" (full of atmosphere). These are powerful examples of the importance of having a voice, a presence, in a variety of contexts. Thus these German words express the subject of the poem in a way that the English language cannot. I was fascinated by this aspect of the German language—how the words are built on so few basic roots, and thus to me, a non-native speaker, seem more obviously connected to one another. The effect in my mind as I started to learn these words and see the connections between and among them was of looking at a multifaceted thing from many sides at once. I saw the different facets as connected and I saw simultaneously how they faced in different directions. Playing with these words in German, I could express a particular set of experiences and insights—a set of assertions and sounds—even in a language that was still new to me, that I could not have achieved in English and do not achieve in the English translation of the poem. Even at this early stage, something was already lost but something else already gained in translation.

At this point I could play with these words in composing a poem, but

I had in no way mastered them as part of my daily mode of expression. Feeling not only inarticulate but also voiceless was both frustrating and intriguing. It was not simply an issue of not knowing the language; it was an issue of not yet being the person who knew and could use the language to communicate. I was fortunate that at this point Lisa and Moritz spoke only in basic phrases about fairly simple things. Therefore, talking with them was a challenge, but it was nothing like trying to carry on a complex conversation with older interlocutors. It eased my movement into a new medium, a new culture, a new version of myself.

Verena Stefan writes of her experience of having to become another person in another culture: "Setting off from one continent and landing on another . . . means to translate myself, my whole existence into another one, without knowing the target language."[24] This issue is one of identity as much as of fluency. I chose to engage in this "act of transformation,"[25] but I am aware that for many who embark on such an educational process this is not a choice and the transformation is as much a loss as a gain. Richard Rodriguez articulates this experience most clearly when he writes about having to learn English at school when his parents spoke Spanish at home: "I couldn't forget that schooling was changing me and separating me from the life I enjoyed before becoming a student." Rodriguez compares himself to a student he reads about in a book: "Here is a child who cannot forget that his academic success distances him from a life he loved, even from his own memory of himself."[26] Perhaps in part because I chose this educational experience, I felt it as an adding and integration of a universe to the one in which I already lived, not as a loss of a previous self and world. I experienced it, as Eva Hoffman explains, as learning to translate between identities and languages "without being split by the difference."[27]

Although I did not feel split, I did feel pulled. As I struggled and played with the points of connection and the disconnects between the two languages and the ways of being that they articulate, these feelings of frustration and inspiration persisted, and they remain a part of my experience to this day. Pulled always in more than one direction between what felt and continues to feel like various versions of my self that are and are not the same, I learned and was aware of that learning because of the contrasts and connections between the different words and worlds that drew me. Complicating the feeling of being pulled in more than one direction was the awareness that within the U.S. and the German worlds was as well a range of different ways to speak and be American and German. Early on I struggled with how both to reconcile and to retain the complexities within and the contrasts between my American English voice(s) and my emerging German voice(s). This is another thread of my experience that is woven through the first two stanzas of the poem. At the early stage of my language learning, when it felt as though I had two competing voices and which my comparison between my English and German voices strives to capture, my main study strategy was to search for correspondences. Having immersed myself in a new element full of unfamiliar sounds, signs, and signals, I needed to find correspondences between ideas and words in English and ideas and words in German. In mid-October, I felt myself constantly trying to make a literal translation from one language—and self—to another. Before I knew enough of the language and way of being that speaking a language requires and entails, I tried to find ways of speaking and ways of being that literally replaced sound/word/way for sound/word/way.

At a particular stage in learning a language, this kind of direct translation is at once necessary and narrow. This phase of my education was certainly trying to my friends and teachers who strove to help me see that one both needs to do this and needs not to do it. Part of the challenge was that, like anyone engaged in learning, I wanted to already know. That I didn't and couldn't already know made me feel vulnerable and insecure. It was hard to trust myself and it was hard to trust my teachers, as they tried gently to lead me forward through my frustrations. So, while all translations and all forms of education require some degree of direct translation—some kind of finding of correspondences or connections between what one knows and what one is striving toward knowing or expressing—neither meaningful education nor meaningful translation can be constituted by only this kind of literal process. One must build on and move beyond transliteration, circle out from and back to it, within every educational experience and every translation as well as across educational experiences and translations. And to do those things, one must trust oneself and others in the process.

As I wrote in my poem, "*wenn ich weiter in meiner neuen Sprache gehe*" (as I made [make] my way further into my new language), I entered a new phase. Feeling the limits of trying to find word for word, I felt a desire to find sense. Schopenhauer argues that we cannot grasp the spirit of a foreign language by "translat[ing] each word into our mother tongue and then associat[ing] it with its conceptual affinity in that language."[28] Moving beyond actual words to seek the spirit of language, I had to find different words to create meaning than any literal translation out of my own language could produce. After a poetry reading that the poet and translator David Constantine gave in Göttingen the same fall that I was there, he said about the process of translation: "*man sucht dann die Äquivalenz, die Wirkung und nicht eine Memesis der Methode oder des Buchstabens selbst*" (one seeks, then, the equivalence, the effect, and not a replication of method or of letters themselves).[29] Complete correspondence between languages is not possible because "every language has words which are not translatable, because they fit into its culture and into that only; into the physical setting, the institutions, the material apparatus, and the manners and values of a people."[30] The goal of translating is to create a text that is "*mit Vergnügen zu lesen in der eigenen Sprache*" (pleasurable to read in one's own language).[31] The text that one produces when one translates from one to another language, explained Constantine, "*kann nicht gleich sein*" (cannot be the same), but rather "*muss analog sein, weil das eine andere Sprache ist mit anderem Geist*" (must be analogous because it is another language with another spirit).[32] When trying to express something known in a new language, one is not engaged in transliteration but rather in the re-articulation of a complex human experience,[33] and this re-articulation must be analogous, not identical.[34] To search for and to speak the spirit of a language, one must build on but move beyond literal translation and toward some sort of larger coherence of meaning.

At the stage during which I first started to feel the desire to find sense rather than only word-for-word correspondences, my efforts at expression had an analogue in my perception and understanding of what others said. Some German words started to seem "transparent"—a word that is written the same in English and German but pronounced quite differently—and familiar English words became "*plötzlich fast unbekannt*" (suddenly almost unknown). By "transparent" I mean that when I heard these words, I didn't have the experience of hearing a *German* word and being able to understand it. Rather, I had the experience of hearing sound and understanding it. I didn't know "*welche Sprache sprach oder hörte ich*" (which language I spoke or heard), but I understood what had been said. The most vivid such moment I recall is of hearing although not exactly watching cartoons on television with Moritz and Lisa. The sound filled my ears, and I understood what it meant, and not until I heard a word that I didn't understand did I consciously grasp that I had been hearing German. The flipside of this experience was suddenly feeling as though I couldn't remember English words or no longer knew some of the meanings of the English words I did remember. There was a way in which I felt as though I was, quite literally, losing my mind. Of course I was also finding it, both again and anew, but I couldn't always remember that when I was feeling disoriented or when I was overwhelmed by feeling reoriented.

In early November, I felt myself at a point in learning German at which I was beginning to succeed at creating the new structures necessary for expressing myself as well as understanding others. I had succeeded in mapping out "several new spheres of concepts" that had not existed in my mind before.[35] It was an exciting and also a sad time. Exciting because I finally felt that it was indeed possible to understand the structures and practices of the language. Sad because I necessarily lost the sense I had before of the utterly new, the utterly unknown. And that is sad because it is precisely the confrontation with the unknown that promises the learning of something new and, as importantly, prompts one to rethink all that is already known. This rethinking of the familiar is essential to learning. As one moves toward greater certainty, one necessarily loses that sense of uncertainty that, as John Dewey said, is the catalyst for striving to learn.[36] When sometimes I discerned in others' speech simply meaning, and I couldn't have said which language it was wrapped in, I wanted both to let this new understanding unfold but also to hold onto the feeling of alienation, what Bertolt Brecht called the *Verfremdungseffekt,*[37] that not only inspired me to learn something new but also, as importantly, prompted me to rethink the familiar.

Even more profound than rethinking the familiar is realizing and rethinking the assumed. I had begun to assimilate, with much practice and almost constant error, some of these German rules and structures—such as the fact that every proper noun begins with a capital letter, is masculine, feminine, or neutral, and for each of the genders one must learn not only definite and indefinite articles but also the endings that go with the adjectives that modify the nouns. Other structures proved more problematic. It was not that I couldn't understand how they were supposed to work. Rather, it was that they challenged on a profound level my ways of thinking and being in the world.

One example of such a challenge is the set of rules about verb placement. In *Die schreckliche deutsche Sprache* (*The Awful German Language*), Mark Twain railed against long German sentences, made up of all kinds of compound phrases, through which one must slog to the very end, at which point the verb appears and "you find out for the first time what the [speaker] has been talking about."[38] What he was referring to, as those familiar with German know, is that in a German sentence the verb must always be placed in the second position in an independent clause: *Ich gehe ins Kino* (I *go* [am going] to the movies). The regular exception to this rule is when the independent clause is a question, in which case the verb occupies the first position: *Gehst du ins Kino?* (*Go* you [are you going] to the movies?). So far these rules are not too different from those of English and some Romance languages. The difficulty came for me when auxiliary (or helping) verbs appeared in sentences or when I began to try to construct dependent clauses. Let me focus on the first example by way of illustration. If one has a helping verb in a sentence, then half the verb (the conjugated, helping part) goes in the second position and the rest of the verb (the action itself) goes at the end of the sentence. For example, *Ich will ins Kino gehen* (literally, I *want* to the movies *to go*). That's not too difficult when the sentence is short, but when it is long, and if one is not accustomed to holding the verb in abeyance, it can be a challenge.

Twain's critique described perfectly my own experience both of feeling startled to hear the action of a sentence plunked down at its end and, when forming a sentence of my own, of having to hold onto the verb—I often had a vague image of myself carrying it in the crook of my arm—and move across the space and time that my sentence encompassed. I felt as though my thoughts had to be dismantled and reassembled in a different order—which they did—and in having to disassemble and reassemble my thoughts, I had to create spaces that could accommodate these different-from-mine notions of how language represents the unfolding of ideas and actions in time and space.

Verbs were and remain a challenge, but the most memorable challenge for me was the struggle I had in deciding when to use *als* and when to use *wenn*. *Als* is used to mean "when" when one is referring to something that happened one time in the past. *Wenn* is used to mean "when" when one is referring to events that happened multiple times in the past, or it is used to refer to the present, future, subjunctive, or conditional. The problem for me was what counts as a single event in the past. An example such as "*als er die Tür aufmachte*" (when he opened the door) makes sense to me: it is clear to me that this event happened only one time in the past. But a construction such as "*als ich jünger war*" (when I was younger) is considered in German to count as a single event (a phase) in the past, whereas I would be inclined to use *wenn* because being younger does not seem to me to be a single event or phase but rather something that occupied quite a long period of time.

I learned from my struggle with *als* and *wenn* constructions that I have a different way of thinking about events, time, and continuity—and the self in relation to all of those—than this component of the grammar of the German language allows. As I was engaged in this educational experience, and at the same time reflecting on it, I saw two ways that I could avoid making mistakes with *als* and *wenn*. I could convert my way of thinking and being in the world, replace my old way of thinking with this new one, and have it become second (or first?) nature. Alternatively, I could always be very deliberate and self-aware, perhaps even self-conscious, about this particular grammatical—and epistemological, existential, ontological, phenomenological—point.

I chose the latter. I decided that "*am besten überlege ich meine Stimme in jedem bestimmten Zusammenhang*" (at best I deliberate over my voice within each particular context). I meant by this not only that I needed to think about the particular construction I chose. I meant as well that I needed to choose that construction not only through a consideration of the structures of the language and the expectations of the culture but also depending on with whom I was speaking. Working through this particular point of grammar within the context of my larger educational experience,

I reinforced for myself that only in this way can real listening, real communication, real learning happen—when *"der Sinn des Gesagten und des Ungesagten wird zwischen den Sprechern fortwährend gemacht"* (the meaning of the spoken and the unspoken is perpetually made between the speakers). As Paulo Freire argues: "Without dialogue there is no communication, and without communication there can be no true education."[39] Dewey also highlights the relationship between the words "communication," "community," and "common"[40]—words that have to do with meaning made through interaction among living beings, and Steiner goes so far as to assert that communication is translation.[41] Texts can also evoke a dynamic, reciprocal communication. Quoting Fischer, Seyhan explains: "Texts that call for a dialogue foster an ethical disposition, for they awaken in the reader 'a desire for *communitas* with others, while preserving rather than effacing differences.'"[42] This was the process in which I was engaged with Moritz and Lisa, with my classmates and teachers at the Goethe Institute, and with my friends.

Out of my struggle with *als* and *wenn* constructions and many other moments of frustration, of insight, and of evolving fluency, I reinforced from my position and perspective as student how anyone engaged in education must be: *"Sicher und offen, sprech' und hör' ich zu von neuem"* (Certain and open, I speak and listen anew). To be at once certain and open is far from impossible. I mean certain enough to speak, to hazard interpretations, to make a claim, to make meaning. And I mean open to the voices, interpretations, claims, and meanings of others as well as to what might be going on unconsciously, coincidentally, or contiguously. In this exchange, I not only discover *"ein neues Verständnis"* (a new understanding), but I am also newly "self-aware"—a word (and therefore also, perhaps, a concept) that does not exist in German. Self-awareness is to me, however, absolutely essential to any educational experience.

Compounds such as "self-aware" and words such as "resonate," which I retained in English in my poem, are central to my ways of thinking about the world. I felt that I needed to retain certain aspects of my American-English language and ways of thinking, even as, at the same time, I was compelled by some of the German ways of thinking and speaking I was learning. I was at that point living the paradox that I had been made by the language—something that was inexpressible in it. It was at the moments when I felt that there was no space in the German language and ways of thinking into which to carry myself that I became particularly aware of aspects of myself I had not so carefully considered before. And yet the paradox was generative for what it taught me about who I already was and who I might become.

I had become a paradox in another way as well: I was a teacher who had become a student again. Although my pedagogical practice is premised largely on the conviction that roles are not fixed, that a teacher must always be someone open to learning as well as open to learners, my formal role had changed. I was no longer a teacher, although of course I still was, and my teachers at the Goethe Institute knew it. They and I engaged in another paradoxical activity: we enacted our formal roles during class time, and we engaged in discussions of pedagogy outside of class. Allender argues that to develop our teacher selves "requires constantly remembering what it feels like to be a student,"[43] and as a teacher-student, I had a unique opportunity to learn from and with my three teachers at the Goethe Institute. From my double perspective I was aware both as a learner and as a teacher of the pedagogical approaches each of them used, and reflecting on these approaches and talking with my teachers about them enriched my experience as a student and gave me much to think about and rethink as a teacher.

My teachers used a wide variety of very effective approaches, of which I mention here only a few. My first two teachers split the teaching of the basic course in which I enrolled. The teacher who taught the first part of the course was particularly good at engaging us as students very actively to apply what (little) we knew at the basic level and to play with and build on that. Although many of the texts with which we worked were in our textbook and handouts, we were active in making sense of them, talking with one another about them, reviewing them. Thus this teacher both expedited our learning and inspired us to forge ahead in what felt to us like the chaos of an unfamiliar medium. The teacher who taught the second part of the basic course was exceptional for her use of our own work to deepen our understanding of and engagement with the language. Ensuring that we were active not only in engaging others' texts but in composing our own, she moved us to a new level of creativity and understanding. For instance, she once took stories we had written, typed them up with the verbs in one version and blank spaces for the verbs in the other version, and asked us to fill in the verbs in the blank spaces, properly conjugated, without looking at the originals. This approach both provided us with practice and celebrated our creativity. The teacher of my middle level course offered particularly lucid and illuminating explanations of grammar rules, clarifying not only the particular grammatical points at hand but also the way the entire grammatical structure functions as an integrated system. These meta-explanations put into a coherent perspective the various elements of the language and the culture in which the German language is spoken.

The pedagogical strategies my teachers used were particularly appropriate, and effective, for the stage of learning German at which I found myself when (*als*) I was in each course. All three teachers also engaged in another particularly effective approach: they immersed us as students in the medium we were striving to learn by speaking only German and doing so in a way that ensured that they were understood by students. When someone didn't understand a word or an idea, the teachers used other words to talk around the word, until by context and by coming at the word or concept from various angles, it became clear. As a teacher and as a student, I was inspired by this deliberate and thoughtful saturation process that neither drowned us nor kept us merely damp.

The pedagogical approaches my teachers used contributed to the building of a structure within which we as students could learn the language and transform ourselves through that process. Immersed in the element in which we were trying to learn to live and pushed to make our own meaning out of what we were experiencing, we moved through inextricably connected aspects of the education process—literal translation, looking for sense, and reconstituting selves.

I also experienced moments of frustration as a student and as a teacher, intensified by the newness for me of being entirely in the formal student role and by the familiarity I have with teaching from the other side of the desk. One frustration was the discrepancy I sometimes experienced between what I felt that I wanted and needed to know at a certain point and what my teachers felt that I—and others in the course—needed to know. In all educational processes, some things need to come before others; one needs to understand certain things before one can understand other things. This may be particularly true in language study, but it is true generally as well. Sometimes when I or a classmate would ask a question about grammar, our teachers would tell us that we should not worry about that at this point. This observation is not a criticism of my teachers but rather a highlighting of the fact that there exist these discrepancies between what teachers think learners need to know and what learners feel they want and need to know. This issue is, again, one of trust—trust that learners do (or do not) have in themselves and trust that learners do (or do not) have in their teachers (and vice versa). No easy solution to this dilemma exists, but it is an important one, because if learners feel they cannot understand—that they cannot translate either an idea or themselves—they have trouble moving forward with their education. And yet teachers know from educational theory and from teaching experience that certain approaches to learning a particular concept or practice work better for most students most of the time. Regarding this particular frustration, I had a double awareness: my awareness as a student was born of my experience of and perspective on feeling frustrated and challenged in learning, and my awareness as a teacher was born of my experience and understanding of striving to help others learn. I felt myself and watched others approach and sometimes move beyond the edges of what Vygotsky called the zone of proximal development[44]—

the space within which students feel both capable and challenged enough to learn. The tension between comfort and discomfort is a tricky one to maintain, and yet it is within and out of that tension that education unfolds.

Another kind of frustration I experienced emerged in relation to the way we as students were invited to participate in class. In my first course, we were extremely active as students; both teachers ensured that we engaged regularly in a great deal of individual as well as group work so that all of us were constantly talking as well as listening, reading, and writing. In my second course, however, our teacher had a different notion about our participation. We did very little group work, rarely wrote in class, and spoke much less because we remained primarily in our larger group (17 students) with the teacher leading the discussion. I found this situation, as both a student and a teacher, problematic. As a teacher I find it imperative that students be as active as possible in their own educational processes. I believe that their being active is, in fact, the only way they will really learn, and that means that I cannot cover as much material or control as much of the process. This conviction that I held as a teacher was reinforced through my experience as a student. The teacher of my second course was convinced, however, that his role was to carefully control and monitor our education. When I spoke with him about my feeling that I needed to be more active in his class—that I wanted more group work, more creative compositions, more participation—he explained that if he sent us off into groups to talk amongst ourselves, he could not monitor and correct our German, and that we might reinforce errors and misconceptions. My conviction as a teacher and my experience as a student clashed with this view, and this experience clarified and reinforced for me what I see as one of the most basic problems in the way much education is conceptualized: as something done to or for someone (students) by someone else (teachers).

I spoke with my teachers throughout my time at the Goethe Institute about what inspired me and about what frustrated me about their courses. As part of these ongoing conversations, my teachers shared with me texts they found interesting and their thoughts on teaching and learning. Toward the end of my time in Göttingen I invited all three teachers to meet together with me outside of class to talk about their pedagogical approaches and the book I was planning to write. I asked my friend and colleague, the father of Moritz and Lisa, to join us in this conversation, since I knew I could not say everything I wanted to say or understand everything my teachers would say, and I knew he would be able to work as a kind of translator. We talked about the difference between education that focuses on the product and education that focuses on process and the difference between education that is a one-way transfer of knowledge and education that is a two-way process through which understanding is co-constructed. We talked about teaching and learning as a form of communication—"*ein Zyklus oder eine Schleife, an dem ein oder wenigstens zwei Menschen beteiligt sind*" (a cycle or a loop in which at least two people take part).[45] We explored different metaphors for teaching and learning such as "*eine Brücke zu bauen*" (to build a bridge), which could imply different things depending on who builds it and how. Each of the ideas and metaphors that we discussed implied something different about the education process and those involved in it.

As a student in the courses of these teachers and as a teacher in conversation with them, I had a unique opportunity both to experience and to discuss the processes of teaching and learning. From both these perspectives I clarified for myself the educational principles I embrace and attempt to put into practice—those that I brought with me consciously and unconsciously as I re-embraced the formal role of student and those that were thrown into a different kind of light through the double perspective I had while at the Goethe Institute. Before I enumerate the qualities of formal educational experiences that generalize across contexts, I want to reflect on what I learned and re-learned as a student and that made my formal understanding as a teacher more complete.

- Once again, I do not intend to privilege the learning of a language as the quintessential form of learning; rather, I wish to emphasize that all education is local, and this instance of education was circumscribed by local circumstances.
- Through a formal educational experience, one does not become an entirely new person but rather a new version of one's self.
- In terms of the particulars of the educational process, perceiving meaning is not the same as producing it.
- Uncertainty, but trust in one's self and others to move through that uncertainty to a new place of understanding, is what drives us forward and gives us the confidence and the strength to integrate the known and the new.
- Adults engaged in education must be more deliberate than younger learners because there is more new to integrate with the known and there is a greater sense that one's identity is already established.
- Striving to find correspondences between ideas and words, to be patient, to expect and accept loss as well as gain, to feel disoriented and reoriented, to choose, at times, not to learn something and to accept or not accept ways of thinking, speaking, and writing—these are all aspects of education.
- The process that is education should have no end beyond itself, nor should it be done to or for someone by someone else; to be most

effective, it must be chosen and enacted by students for themselves, with the support and guidance of teachers.

These lessons I relearned as a student connect with the convictions I carried as a teacher. One of the most foundational of my convictions about education is that it must be based on constructivist principles. A wide variety of pedagogical practices aggregate under the term "constructivism," and I am referring here to what all constructivist approaches have in common: the belief that students actively create their own understandings. Premised on "the continual and sympathetic observation" of students' interests[46] and the development of pedagogical approaches that give students "the opportunity to explore their ideas and to try to make more sense of them,"[47] constructivism positions students as active creators of their knowledge rather than recipients of others' knowledge. My ongoing conversations with Moritz and Lisa, my writing and rewriting of my poem, the many active ways I engaged with texts and with other people both within and beyond the walls of my classrooms at the Goethe Institute, and my analysis of those experiences in this book are all examples of my constructing my understanding. What I am adding to the notion of constructivism is that not only do learners construct knowledge within an educational context, they also construct selves.

A second basic conviction I have is that education must be critical. Critical pedagogies not only position students as active in their own knowledge construction but also foreground the political nature of education. Critical pedagogy calls for the empowerment of students "to critically appropriate knowledge existing outside of their immediate experience in order to broaden their understanding of themselves, the world, and the possibilities for transforming the taken-for-granted assumptions about the way we live."[48] Within this framework, "the learning process is negotiated, requiring leadership by the teacher and mutual teacher-student authority."[49] This set of values was something I brought to my educational experience at the Goethe Institute. I situated my own learning within context, historical and social, and on a personal as well as broader educational level, I explored and questioned the taken-for-granted ways we think and live in a negotiated process with my teachers.

A third set of convictions I hold has to do with power and risk. Learning to participate in any new discourse, to use a new language within a new context, is to gain "the ability to take one's place in whatever discourse is essential to action and the right to have one's part matter."[50] This ability is not simply a matter of learning a particular set of discourse practices; it is a matter of becoming a person who recognizes herself and is recognized by others as a legitimate participant within that discourse. This ability can only be developed if teachers make space for students and inspire trust, and if students trust themselves to take risks within those spaces. The balance between challenge and support, between guidance and response, is one that, like the content of what is learned, must be continually negotiated between the teacher and the students.

A fourth conviction I hold about education is that one brings one's entire self—one's values, tendencies, and needs, as well as a language in which to express them—to any educational endeavor. The fact that words and concepts such as "self-aware" are central to my beliefs about being as well as learning means that I will recognize certain contexts and practices as educational and others not. The fact that the compound "self-aware" and perhaps the concept to which it refers do not exist in German means that education will be conceptualized and engaged in differently by a person whose values, tendencies, and needs are primarily German.

Fifth, a central component of any educational experience must be time for reflection upon and analysis of it. Connected for me to the notion of self-awareness is the notion of critical reflection. It is only in the critical contemplation of experience that one can really make sense of it—make a meaningful connection between what was lived and what was learned. To have the experience but miss the meaning, as T. S. Eliot put it,[51] is to not learn. In my own experience I achieved this critical reflection through writing and rewriting the poem, and through writing this book, sharing my writing with colleagues, and then revising.

The final conviction I want to mention, and that ties together and underlies all the others I mention above, is the importance of placing students at the center of any experience or analysis of education. Students should be the starting point and reference point for planning, practice, and analysis. Furthermore, as much as possible, we need to try to understand students' own perspectives on their learning, not simply apply theories to them and interpret for them the results of that application. Thus, educators need to provide opportunities for students that invite constructivist, critical, risk-taking, self-informed, and reflective engagement.

Throughout the chapters of this book, in which I analyze the educational experiences of students in educational contexts that I co-designed and co-facilitated, I discuss these six sets of values in terms of creating spaces of imagination and action and fostering collaboration within those spaces. The spaces of imagination can be between and among disciplines as well as spaces between what is considered personal and what is considered academic. They can be spaces created outside of the regular flow of time and place, liminal spaces between "the indicative (what is) and the subjunctive (what can or will be)."[52] They can be spaces created by the juxtaposition of old versions of oneself and evolving versions. Within these spaces, students engage in formal education that can "reorient consciousness" and "move [them] from a kind of confinement

to something wider."[53] The spaces within which students make these movements constitute and create "moments when the self is on the threshold
of possible intellectual, social, and emotional development," and the
"texts" that these students produce—whether written texts or modes of
interacting with one another—are "sites of self-translation."[54] Like the
space that German juxtaposed to English, and the country of Germany
juxtaposed to the United States, opened up for me, the new places, cultures, languages, and practices in and through which students worked in
the contexts about which I write allowed them to bring together various
"separated realms of experience"[55] and to find or formulate new connections and insights.[56]

The fostering of collaboration is the second theme that I trace throughout the chapters of this book. To collaborate—literally, to labor together—
means bringing more than one perspective, more than one way of seeing
and acting, together to work toward a new vision and set of practices. As
I wrote in my poem about making meaning, "*der Sinn des Gesagten und des
Ungesagten wird zwischen den Sprechern fortwährend gemacht*" (the meaning
of the spoken and the unspoken is perpetually made between the speakers). The generative work of meaning making unfolds in the spaces between people and ideas. All of the educational contexts I discuss in the
following chapters were collaboratively designed by me and other educators, and each of these collaborations spanned fields or realms, literal
as well as semantic spaces, cultures, and contexts that are often kept separate. Within each context, collaboration was the modus operandi as
well. Learners in each context worked in various collaborative configurations, all of which became spaces "in which to construct shared understandings, knowledges, claims on the world."[57] This kind of collaborative
process embodies what Sfard calls learning as participation[58]—it is an
active, co-construction of meaning and identity.

These basic educational values that I hold were re-illuminated for me
through my application of the metaphor of translation. This basic concept, which I have already introduced in my discussion of the poem and
upon which I elaborate both theoretically and through several concrete
examples in subsequent chapters, is that when one engages in education,
one engages in both the literal and metaphorical processes of translation. The literal and the metaphorical levels are always working together;
they are inseparable. On the literal level, one must learn to recognize a
new vocabulary, think in new ways, and speak and write using these new
ways of thinking and these new words. There are stages as well as recursive qualities of this kind of translation. Through working with language
and ways of thinking, if one engages in that work fully, one translates
oneself in a more metaphorical sense: one makes a new version of oneself—one integrates the old and the new into a renewed self that has

elements of both. In both the translation of language and the translation of self, one preserves something of the original or previous versions, and one renders a new version appropriate to a new context and to the relationships with oneself, with others, and with the content one explores within that context.

Essential to my formulation of this process is the notion that the student, the person who is engaged in the formal process of education, is both the translator and the thing translated. This assertion is part of what takes the notion of translation out of the literal realm in which it is usually applied and into the realm of metaphor. Such an assertion prompts us not only to rethink what translation is, it also challenges the tendency in education for teachers to try to transform learners—to make them into versions of knowers that the teachers themselves have in mind. The metaphor of translation as I use it here not only argues for a new way of understanding education, it also shifts these relational dynamics. As Bassett and Trivedi argue, "Translation is not an innocent, transparent activity but is highly charged with significance at every stage; it rarely, if ever, involves a relationship of equality between texts, authors, or systems."[59] By reconceptualizing education as a process of translating languages and selves, and by shifting the locus of control for that education, for that translation, to students, we can shift these unequal power dynamics. By defining translation as I define it and by altering our notions of the participants in and the processes of education, we re-understand both translation and education.

Constantine has argued that the desire to translate is born of the impulse to preserve, and at best results in the preservation of the human. It embodies the belief that "translating is the practice and the proof of that statement by Terence in the second century B.C.: 'I am a human being. I count nothing human foreign to me.'"[60] This sense of connectedness to other human beings, the willingness to find words and ways of being with people, makes the translator engaged in a profoundly human activity. It is for that reason, as Constantine explains, that every reader, every translator, brings to every text "*etwas . . . aus der eigenen Erfahrung, aus dem totalen Leben bis zu dem Punkt hin . . . nicht beim Interpretieren, sondern beim Lesen, beim Fühlen . . . ob man das merkt oder nicht*" (something out of one's own experience, out of one's entire life up to that point, not through interpretation, but rather through reading, through feeling, whether one is cognizant of it or not).[61]

The sense one makes at each intersection of the familiar and the new, to which one brings one's entire life as to the reading or translating of a text, becomes educative, becomes a learning experience, when one is conscious of the process and through it becomes a richer, more integrated person. As I engage in this analysis as a teacher, I continue to pursue my own most recent engagement with formal education as a student; my efforts to translate language and myself through learning German are ongoing. Because my educational experience was of learning a language, the two levels at which I discuss translation—the literal and the metaphorical—were obviously intertwined for me. But I want to state clearly that in analyzing educational experiences in which the subject matter under study is not language, as in the examples in the rest of this book, these two levels—the literal and the metaphorical—are less obvious but no less present and also inextricably intertwined.

My experience of translating the poem I wrote to capture my understanding of my experience in Germany foregrounds yet again my themes. I wrote the poem in German and then translated it into English for this book. Writing the English version of the poem, I had to revisit repeatedly not only the meanings of the German words I was just learning but also the meanings of the English words I thought I knew. It was, in fact, working between the two languages that brought me to the point of feeling that I had expressed what I wanted to express, although I still feel as though it is expressed better in the German version than in the English. That fact is not because the original has some sort of magic quality about it—Bassett and Trivedi quote Fuentes's claim that "'originality is a sickness,' the sickness of a modernity that is always aspiring to see itself as something new."[62] Rather, it is for two other reasons. The first is that I feel as though I have not yet engaged for a long enough time in this particular formal educational experience to be able to translate my words or myself "back" (I prefer forward) into English. Verena Stefan, a native German speaker, writes about a sentence she wrote to capture a deeply rooted experience: "I already no longer know how to translate this sentence into German. I would have to write it entirely differently in German to begin with, and right now I wouldn't know how to do it. It has slipped my mind, yielding to something to come."[63] The second reason the poem is better in German is that the translation uses only one language: English. It does not profit from the juxtaposition of two languages, of two semantic spaces and worlds that the German original does. "A textual space 'will support more life,' that is, generate more significant meanings, 'if occupied by diverse forms of life (languages).'"[64]

Translating my poem from German into English, I was both the author of the "original" and author of the new. Rendering the poem in English was harder in some ways than writing it in German. The poems are not the same. They cannot be if they are to carry meaning in two different languages, two different realms of knowing and being. I am not the same person now as I was before I started to learn German or that I was when I wrote the poem. Nor am I an entirely different person. As one of my teachers put it, through the educational process one changes one's condition, but "*der alte Zustand ist in diesem neuen Zustand enthalten*" (the old condition or state is contained in this new condition or state).[65] When one becomes an integration of more than one universe—more than one language system and way of looking at the world—one is enriched, widened in a powerful sense, but also aware of the limitations of both languages and worlds, thrown into relief as they are by juxtaposition to one another. The English translation was more difficult because English was no longer transparent to me, German had complicated it, and because the self that wrote the German poem was striving toward being a different, richer self, not renderable in a single language.

In engaging in this educational experience I have engaged in a process that is at once duplication, revision, and re-creation, with meaning lost, preserved, and created anew. And like a new translation of a text, responsive to a new context and audience, this new translation of my self is a richer entity—more vital, resonant, and open to expression and to interpretation. Schön suggests that new metaphors can be triggered when one is immersed in an experience of a particular phenomenon; at the same time that one is reflecting on the phenomenon one is experiencing it.[66] The process of translation I experienced—literally in writing the poem and metaphorically in what the poem is about—is the process of education.

To switch between languages is to switch between relationships, for one cannot be exactly the same person in different languages, and the people with whom one converses and the contexts within which those conversations take place are also necessarily not the same. Now back in the United States, continuing to learn German both formally and informally, I must engage in a different translation process than the one in which I engaged while in Germany. Moritz and Lisa are also learning to speak differently and be different. As they begin to speak English in order to be understood by people who do not speak their first language, they appear to me to be different people, not just to be speaking a different language. Between us we bring together the two and more than two universes in which we have all been moving and we transform ourselves. As Cohn points out, learning a language "is a transformative rather than an additive process": learning a new language is not simply a matter of adding new information and vocabulary; rather, it initiates the learner into a mode of thinking about people, power, and relationships.[67] This is true as well of any educational experience. The ability to change our mode of expression and interpretation, and the awareness of what such change requires and entails, is the ability and awareness we should bring to or develop for our own experiences of education and our facilitation of others' education.

Chapter 2
A Metaphor for Change in Learning and Teaching

> The most fundamental values of a culture will be coherent with
> the metaphorical structure of the most fundamental concepts
> in a culture.
> —George Lakoff and Mark Johnson, *Metaphors We Live By*

During the months that I lived in Göttingen, occupying the formal role
of full-time student for the first time in many years, I was starting again
"where the learner is,"[1] embodying rather than only imagining that place.
I was also experiencing the metaphor for education I had conceptualized
before I left; I was living translation. When I returned to the United
States, I attended a lecture in which Verena Stefan discussed the particular challenges of learning to live in new languages and cultures that she
experienced when she emigrated from Germany to Canada.[2] Throughout her talk she repeated a phrase that struck me as representative of the
very translation processes she described; she kept saying: "I made an interesting experience." Because my study of German was so recent, I not
only knew what she meant but also why she said it the way she did. Whereas
in English one has experiences, in German one makes them. Stefan's direct translation of "*ich habe eine interessante Erfahrung gemacht*" into "I
made an interesting experience" threw into relief for me not only the different linguistic structures of German and English but also how these
particular structures yield very different notions of experience and
agency in the world.

The reason one "makes" an experience in German is that the original
root of the Middle High German word for experience (*Erfahrung*),
which is *ervarn,* means to make a journey, to move from one place to
another.[3] In my mind, always drawn as it now is between (at least) two
languages and ways of thinking, I connect the word *Erfahrung* to the two

central words that carry my analysis of education, "metaphor" and "translation," because they all signal for me certain kinds of movement, either mental or actual, from one place (conceptual or literal) to another. The root of the word "metaphor" (*Metapher* in German) is the Greek *meta phorein*, which means to carry over or to transfer. The root of "translation" is the Latin *translatio*, which also means to carry over or to transfer.[4] The German word for translation, *Übersetzung*, has at its root *über* (over or across) and *setzen* (to set or place). Thus my metaphor for education echoes in English and in German both the action of experience and the action of metaphor: the action of moving from one place to another, the action of carrying over. That it echoes and embodies the action it calls for makes this metaphor practice what it preaches.

To "carry over" one needs at minimum two different "places"—realms of understanding and action that, when they are juxtaposed and when one tries to bridge and move between them, one can gain new understandings of both. The metaphor *education is translation* lets me think of students carrying meanings and selves from one "place" to another— through *Erfahrung*, through metaphor, through translation. This experience is not "made" one time once and for all. When we fully engage in education—as when we engage in translation—we carry over words and selves again and again. Furthermore, to be a vital process, this cannot simply be the moving of an idea or a practice unchanged from one realm to another. Constantine's claim about language holds true for any vital thing: it is living "only in so far as it can move and change."[5] Similarly, education "is a process of enabling a person to become different."[6] Thus the metaphor that underlies all the metaphors I discuss here is that *education is change.*

When we return to the roots of things, such as words, we find out what human impulse motivated their invention. Paul de Man suggests that "it is no play of words that 'translate' is translated in German as 'übersetzen' which itself translates the Greek '*meta phorein*' or metaphor."[7] The fact that the different branches of this system of meanings across and within languages have the same root reinforces for me the importance of getting at the roots of our beliefs and practices, in this case, in education, not only to uncover what meaning has been previously inscribed in them but also to complicate assumptions that have evolved and to open us to fresh interpretations of old meanings.

The roots of several other words are relevant to this discussion as well: education, teach, learn, and student. The root of the word "education" is the Latin *educare*, which means to lead out or bring up. "Teach" and "learn" have the same root meaning in English and in German ("*lehren*" and "*lernen*")—the roots are *tæcean* and *læran*, respectively—both of which mean to lead or show the way. The root of the word "student" (*Student* [male] or *Studentin* [female] in German) is the Latin *studere*, to study, which means to be zealous and to strive after.[8] These roots are as relevant as those of "metaphor" and "translation": they trace these educational processes back to movement and change.

Metaphor as Root

Pepper applies the metaphor of roots to the trope of metaphor itself, explaining that a root metaphor is a commonsense fact whose structure, when understood, can appear to explain a variety of related phenomena.[9] As the word "root" suggests, such a commonsense fact exists under ground; it is out of sight, but it nevertheless constitutes the most basic support system for what branches above the surface. Because it is not necessarily visible, a root metaphor must be dug up to be discerned. So too with the workings of metaphor; we must dig below the surface to discover why metaphors are an innate and ubiquitous feature of human thought.

Anthropologist James Fernandez suggests that there may be something particular about the intersection of the human mind and the physical universe in which we live that makes metaphor an obvious, perhaps ineluctable, vehicle for carrying human meaning. He writes: "our minds organize our perceptualized experiences by reference to their relative distances from each other on some prelinguistic quality space which arises out of the very nature of life in a world defined by gravitational forces."[10] Following Fernandez's logic, we can think of concepts and words as occupying and embodying "semantic spaces."[11] These semantic spaces are constituted by what we like to believe are internally coherent ways of thinking, lexicons generated out of those ways of thinking, and contexts within which both the ways of thinking and the lexicons are meaningful. A metaphor brings together two terms that are drawn from and evoke very different semantic spaces. The juxtaposition of the seemingly unrelated terms of a metaphor prompts us to rethink both terms, to re-conceptualize both spaces,[12] to think about what the pull between the two might be. Metaphors "always define a relationship between terms,"[13] and it is in such relationship that meaning is made.

To make meaning, then, one looks for relationships—selects "aspects of the phenomenal field" that seem "to call out," that seem to "hold potential meaning."[14] The relationship in metaphor is constituted by the combination of familiar and strange features, or the unfamiliar combination of familiar features, which formulates for us "some similarity antecedently existing,"[15] expresses to us "significant and surprising truths,"[16] or "provides us with new perspectives."[17] Because of its ability to prompt this kind of vision and re-vision, metaphor is a particularly powerful catalyst for learning, which requires a "break with the taken-for-granted."[18] A metaphor is a "device of representation in which a new meaning is learned" and which "makes a movement and leads to performance."[19] A metaphorical characterization bears "no physical resemblance to the process being described," yet it does make that process "graphic" or "visible."[20] Through the leap of imagination required to make a connection between already related things or to create a relationship anew, our understanding is dislocated into meaning: we are temporarily released from and then pulled anew back into the gravity-guided spaces in which we live.

"Dislocate"—to dis-place—is an essential word here, extended from T. S. Eliot's notion that we must dislocate language into meaning.[21] Metaphor effects dislocation by "asserting something to be what it is plainly known not to be."[22] Through its use of the language of "seeing through"[23] or "seeing-as," a language that highlights the space between two things, rather than the language of "describing,"[24] a language that focuses just on one thing, a metaphor prompts new insights. People can see something *as* something else because it is not, in fact, that other thing.[25] In the face of this seeming contradiction, the "reader" must engage in a kind of "imaginative workmanship that perceives correspondences, that discerns analogies, that brings 'severed parts together.'"[26] So, when we encounter metaphors such as *schools are sorting machines, education is banking,* or *teachers are saviors,* we do not interpret these assertions as literally true. Rather, the words are "felt by the reader or hearer *as* a metaphor,"[27] and between the realization that the words are not meant to refer to a literal reality and the conclusions we come to about what they are in fact meant to evoke, a space of imagination opens up.[28] This is, to borrow an anthropological term, a liminal space—an "in-between place which bridges the indicative (what is) and the subjunctive (what can or will be)."[29] Metaphors dislocate and re-locate us in our minds first to a kind of space outside of regular time and place and then again when we return to "reality." Through this movement we can "carry" meaning from one "place" to another by fusing "two separated realms of experience into one illuminating, iconic, encapsulating image."[30] As Kaplan puts it, "metaphor happens in the split second of one word substituted for another."[31] Thus when metaphor works, it is metamorphic; it is transformative,[32] it effects change.

In any intellectual realm or practical exchange, we analyze the extent to which a metaphor intensifies our sense of reality; we judge a metaphor "by 'the quality of the transformation that is brought about.'"[33] Dickmeyer suggests that "any metaphor has merit if it makes an aspect of a system more clear."[34] At best, the two terms that are brought together in a metaphor "ignite each other but [do] not completely destroy each other."[35] Through a particular kind of "linking of extremes," metaphors can give us "a sense of sudden liberation."[36] Many metaphors can do this, even if only temporarily or partially. But we can also decide that a metaphor is "trivial or sterile," that the points of relationship thrown into relief by the metaphor are unimportant, limited, or unsustainable.[37] These are what many call dead metaphors; the illumination they offer, if it was ever significant, is no longer so.

Alternatively, metaphors can function in significantly detrimental ways: to formulate and fix thoughts and actions within prescribed, rote, and unreflective patterns or to exploit for purposes of manipulation, control, or particular interest the way metaphor—and, more broadly, language—foregrounds particular qualities or attributes and obscures others. What Lakoff and Johnson call the conduit metaphor is a good illustration of a root metaphor that formulates thoughts and actions within prescribed, rote, and unreflective patterns. Examples they offer of how speakers of English use this metaphor to talk about language include: "It's difficult to *put* my idea *into* words"; "Try to *pack* more thought *into* fewer words"; and "Your reasons *came through* to us." As Lakoff and Johnson point out, this way of talking about language is absolutely commonplace. It therefore masks the conduit metaphor's assumption that words and sentences have meanings in and of themselves, that meanings have an existence independent of people and contexts, that meanings can simply be passed from one person to another, and that, therefore, sense of context, relationship, and interpretation are all unnecessary.[38] None of this is true, however, and to act as though it were is to risk serious misunderstanding. Nevertheless, some people prefer embracing prescriptive, rote, and unreflective ways of thinking and being to the more difficult work of analysis and interpretation.

An example of an even more detrimental metaphor is the metaphor *argument is war.* Examples Lakoff and Johnson offer of this metaphor include: "Your claims are *indefensible*"; "I *demolished* his argument"; "Her criticisms were *right on target.*" Like the conduit metaphor, the war metaphor not only "structures the actions we perform,"[39] in this case, in argument; it also normalizes and masks underlying assumptions: that disagreements must be fought over, that there must be winners and losers, that there are, by extension, bad and good sides to be on. Such underlying assumptions sanction a way of being—bellicose and righteous—that encourages and even celebrates attacks on others.

Although less thoroughly—and unconsciously—woven throughout our daily speech, and although (perhaps) less likely to lead us to international, intercultural conflicts, the metaphors for schools, education, and teachers that I mentioned earlier are also detrimental. When schools are sorting machines, students are inanimate objects to be produced, and schools cannot strive for or effect a mixing or equalizing of students. When education is banking and learners are empty accounts to be filled, then those learners are passive receptacles and cannot generate their own knowledge or question the knowledge they receive. When teachers are saviors, students must be in physical, psychological, or spiritual danger, or all three, and in need of rescue or redemption. Each of these metaphors casts students as without variety or different strengths, without their own resources, and without agency. Because metaphors not only foreground certain qualities but also obscure or eliminate others, they can lead people to assume or accept that one particular way of thinking is the only way to think and one set of particular practices the only possible set. In other words, metaphors can be taken as literal and conclusive, thus they can close down the space of imagination they initially opened up.

When in our minds schools become sorting machines, how do we re-understand and hence design our schools? When in our minds education becomes banking, how do we re-understand and hence facilitate education? When in our minds teachers become saviors, how do we re-understand teaching and hence teach? Central to each answer is a process of change. What kind of change and to what end determine what kind of metaphor one is dealing with and what the implications are for education in the United States. When schools are sorting machines, the desired change is from students out of order to students in order. When education is banking, the desired change is a movement from intellectual poverty to wealth through a process of accumulation in what are presumed to be the initially empty minds (accounts) of students. When teachers are saviors, the desired change is from lost, helpless, or hopeless to redeemed creatures. Each of these fosters one set of notions and facilitates one set of actions at the same time that it excludes or renders remote others.

As these examples illustrate, the process of sense making in which we continually engage not only unfolds within a metaphoric structure but is also always "value constituting"[40]; it is "making sense in a particular way, privileging one ordering of 'facts' over others."[41] Because any metaphor frames our understanding in a "distinctive yet partial" way,[42] and because metaphors bring with them "certain well-defined expectations as to the possible features of target concepts, the choice of metaphor is a highly consequential decision."[43] Every metaphor assumes or generates a lexicon, a vocabulary, a way of naming with the conceptual framework of the metaphor, which embodies and reflects underlying cultural values, and which has the potential—if taken as totalizing—to eclipse other ways of thinking and behaving.

Because of their potential both to open up and to close down spaces of imagination, in taking up or in creating metaphors we need to be clear on what the terms of the relationship are, what we are privileging, and what the results of such relationships and privileging might be. Metaphors can "reorient consciousness" and "help us move from a kind of confinement to something wider,"[44] they can give us access to "the taken-for-granted assumptions that characterize differing cultural and institutional contexts as well as self,"[45] or they can limit and hinder our notions and practices. Because metaphors are "fabrications," they are "a prime means of seeing into the life not of things but of the creative human consciousness, framer of its own world."[46] But only if we become aware of "these almost unconscious allegories and assumptions that drive our perception and behavior."[47]

As "products of the human mind," metaphors are "open to appraisal and criticism, adoption, rejection, or modification,"[48] but that does not mean that people engage in these critical processes. Part of the problem is that the metaphors that guide our thinking and practices are not necessarily "on the tips of our tongues"[49]—they are "'not usually consciously articulated without assistance.'"[50] Even if one is able to consciously articulate a guiding metaphor, when one does not recognize or acknowledge the premises underlying that metaphor, or when one not only embraces but also takes literally only one or another metaphor, then the metaphor is more dangerous than useful. This is so because the very same human mind that searches for metaphors to broaden understanding and guide practice can directly narrow that understanding and practice once again by turning metaphors into literal statements and, if one goes further, into orthodoxies.

One of the reasons for this narrowing, I suggest, is that the kind of critical analysis that one ends up bringing to many metaphors for schools, teachers, or education—in part because they invite such analysis—focuses on how one understands an already defined institution, role, or process. In other words, the terms are already not only defined but also enacted; they have clear parameters; they evoke comprehensible images in a way that reifies what is already understood in a particular way rather than moving to another place of understanding and action. Metaphors are reassuring in this sense: they tell us what we should do.[51] It is not surprising that metaphors evoked for schools tend to be institutional, metaphors evoked for teachers tend to be role-based, and metaphors evoked for education tend to be more process-oriented. Schools are institutions, teacher is a role, and education is a process. These are metaphors that have become literally "true." But we need to get outside of these matrices because they keep us from changing our limited way of thinking and acting. As a basic mechanism behind any conceptualization, metaphors make our abstract thinking possible, yet many of them "keep human imagination within the confines of our former experience and conceptions."[52] I suggest that many metaphors do this—in fact, any metaphor *can* do it—but the efficacy and effect of a metaphor depends as much on its use as on the formulation itself.

I dwell on the danger of metaphors because they have had a profound effect on our thinking about and practices within schools, teaching, and education in the United States. If we allow the verb "to be," which is at the center of every metaphor, to be taken as exclusive and definitive, for all times and across all contexts, we lose the generative power of metaphor to dislocate, transfer, and transform—to change—thought and action. Perhaps this is a danger particular to the English language as well as U.S. American culture—to have only one word for the notion of "to be"—and to totalize rather than to modulate and continually redefine. Compare English to Spanish, for instance, which has two verbs for "to be": *ser* and *estar*. The most basic guiding principle about when to use one or the other form of the verb is that *ser* must be used if what follows the verb is a noun, but when adjectives follow it, one uses *ser* when referring to permanent states and *estar* when referring to temporary conditions.[53] These differences illustrate an awareness of different forms of be-ing, and they create, in both language and action, spaces for those different ways. Working within the English language, which is for me now clarified and complicated by my recent learning of another language, it is possible to find metaphors that keep spaces of imagination and action open.

When Education Is Translation: The Potential and the Danger of the Metaphor

There are multiple meanings inherent in the word "translation." Translation is most often used to mean the making of a new version of something by rendering it in—carrying it over to—one's own or another's language. But the other meanings must be kept in mind when one uses the metaphor of translation to characterize the process of education. To translate can mean to bear, remove, or change from one place or condition to another; it can mean to change the form, expression, or mode of expression of, so as to interpret or make tangible, and thus to carry over from one medium or sphere into another. And to translate can mean to change completely, to transform.[54] When I conceptualize education in these terms, I emphasize its primarily language-based nature, I foreground interpretation, expression, and communication as rich, complex human processes, and I argue for ongoing transformation—ongoing interpretation and articulation not only of meaningful words but also of meaningful relationships and selves—rather than a static state or relationship, as its desired goal. A student who genuinely engages in well-designed formal education changes her condition, makes herself comprehensible to others in a new sphere, makes a new version of herself, is transformed. These processes are never finished; they are always open to further revision and always lead to further re-renderings.

This metaphor challenges traditional conceptions both of translation and of education. In terms of translation, I argue with Steiner that the same model we use to understand translation between languages should be applied to interpretation within languages, particularly as words within a language are juxtaposed over time. Thus, any act of communication, any effort at understanding, is a translation.[55] Steiner puts it this way: "*human communication equals translation.*"[56] In terms of pushing traditional conceptions of education, this argument displaces the notion that a student is "passive, isolated, and rightfully dependent on the expertise and experience of others"[57] and asserts instead, in the spirit of constructivist notions of learning, that the student is the one who actively effects her own education. The teacher is also a translator of herself as an ongoing learner, but her main goal is to facilitate the translations of her students. Thus with this metaphor I do not argue that the teacher translates students. Rather, the teacher creates a context in which she can facilitate, support, and encourage the students' translation of themselves. Within this conceptual framework the school is a site of translation, one context among many in which students learn, but the one whose specific responsibility is formal education.

Within schools and with the support of teachers, students engage in a process of finding and forging new languages and selves. However, the words and selves students find and forge do not replicate or replace students' former words and selves. Rather, students draw on "original" words and aspects of themselves to render new versions that resonate within a new context and set of relationships[58]—a process that moves "in concentric and ever-widening circles"[59] and also is always ongoing. They translate what is not said as well as what is; they struggle to produce words and selves that "will have a meaning . . . will have an echo, will have a sound"[60]—what Walter Benjamin called an "echo of the original."[61]

It is important to clarify here what I mean by "original" in reference to "self." I do not mean to suggest that there is an essential, fixed self that existed prior to the challenges posed by a new formal educational experience. Rather, with "original" I refer to the consciously constructed narrative of self that was composed by an individual as soon as that individual had the cognitive capacity to engage in such composition and be metacognitively aware of the composing process.[62] This "self" or self-concept, as some psychologists call it, is "the sum of an individual's beliefs about [her] attributes such as [her] personality traits, cognitive schemas, and [her] social roles and relationships,"[63] and the consciously constructed narrative of self that I am calling original is the reference point for past, present, and future engagement with situations and people. This original self is first constructed at a certain stage of development when individuals are able to integrate seemingly contradictory aspects of themselves into a more unified notion of self.[64] This self is "storied" by children initially constructing their identities, and "[t]hrough joint reminiscing one learns to evaluate one's past, to interpret one's experiences, and at the same time to own them as part of oneself, indeed, as the very heart of who one is."[65] School begins for most children around the same time they are composing their original narratives of self, although most schooling experiences unfortunately do little to name explicitly and foster intentionally the self-aware construction and reconstruction of a self. We nevertheless carry those original versions of ourselves with us, and so when we return to formal educational contexts as adults, these original selves are re-evoked.

The original self we compose as young people is actually re-composed many times and for many reasons because the development of self is, in fact, "a lifelong project."[66] Because "none of us is the same either as we were in the past or as we will be in the future,"[67] we develop what psychologists call the "temporally extended self" (the self extended in time), which entails making connections between self-representations from different moments in time and a certain kind of cognitive processing that allows a self to remember previous experiences and re-experience them.[68] Holstein and Gubrium argue that we need to "restory" the self "so as to provide it with opportunities for being diversely constructed";[69] we need to re-compose ourselves in order to maintain and further the relational identities that constitute the temporally extended self.

By the time we engage in formal educational experiences as adults, we have restoried our original selves many times. What I am suggesting here is that we define the formal educational process in terms of this re-rendering process. I suggest that education be the process through which students take up the composed and readable versions of themselves that they have constructed and carried with them and that they consciously and deliberately translate those versions with the support of teachers and other students. Like translations of texts, the new versions of self students compose create a dynamic tension between the familiar and the new, both resonate and surprise, and capture some vital essence of the human experience, which we are compelled, and able, to interpret.

I am suggesting that a student engaged in the deliberate, conscious, and systematic process of education engages in such translation. Striving always to connect the known with the new, a student cannot simply seek one-to-one correspondences between the familiar and the strange. Rather, in the texts, the situations, the people she reads, and the interpretations of those texts, situations, and people that she produces, a student must find new ways of naming that both preserve something of what is already there and create something new. Such a translation must resonate; it must be pleasurable to "read" in one's own language.[70] At the same time, however, it must preserve some sense that it has been translated. There must be a balance in translating: on the one hand, "the artistic impulse to take over a text, to overcome its otherness and force its assimilation to one's own language," and on the other, "that scruple which begs to preserve the integrity of that otherness."[71] Go too far in one direction, follow our "desire to translate everything . . . into our own Procrustean grid of priorities"[72] and follow the lead of Latin translations of Greek texts—a process of translation that meant "transformation in order to mold the foreign into the linguistic structures of one's own culture"[73]—and we lose some vital sense of what is being translated: "Translation that fails to maintain alterity, or succumbs to 'the danger of killing the dimension of the foreign'—translation that . . . erases all trace of foreignness, otherness, alterity—is impure or 'bad translation.'"[74] Go too far in the other direction and render something completely other, and something equally vital is lost—or more precisely, not gained. Thus, "the ideal model for translation becomes that which creates the simultaneous experience of both proximity and separateness, intimacy and alterity."[75]

The challenge of how to balance these two impulses emerged early on in my process of learning a new language, and it persists. The desire not to develop a second-nature understanding of where to place the verb in a sentence and when in German to use *als* and when to use *wenn* was only the beginning of my struggle with this aspect of education, of translation. I continue to write and to speak what my German and German-speaking friends tell me are English constructions. I do this not only because I still do not have a firm grasp on all of the constructions in German but also for the same reason that I kept some English words in the German poem I wrote: to preserve what resonates for me in English and to create both intimacy and alterity. At the same time, I am also told, many of my English sentences seem to be constructed according to German grammatical rules. This aspect of education is the less conscious and deliberate, the learning that happens as a result of the experience and that changes not only the language spoken but also the self speaking. This new version of myself blends German and English in two directions. I make choices about how I render myself, but I am also rendered by the languages I have learned.

I have dwelt upon the notion of students as active agents in their education, and the question of who has what kind of agency in translation is also a significant one.[76] Although translation can be something done by someone (a person) to something (a text), it can also be something beyond this literal sense of the word. Levy argues that there are two points of view in translation: teleological and pragmatic. From the teleological point of view, translation is a process of communication. From the pragmatic point of view, it is a process of decision making.[77] As I experienced it as I learned German and as I apply it to the experiences of the students about whom I write in the following chapters, it is both. Students must be at once characters, authors, and critics; at once text, translator, and reader. Occupying these multiple positions in relation to the spoken and written texts they produce helps students see how all of us occupy multiple, relational positions in life.

Making and rendering some kind of ultimate meaning out of thinking, speaking, and writing is impossible. It is impossible to achieve a complete and fixed interpretation that will remain generative over time. That is a good thing. The same goes for teaching. Ellsworth argues that teaching in particular is impossible in the sense we tend to mean it (that is, as transferring our ideas into students' minds); she suggests that if teaching could be made to be possible, "the moment of having been taught would be a moment of closure, return, self-sameness, stasis, rigidity."[78] It is, then, impossibility that we are after—an unending series of efforts to make meaning, which will succeed and fail to varying degrees, but which are always understood as ongoing and productive: a generative process of *attempting* to retain, re-make, and carry forward meaning.

The impossibility of the task of translation is part of what animates it as a metaphor for education. When students are active agents engaged in this impossible task, everything is called into question and they must critically reflect on what they think they know and who they think they are. I am thus referring in part to a reflexive as well as metaphorical process when I assert that students are themselves both the translators and the thing translated. Highlighting the relationship between the literal practice of translation and its use as a metaphor, Eva Hoffman argues that "you can't transport human meanings whole from one culture to another any more than you can transliterate a text."[79] Substantiating the reflexive process I describe, she writes of the process of learning to interact with and understand others after her emigration from Poland to the United States: "I must translate myself . . . by the motions of understanding and sympathy . . . by slow increments, sentence by sentence, phrase by phrase."[80] Varena Stefan describes her experience in the same terms: "Setting off from one continent and landing on another . . . means to translate myself."[81]

Dorinne Kondo engaged in a similar translation when she conducted fieldwork in Japan. As a Japanese American, she was "a living oxymoron" who caused both herself and her hosts significant stress as they "had to strain to make sense of one another."[82] Kondo explains that "in the face of dissonance and distress," and in an attempt not only to make sense of but also to make livable the tension between the Western sense of self as an individual and the Japanese sense of self as "inextricable from context," she learned to speak of "selves in the plural."[83] Kondo, like Hoffman and Stefan, integrated the different aspects of her self and her relationships not into a single, monolithic whole but rather into an evolving, dynamic (id)entity in context. She learned to translate between identities and languages "without being split by the difference."[84] I learned and continue to learn to do the same: In the context of living in Germany, I had to translate myself in one way; now, living again in the United States, I must translate myself in another.

Anyone engaged in a deliberate, conscious, and systematic process of formal education also experiences a change of cultural context. She may literally enter a new country, but she certainly enters a new country intellectually, psychologically, emotionally, and in other ways. Any area of study has its own values and practices, its own ways of thinking, acting, and interacting, its own culture. Thus when someone enters the new country and culture of a new area of study, she must engage not only in literal forms of translation but also in the kind of metaphorical translation process that Hoffman, Stefan, and Kondo describe and in which I engaged and continue to engage as I learn German. It is not simply that one learns to speak a new language; it is that one makes oneself a different person. Proefriedt argues that "the immigrant, the outsider, the person moving from one society to another and, importantly, undergoing the experience in a reflective fashion, becomes the model for what it means to be educated in the modern world." He suggests that this is the case because "what is needed henceforth is a capacity to measure the values of one society against another, to embrace the radical decentering of the world brought home by the movement from one culture to another."[85] This is the work of education.

Translation as I use the term is both a responsive and a generative interpretive act; it refers to a kind of education that unfolds between as well as within people, and it is premised on the belief that we must continue to create new interpretations for each new context and group of people. Within the dynamic tension between the familiar and the new— what we already understand and what we are striving to understand— education is a process of rendering interactions and selves that both resonate and surprise. It is a process of rendering and re-rendering some vital essence of the human experience in relationship and in context. These processes are backward- as well as forward-referenced, and thus both produce something new and acknowledge that something of previous versions is preserved in the change. Translation is a process that is at once duplication, revision, and re-creation, with meaning lost, preserved, and created anew with different textures, boundaries, and resonances. And like a new translation of a text, responsive to a new context and audience, a new translation of a self is a richer entity more vital, resonant, and open to expression and to interpretation.

If we live by metaphors because we live in relationship in real and imagined spaces, then some of the words we use to define the relationships between things located at "relative distances from each other"[86] run the risk of fixing those things in a specific relation to one another. This is a particular danger if in our metaphors we evoke already defined institutions or roles. If we consider the word used to constitute metaphors—"is"—we can see that every "is" assertion can easily become a "must be" and thus forget about what can or will be.[87] Every "is" assertion can make the original metaphor a literal assertion, thus closing down the space of what can or will be.

Thus translation as a metaphor is "as susceptible to abuses and undesirable interpretations" as any other conceptual framework; "we can only protect ourselves . . . by constantly monitoring our basic beliefs."[88] If one evokes only one part of the definition of translation, it can be as dangerous as it has the potential to be generative. For instance, taking up only this meaning of translation—to make a new version of something by rendering it in one's own or another's language—translation can be interpreted as a literal process, a transliteration, a carrying over without deep change. Alternatively, taking up only this meaning of translation—to bear, remove, or change from one place or condition to another—suggests that translation is simply carrying something over in its entirety, not revised or reconstituted. And if one takes up only this meaning of translation—to change completely, to transform—then translation can be interpreted as meaning everyone needs to be changed completely with nothing of previous versions discernable.

Only when I keep in mind the many meanings of translation and only when I keep in mind as well that I am using translation as a metaphor does it have the potential to keep open the spaces of imagination and action that it opens up.

Historically Powerful Root Metaphors

It was in part my dissatisfaction with the existing metaphors for educational processes that led me to conceptualize *education is translation*. To locate this new metaphor in relation to both dominant and less common ones, I analyzed various metaphors that teachers, educational researchers, and the population in general use to describe or to prescribe educational roles and practices. (See Appendix for a complete mapping of the metaphors I found.)[89] This review of metaphors is not exhaustive, in part because it cannot be; as Wheelwright points out, compiling a dictionary of metaphors would be an impossible task.[90] The use of metaphors in discussions of education is like our use of metaphors in daily life: ubiquitous and largely unconscious. My goal was rather to look across a variety of metaphors for general tendencies of thought, for patterns of framing experience, for common impulses toward (or against) movement, growth, and change.

A powerful metaphor can encompass a worldview and institute—and sometimes institutionalize—a set of practices. The two root metaphors that have proven the most powerful and enduring in shaping dominant notions and practices of education in the United States since early in its history are *education is production* and *education is a cure*. They have co-existed in the field of education at least since the industrial revolution in the United States, although the latter metaphor has been in evidence since shortly after the founding of the nation. They apply primarily to elementary and secondary schooling in the United States, although it is not difficult to see their influence in many higher education contexts. Each assumes and generates a lexicon, a vocabulary, a way of naming within the conceptual framework of the metaphor, which embodies and reflects certain underlying values.

These two metaphors have powerful implications for the student's role in formal schooling, but they do not foreground that role. Although metaphors may have as one of their focal terms "education," "teachers," or "schools," and not "students" per se, any educational metaphor implies a particular way of conceptualizing and treating students. The ways that these metaphors cast students stand in stark contrast to my emphasis on attending to students' perspectives and needs; they represent the dominant ways of thinking and acting against which *education is translation* strives.

Education Is Production

Embodying what Callahan termed a "cult of efficiency"[91] that was born of the industrial revolution in the United States, the conceptual framework that the metaphor *education is production* provides includes reference to the roles, lexicon, and the actions and interactions of the nineteenth-century business of production: the manager, the factory worker, "the sorting machine."[92] Critics coined the metaphor, *a school is a factory*,[93] to illuminate how, during the early nineteenth century, urban schools in particular "came to be viewed as institutions to be managed and a set of educational experiences to be organized."[94] Within these institutions, "school leaders, like the industrial leaders they looked to as models and guides, sought the Holy Grail of scientific management." By the 1850s public discussion about educational policy illustrated the "complete acceptance of the industrial model by educators."[95] The graded school that was conceptualized at that time "was to be one of the chief tools used in the process of manufacturing good Americans."[96]

Within this manufacturing process, curriculum is "an assembly line down which students go," and students themselves are "products to be molded, tested against common standards, and inspected carefully before being passed on to the next workbench for further processing."[97] Such a concept of school led to "reductionistic, 'parts-catalog' approaches to teaching and learning."[98] This "bureaucratic model" is characterized by, among other things, its "allegiance to behaviourism and what Macdonald has termed a 'technological rationality.'"[99] Obsessed with efficiency and scientific management, both educators and the general public not only embraced but also idealized production as the model for education. The metaphor "pervaded the larger culture"[100] and continues to do so, as evidenced by the increasingly frequent imposition on students of standardized tests.[101]

Within the conceptual framework of *education is production*, teachers can be workers, machines themselves, or managers. When *a teacher is a factory worker*, she is assumed to be "not very skilled, not very insightful, and, within the context of 'real' professions such as law and medicine, not very bright." Furthermore, "the control structures of the school are the control structures of the factory: tight supervision and product inspection. Curriculum design and the quest for teacher-proof materials dominate the thinking of many center office functionaries, but the curriculum guides must be made simple for teachers as well as students. Above all, the curriculum must be articulated with the tests that will be used to inspect the students who are the products of the controlled and rational process."[101] An underlying premise here is that there is limited utility for teachers to fashion the curriculum; like workers in a factory, they are thought to be best off following directions. The class bias—the considerable degrading of teachers—is most evident in this metaphor. Classic examples of control structures for teachers aimed at efficient production are packaged curricula, readers, and textbooks organized into tightly sequenced units and accompanied by teachers' guides—forms of highly structured, step-by-step instructions that actively discourage creativity, critical thinking, or any kind of deviation from the standard set forth in the manuals.

Within this construct of *education is production* teachers can also be mechanical themselves. One teacher describes himself as "a well-ordered machine," explaining: "'My job seems to be like an engine that is well taken care of. Everything works the way it is supposed to work. There is a set rhythm and reason to why things work in the way they do.'" This machine works within "'a time frame in which you have a set of goals and objectives that need to be accomplished. You take a student from this point to that point.'" As Efron and Joseph suggest, this teacher is "a technician" who keeps the "factory—the educational machine—operating."[103]

Finally, when the teacher is the mastermind that oversees the work of production, *the teacher is an executive.* Here the teacher is the manager of a system located not "inside" the process of teaching and learning but rather "outside," a position from which he "regulates the content and the activities on the learner."[104] In this model, teachers are "highly skilled technocrats: professionals in the sense that engineers, accountants, and architects are professionals."[105] Within the conceptual framework of this metaphor, the teacher appears to be "the manager of a kind of production line, where students enter the factory as raw material and are somehow 'assembled' as persons."[106]

The root metaphor *education is production* and the multiple branches that spring from it—school as factory; curriculum as assembly line; teacher as factory worker, machine, or executive; and students as products—create a strikingly inhumane model. Rice sharply critiqued the factory model of schools at the time of its emergence: "The school has been converted into the most dehumanizing institution that I have ever laid eyes upon, each child being treated as if he possessed a memory and the faculty of speech, but no individuality, no sensibilities, no soul."[107] Although *education is production* includes three different metaphors for teachers, each of which accords teachers a different degree and kind of authority, all three cast students in basically the same role: they are marched through drills and hurried through worksheets that test them on discrete, disconnected, and deadly boring bits of information; they are taken "'from this point to that point'";[108] they are "'assembled' as persons."[109] Within this metaphorical framework and the practices it engenders, there is no place or incentive to "attend to whether or not learning is meaningful or satisfying for the students."[110] And as Dewey queries, "What avail is it to win prescribed amounts of information . . . if in the process the individual loses his own soul?"[111]

The experience of students, even at privileged and ostensibly "good" schools at the beginning of the twenty-first century, is indeed one of being shuffled along a conveyor belt. One student describes his life: "6 o'clock in the morning my alarm goes off and I go to school all day long, and then I go to work for five hours, I don't get home until eight o'clock, and then I do four hours of homework, and then I wanna just sit back and just do nothing, and I can't, I gotta hurry up and fall asleep but I'm so wired from the day that I can't fall asleep and before I know it, the alarm, and I gotta do it all again, and the next day."[112] Pope suggests that "we are creating a generation of stressed out, materialistic, and miseducated students,"[113] and this student's description of his life bears it out. According to this model, students are trained to enact highly scripted, grueling, pre-set motions that are going to lead them to prescribed ends.

By making arguments for the betterment of the economic state of the country and the maintenance of the United States as the primary world power, proponents of education as production actually effect a worsening of the human state. Students enact the production metaphor themselves: they study to compete and complete rather than explore and examine, and they wear themselves out in the process. Any innovative thinking or behavior, although it might invigorate students, would hinder production. Thus, such a metaphor, under the pretext of advocating advancement, argues for and effects ways of keeping the social structure the same.

Education Is a Cure

The root metaphor *education is production* eclipses the human with the mechanical; the root metaphor *education is a cure* calls attention to the human—but to human weakness. Just as production in the educational realm was seen as inefficient, this second root metaphor is premised on another perceived problem that needs remedy. The centrality of sickness, as a constituent and also an obsession, is clearly manifest in this second root metaphor for education in the United States.

Schlechty suggests that the notion of the school as a hospital was an outgrowth of "the perception that the legitimate purpose of schools is to redress the pain and suffering imposed on children by the urban industrial society."[114] But the reaction against industrialization was not the first manifestation of the root metaphor *education is a cure*. The original ill that schools were established to remedy was one that colonists brought with them to the "new world": children's innately sinful and evil nature. In colonial America children were thought to be "'born into sin and creatures of Hell, Death, and Wrath and therefore corrupt natures.'"[116] Characterized as "'depraved, unregenerate, and damned,'" children "had to be broken so they could be taught 'humility and tractableness.'"[116] Among the first laws passed in the United States requiring the establishment of schools was the Old Deluder Satan Act passed in 1647 in Massachusetts.[117] The purpose of the law was to ensure that young people learned how to read the Bible and thereby be "treated" for their innate ills and immunized against future depravity.

Words such as "illness" and "remedy" need not appear in the discourse for the root metaphor, or what Schön calls the generative metaphor, to underlie the story.[118] Throughout U.S. history the root metaphor *education is a cure* has taken different forms:

some nineteenth century supporters of education argued that crime could be eliminated in a society only through the proper education of children. Thus, public education assumed the burden of moral and social training. In the twentieth century this impulse continued and expanded as schools adopted programs designed to end drug abuse and alcoholism, reduce traffic accidents, and improve community health. . . . Some advocates of public schooling contended that mass education would increase the wealth of the entire community, eliminate poverty by giving all citizens job skills, and reduce tensions between the rich and the poor by providing equality of opportunity.[119]

If education is a cure, the job of educational institutions, personnel, and processes is to assess perceived illnesses or deficiencies and to implement a regimen to remedy them. Within this metaphorical framework, the curriculum becomes a prescription, with the ideal prescription being highly individualized—administered to each student depending on her needs and deficiencies and capitalizing on her strengths. These deficiencies and needs are assessed and treated through diagnostic testing, the use of scientific instruments, and "intervention strategies (treatments) based on research and derived from clinical trials."[120] This metaphor privileges faith in rigorous medical practice, and it assumes and asserts that such practice is the answer to persisting problems in the United States.

Within the realm and lexicon of the metaphor *education is a cure,* two metaphors drawn from clinical practice cast the teacher as clinician. One is that *a teacher is a diagnostician.* In the late 1960s, David Hawkins suggested that the function of the teacher "is to respond diagnostically and helpfully to a child's behavior, to make what he considers to be an appropriate response, a response which the child needs to complete the process he's engaged in at any given moment."[121] Thirty years later, Mildred Solomon wrote: "[A] diagnostic teacher is one who casts oneself as an observer, scrutinizer, and assessor, as well as an engaged leader."[122] Diagnostic teachers "seek to know students' current understandings and misconceptions." They aim also to "deepen their own subject-area knowledge and make judgments about what concepts are worth teaching." Furthermore, they "assess their own beliefs and practices, selecting, designing, and redesigning appropriate pedagogical strategies and curriculum materials that make sense given students' understandings and the concepts and skills they want to promote"[123]—like a doctor assessing the needs of a sick patient. A diagnostic teacher assumes "a stance of critical scrutiny."[124]

Depending upon how this metaphor is used, it might or might not be more empowering to students than the industrial metaphor. Hawkins argued that the goal of the teacher should be to make himself unnecessary: "the child should learn how to internalize the function which the adult has been providing." The goal of education, according to Hawkins, should be "the child's ability to educate himself."[125] In this sense, the metaphor *education is a cure*, with teacher as diagnostician, might well be understood to put the child at the center of his own education, although the language of diagnosis, as tightly associated as it is with medicine and the premise of illness, might still render the lexicon problematic.

A second metaphor for teacher within the lexicon of education as cure has its roots in progressive models of education and in the advent of various forms of psychoanalysis, where these work to humanize education: *a teacher is a therapist*. A teacher is "an empathetic person charged with helping individuals grow personally and reach a high level of self-actualization, understanding, and acceptance."[126] According to this model, the teacher does not impart knowledge and skill to students; rather, he helps students gain their own knowledge and skill.[127]

Teachers in the role of therapist are certainly situated in greater proximity to students and the learning process than those who are guided by industrial metaphors, but the persisting underlying assumption of illness needing remedy is troubling. The premise of illness keeps students passive and ailing (or potentially ailing) with the only remedy being the active intervention of educators. Furthermore, this metaphor can prompt some teachers to feel a conflict regarding their responsibilities. Many teachers see themselves as "providing emotional support for their students."[128] But some feel that "balancing their major role of educating with that of therapist or counselor" is a challenge.[129]

The root metaphor *education is a cure* and the multiple branches that spring from it—the school as hospital, curriculum as prescription, the teacher as diagnostician or therapist, and the student as sick patient—create a version of reality that, although ostensibly more humane, casts students as ill and in need of remedy. The positive face of this metaphor is that education can be understood as care: caring for students and caring that they become healthy—or using their strengths to help overcome weaknesses. But the assumption that they are unhealthy and the schools' prescribed courses or remedies constitute the only possible cure is problematic. Theoretically, the metaphors of school as hospital and education as cure elevate the student from the role of "product," which students occupy within the education as production metaphor, but they keep the student in a dependent role: "the role of client dependent on the expert."[130] Students are patients who accumulate records of tests and regimens of treatments. It is these records and regimens that define students and what happens to them. Nowhere is the language of this metaphor more pervasive than in special education and remedial programs—two places in school where one is most likely to find academic "'casualties.'"[131] The "at-risk" student who needs the "remedy" of a remedial program is cast as sick or at risk of falling out of society unless ministered to by the school and its personnel.

The recent proliferation of possible diseases with which students can be diagnosed—multiple forms of attention and physical "deficits" and "disabilities"—as well as the rise in the prescription of drugs, such as Ritalin, and of programs of treatment, such as Individualized Educational Plans, clearly illustrate U.S. culture's construction of student disability.[132] If students want to receive the services and interventions of the school, they must be sick, and if they want to keep receiving attention, they must get sicker and sicker. Therefore, students' restlessness of body as well as mind, for which we generate ever-new diagnoses, suggest that the cure we offer students called education is actually intensifying their supposed illness.

Although the root metaphors *education is production* and *education is a cure* are premised on different lexicons and engender different notions of educational practice, they have similar effects on students. Both keep students passive, as products or patients, confined within institutions that contain and control, like factories and hospitals, and managed by teachers who are technicians or managers on the one hand or diagnosticians and therapists on the other. Adhering, either consciously or unconsciously, to metaphors such as these keeps the power and responsibility for education in the hands of those policymakers, theorists, and practitioners who have always dictated what forms education should take and how education should be reformed. Yet there is something amiss about a system that does not consult the constituency it is intended to serve;[133] we need to make a difference with, not for, students.[134] With Maxine Greene, I am interested in education, "not in schooling . . . in openings, in unexplored possibilities, not in the predictable or the quantifiable, not in what is thought of as social control."[135]

Alternatives to Dominant Root Metaphors

Some metaphors, with which progressive educators have struggled for years against the dominant ones, argue for ways to conceptualize and practice more "natural" and nurturing education. Other metaphors, which both parallel and contrast *education is production* and *education is a cure*, reflect values or developments during particular historical periods in the United States. I touch briefly on three groups of such metaphors both to acknowledge some of the other ways of thinking educators have developed but also to highlight what is problematic about these as well.

Education Is Growth

Although this metaphor has been around longer than either production or cure, it has never been able to displace them as the dominant metaphor for education. Informed by thinkers such as Rousseau and Herbart, it argues that students should be nurtured and let to learn in their own ways at their own pace and, if properly nurtured, will act morally according to their own free will. Dewey built on these premises, arguing that continuity of life means continual re-adaptation of the environment to the needs of living organisms. He proposed a model of learning-centered or progressive education and rejected the notion that children are blank slates or empty vessels to be filled. Many proponents of progressive education embrace this metaphor and design educational experiences, such as those in Waldorf and Montessori schools and in pockets of progressivism in all school systems, in which students can build their own knowledge—in which students can grow themselves.[136]

One particular form the metaphor *education is growth* takes casts the teacher as a gardener.[137] Scheffler contends that "there is an obvious analogy between the growing child and the growing plant," specifically in the sense that "in both cases the developing organism goes through phases that are relatively independent of the efforts of gardener or teacher." This metaphor constructs the teacher's role as one of studying and then indirectly helping the development of the child rather than shaping him "into some preconceived form." Growth and development "may be helped or hindered by [the teacher's] efforts," but growth and development is the focus.[138] This development is based on "an inner growth principle"—the notion that something simple grows into something complex "through various preordained stages."[139] A prospective teacher in an education course describes how this metaphor works for her. She writes an extended story within which she describes students as a "mixed bag of seeds" that the teacher "has to find a way to nurture." She "wants the best for the seeds" that she plants; to be the best teacher she can be, she learns "how to learn from the seedlings"; and "watching the stems, the leaves, and the blossoms dance in the breeze, the gardener too began to dance."[140]

Although nurturing and fostering life seem to be at the heart of this metaphor, there are problems with it as well: a gardener tears out as well as plants, destroys and manipulates as well as nurtures, and generally grows living things for his own or other's pleasure, need, or profit, not for the benefit of the growing things themselves. Furthermore, while this metaphor has growth at its center, that growth can have only a single outcome, it assumes that everything is already inside the learner and the teacher's job is to bring out what is already contained. In short, it assumes a predestined trajectory that can be helped or hindered, but it does not allow for the possibility that a learner might be self-directed or might change directions.

Education Is Consumption

The metaphor *education is consumption* illuminates a particularly U.S. American set of values. During a phase of relative prosperity and complacency in the United States, after the turbulent, alternative, and powerful movements of the 1960s and 1970s, Powell, Fararr, and Cohen described secondary education as a "consumption experience," writing: "If Americans want to understand their high schools at work, they should imagine them as shopping malls." They explained that "[b]etween periods students go outside to find their next destinations, entering and leaving classrooms as if they were adjacent stores." The consumers vary greatly: some know what they want and "efficiently make their purchases"; others "come simply to browse"; and still others do neither: "they just hang out." Within the shopping mall high school are "specialty shops" for students with particular preferences, "product labeling" for the array of course options available, and special and "unspecial" students to select, or be selected by, those options. The shopping mall high school offers accommodations "to maximize holding power, graduation percentages, and customer satisfaction."[141]

The metaphors for teachers that emerge from this conceptual framework include *the teacher is an advisor*. Shopping malls have directories, and some shopping mall high schools offer courses focused on how "to discuss course options, how to read transcripts, how to compute grade point averages, and other practical concerns"—to help students navigate and negotiate the various offerings and requirements of the mall. Another metaphor for teacher within this conceptual framework is the teacher as entertainer. Powell, Fararr, and Cohen quote one teacher's invitation to a part of one of his lessons: "'Just sit back and enjoy.'" Yet another metaphor for teachers within the shopping mall high school is the teacher as salesperson. Powell, Fararr, and Cohen explain: "[The] business [of teachers] is to attract customers and persuade them to buy. Marketing skills are important; teachers become educational pitchmen. Recognizing that necessity, one teacher lamented, 'It would be nice to believe we had a culture that so endorsed the products we have to sell that we don't have to do that.' But lacking cultural endorsement, many strive to build up 'a constituency of buyers.'"[142]

Within this metaphor students ostensibly have significant power because of their choices as consumers. But in fact they "choose" from a very limited and monolithic notion of what education is—a questionable benefit of acquisition and a questionable regimen for health.

Education Is Banking

Freire explains this metaphor he coined: when the teacher is assumed to know all and the students nothing, education "becomes an act of depositing, in which the students are the depositories and the teacher is the depositor." The student's role within this model is limited to "receiving, filing, and storing the deposits." As passive recipients of others' knowledge, students are, according to Freire, denied the opportunity to "be truly human"—the ability to engage in inquiry and praxis, to create, not simply receive, knowledge, which "emerges only through invention and re-invention, through the restless, impatient, continuing, hopeful inquiry men [*sic*] pursue in the world, with the world, and with each other."[143]

Learning is acquisition offers a different angle on the theme of acquiring and saving. Like *education is banking*, this metaphor reflects the basically materialistic culture of the Western world. Nowhere is this materialism more fully embraced than in the United States, established as it was in the wide, open space of what was considered free but was in fact acquired land rich in resources. Explicating the metaphor *learning is acquisition*, Sfard explains that concepts are "basic units of knowledge that can be accumulated, gradually refined, and combined to form ever richer cognitive structures." The lexicon of the acquisition metaphor includes words like "fact," "material," "sense," "idea," and "notion," and underlying these words is the impulse toward accumulation of material wealth, signaled by Sfard's use of words such as "accumulated," "refined," and "richer." The actions according to which one makes the commodities of facts and ideas one's own include "construction," "appropriation," "transmission," "attainment," and "accumulation." Within this metaphor, "[l]ike material goods, knowledge has the permanent quality that makes the privileged position of its owner equally permanent."[144]

Acquisition and banking, like consumption, focus on accumulating commodities. They also reflect the underlying assumption in the United States that students are problems rather than potentials and should leave schools as finished products, whether industrial or natural. There is nothing human in these metaphors, and there is certainly nothing about the experiences of the human beings cast within them. Paley argues that "the first order of reality in the classroom is the student's point of view,"[145] and yet none of the metaphors I have discussed here assume the students' perspective. Furthermore, more often than not, when student perspectives are sought at all, it is through "insistent imperatives of accountability rather than enduring commitments to democratic agency."[146] A growing body of research and practice aimed at putting more of the power and responsibility into the hands of students supports the need for "a fundamental shift of the dominant epistemology in our society and our schools to one based on trusting, listening to, and respecting the minds of all participants in schooling."[147] If educators attend to students as knowledgeable participants in the work of conceptualizing and enacting educational processes, students are motivated to participate constructively in their education because they are partners in the process of educational change; they are active creators of their education rather than passive recipients or victims.[148]

Gained in Translation

Education is translation stands in contrast to the metaphors that have dominated common understandings of educational institutions, roles, and
processes in the United States and even in contrast to those metaphors
that have worked against the dominant ones. It neither evokes an already
established institution nor is it tied to a particular historical time period
or national ethos in the way that *a school is a factory* and *a school is a shopping mall* are. It does not evoke a fixed and operative role the way that *a
teacher is a factory worker, a teacher is a therapist, a teacher is a gardener, a
teacher is an advisor,* or *a teacher is an entertainer* do. Finally, it does not cast
students as mass-produced products, sick patients, plants, or consumers
of commodities. Although each version of a self produced through the
process of translation is a "product" in the sense that it is a rendering in
the context of a particular space and time, because any text and self must
be continually re-translated in order to be meaningful in the context of
other particular spaces and times, the temporary products of translation
can be understood as part of the longer, ongoing translation process.
And unlike plants grown in a garden, students who educate themselves
through a process of translation are conscious, deliberate agents in their
growth.

When the purpose of schooling is to support the process of transforming the self through interaction with others, then the school is no
longer a site of production, cure, or cultivation. Rather, it is a space within
which students can actively compose and re-constitute themselves—a revolutionary site that can open up diverse ways for students to understand
and participate in the world. With the metaphor of translation, I aim to
make the messiness, the complexities, and the contradictions of education compelling invitations rather than daunting prospects. Education is
then "less attitude than action: creation and recreation."[149] It not only
accommodates but also celebrates the "perplexing, dynamic nature of
the teaching-learning process."[150]

I do not offer translation as the ultimate metaphor for education—"a
new defining vision."[151] But if it can "provide a rational bridge from the
known to the radically unknown, from a given context of understanding
to a changed context of understanding,"[152] if it can counter traditional
images of students, if it can help me conceptualize education as an ongoing process of making and re-making connections, of making and re-
making meaning, of making and re-making selves, then it seems like a
better choice than the other metaphors I have analyzed.[153]

Although the contexts, subjects of study, age and purposes of the students, and other variables differ across my experience and the experiences
of those I write about in the following chapters, aspects of our experiences

are similar, aspects of the experience of education that are captured and recast through the metaphor of translation. We all encounter something new that prompts an initial sense of confusion and feeling of being overwhelmed. The attempt to engage and grapple with this something new takes the form of slow, faulty, first steps toward finding correspondences and toward discerning deeper resonances between the familiar and the new. These first, faulty steps lead to the gradual development and refinement of the twin faculties of interpretation and expression in a new medium, so that we can begin to hear, speak, read, and write in or through that new medium. Then comes the integration into our own selves of the words, ways of thinking, and ways of being that the new embodies in a way that does not replace the previous selves but rather enriches them. Taken as a whole, the process is one of transformation of the self that preserves previous versions while simultaneously creating new versions—layered or echoing versions.

Chapter 3
Translating Compositions and Selves

Each of us is, to a large if not exclusive sense, the genetic
translation of our biological parents, the psychological translation
of our childhoods, the social translation of our race, gender, and
class, the emotional translation of our loves and losses, fears and
joys, transgressions and personal betrayals. . . . It may be that much
of what we call "sensibility" is, in fact, more a translation of
extrinsic factors than the features of some fixed identity we call
a "self."

—Sherod Santos, "A la Recherche"

Arms enfolding new texts and notebooks, "Is-this-the-right-classroom?" expres-
sions on their faces, one after another college sophomores enter the classroom, take
seats around the long tables that form a square, and cast inquisitive glances at
the tape player that sits conspicuously at the front of the room. I welcome the stu-
dents, twelve young women in all, explaining who I am and introducing the guid-
ing ideas and expectations for the course, "Finding the Bias: Tracing the Self
Across Contexts." The course, I explain, was co-designed by a professor of history,
a professor of literary studies, and me, a professor of education. The goal of the
course is finding and exploring disciplinary as well as personal biases and using
them as perspectives or lenses for defining and understanding the self in context.
The goal is not to find fixed definitions for biases, selves, contexts, or anything else,
but rather to help us all improve our abilities to read, think, talk, and write about
these things. I urge students to strive to maintain an open, inquiring, critical, flexi-
ble attitude, not hesitate to share their perspectives, and also work to understand
others' perspectives. I then ask students to introduce themselves and to say some-
thing about their hopes and expectations for the course, maybe offer their initial
interpretations of the course's title, and say anything else that they feel is relevant.

After this round of introductions, I explain that we are going to do three dif-
ferent "readings" of the same story. I pass out copies of the lyrics to Bob Dylan's
"Tangled Up in Blue," two different versions, one reproduced on each side of a

single page. I am met with a range of responses—from blank stares from those who have never heard of Bob Dylan or the song to exclamations of delight from those for whom this song is among their favorites. I ask students to read the lyrics silently to themselves and to jot notes on who they think the self is or the selves are in this song, what the contexts are, and how the words work to convey those selves, contexts, and the relationships between and among them.

Silence fills the room as the students study the lyrics, some jotting notes all over the page, some simply marking a word or two here and there. Steadying the tape player, I press Play. First the sound of a single acoustic guitar and then Bob Dylan's voice fills the room—a resonant ringing of strings and a raspy voice recorded in a studio in 1974. Again, a range of responses, different expressions like light and shadows cross the students' faces, some students sing along quietly, some feet tap under the table, some bodies are still. I have asked the students again to jot notes about any ways their readings/interpretations change as they listen, and again some make notes and others simply attend. Another silence, more profound this time, as I switch cassettes. Finally, the silence breaks to a live version of "Tangled Up in Blue" performed by the Indigo Girls in concert in 1995. Electric guitars, complex percussion, cheers from fans, and the voices of two lesbian women singing the words to a song composed more than twenty years earlier by a music legend, a heterosexual, and, some would argue, a profoundly misogynistic man. Students jot notes about any ways their readings and interpretations change as they listen to this version of the song. As the final strains of the song and the cheers of the fans fade away, the college sophomores sit quietly, the music still ringing in their ears.

I ask them for their responses to the three reading experiences they have just had. Does it matter who is telling this story (they themselves as they read silently, Bob Dylan, or the Indigo Girls)? Why? What do you know about Bob Dylan? What do you know about the Indigo Girls? How does a different self telling the "same" story change your perception of the story and of the teller? How does the context of the telling affect your interpretation of a story? How do other differences in presentation affect your interpretation of a story (acoustic, studio-recorded versus full band, live)? What do you make of the difference in tones, in melodious-ness, lyrical-ness, emphasis? What is the effect of co-singing and harmony? What is the effect of having two lesbians, although not in a lesbian relationship together, singing this song together, alternating verses as well as making harmony with one another? What do you make of self-consciousness regarding the on-the-road boy story on the Indigo Girls' part—an awareness of appropriating and rendering anew, if also reiterating, an old story? What does it mean for a man to tell this story about a woman as opposed to a woman (or two women) telling it about a woman? What is the difference between an author singing his own song and someone singing a song someone else wrote? These are some of the questions we address as we work through the personal, textual, and contextual interpretations each student brings to this experience.

After we go over the details of the syllabus, students leave the classroom with the assignment to read Linda Brodkey's essay "Writing on the Bias" and to compose a short, informal analysis of their own strengths and weaknesses as thinkers, readers, and writers. We will discuss Brodkey's essay during the next class meeting, and we will use the analyses the students have written to form writing groups composed to build on students' strengths and address their needs.

As this opening vignette suggests, participants in "Finding the Bias: Tracing the Self Across Contexts" are confronted immediately with a new context and a new set of questions for making sense of what are at once familiar and foreign words. The multiple perspectives evoked, the multiple media used, and the multiple approaches to reading and analyzing are the core of the course. This approach is a surprise to many students; most come to the class expecting to explore "bias" in the way it is more commonly used: as a pejorative term meaning a non-objective, problematically partial, inappropriately judgmental attitude toward or treatment of others. Specifically, students expect a version of current critiques of race, class, and gender inequities. The course touches on these issues by extension, but its primary focus is on the root of bias—a diagonal line cut across something, a tempermental inclination, a determining influence or impulse[1]—as applied to various texts (written, spoken, composed in other media) and as applied to various selves (both the selves being composed and the selves doing the composing). The course takes up the idea of bias, therefore, primarily in terms of composition; it explores how every representation of ideas or experiences is rendered from a particular angle with particular purposes and toward a particular effect.

As the title of this chapter suggests, "compositions" and "selves" are the subjects of translation I analyze in this context. I have defined self as "the sum of an individual's beliefs about [her] attributes"[2] and an entity "with a continuous existence through time."[3] The sense an individual has of her self is constituted by the "cognitive generalizations about the self, derived from past experience, that organize and guide the processing of self-related information contained in the individual's social experience."[4] I use "composition" to refer to something formed from two or more things; to "compose" is to fashion; to construct by mental labor; to design and execute or put together in a manner adopting forms of expression to ideas or to laws of harmony or proportion. A related word, "composed," is not only the adjective form of the noun and verb definitions offered above; it means as well to come to terms: to reconcile, to settle. It means put together well; still; self-possessed.[5] Like a translation, then, a composition can seem as though it is complete and balanced, but it is really a partial representation, a selection, an interpretation, a rendering at a moment in time and in context. And, as with translation, I am most interested in the active and ongoing process of composition; I am interested in the finished or final versions only as temporarily so—to be celebrated and enjoyed but then built on and moved forward from.

The compositions upon which I focus in this chapter include formal and informal written analyses, spoken words, relationships, understandings, identities. I focus on how the students in the course engage in composing processes that include remembering, narrating, evaluating, interpreting, and imagining. The selves—the students—are college sophomores.[6] They are at a relatively early point in their college careers, and the course aims to provide them with a space and a set of structured activities within which to make new meaning out of their own and others' experiences, beliefs, and ways of being. They do this alone and in collaboration: in their own minds, with other students in the course, and with me.

My focus on students as the primary agents in composing texts and selves is evident here; I use the terms of translation to interpret the critical analyses these students offer of their educational experiences in the course. In portfolios these students compose at the end of their semester in the course, they articulate these versions of their experiences, in which I discern both the difficulty and the revitalizing quality of finding and forging words to capture lived experience and the ways that selves are changed in the process of that finding and forging.

The Context and the Customs

"Finding the Bias" is one among many courses offered through the College Seminar Program at Bryn Mawr College. In the mid-1990s, Bryn Mawr, like many other colleges across the United States, replaced its traditional freshman and sophomore reading and writing course housed in the English department with an interdisciplinary approach to the development of critical thinking and writing skills. In part a response to the challenges that interdisciplinary teaching and scholarship have raised regarding how we conceive of liberal studies, this program aims to give faculty and students an opportunity to explore essential human questions posed and explored by scholars, scientists, and poets alike. The courses taught through this program are co-designed by teams of faculty from different disciplinary fields who collaborate to produce common syllabi. The teams of faculty meet regularly during the semester to plan the details of each class meeting, but each faculty member teaches his own section of the course in which 12 to 18 students enroll.

During the summer of 1998, two colleagues and I designed "Finding the Bias." Coming together from the fields of history, education, and literary studies, our goal was to draw upon but also to complicate traditional disciplinary distinctions and to produce a course that would challenge students to explore and to problematize the traditional separation of the personal and the academic in college study. We brainstormed texts from our respective fields that we felt were particularly compelling, and we talked together through how we might craft a course that would challenge students in various ways to identify, trace, and account for the biases that crisscross disciplinary as well as personal realms. During the semester, we met weekly to debrief and to confirm or revise our plans for the next class meeting. It was an intensely collaborative experience in this sense: co-planned while teaching as well as co-planned in advance, our execution of the course was a work-in-progress that each and all of us helped to shape. The subsequent two years that I taught this course my colleagues and I rethought and revised together in a similar fashion, adjusting the course both in response to student feedback and to reflect our own evolving interests.[7] Colleagues who continue to teach the course engage in comparable, ongoing revisions.

The title of the course signals the lexicon that guides thought, discussion, and composition during the semester that students spend in this world; it includes the key words "bias," "self," and "context." These are words that we define and redefine throughout the course as students define and redefine their understanding of compositions and of selves that constitute and are constituted by different biases. The course title is adapted from the title of a personal essay published in a prestigious academic journal in which Linda Brodkey uses the metaphor of bias in sewing to analyze her development as a thinker, writer, and person.[8] In "Writing on the Bias" Brodkey begins with the literal meaning of bias— a line cutting diagonally across the weave of a piece of fabric. In "Finding the Bias: Tracing the Self Across Contexts," we begin with the figurative meaning: a slant, a preference, a perspective, a prejudice. In academic practice and in life, finding a bias is the process of deciding how one will cut across various facts, ideas, experiences, and contexts—and discerning how others have done so. Just as Brodkey argues that finding and following the bias is as critical to writing as to sewing, we develop the course around the premise that when students engage in thinking, reading, talking, and writing along a particular bias, they continually see one thing in terms of another—the essence of metaphor and of critical thinking.

In challenging students to develop their critical and creative abilities, we ask them not to separate and distance themselves from what they study and who they are but rather to recognize, name, and trace a variety of biases along which they and we live, think, and write. The texts we assign all productively violate the boundaries of academic and personal writing and of specific disciplines. The writing assignments for the course use these texts as models of how to complicate any simple delineation between the personal and the academic, and between the genres of fiction, history, educational theory, autobiography, and anthropology. Early assignments challenge students to see that selves, including their own, always interpret the world from specific angles of vision.

The first assignment is to write a short essay on a defining family myth. This activity helps students see that every self has tendencies, interests, preferences—biases—even if they are implicit, unrecognized, or externally generated. Moving on from an analysis of a single bias, we ask students to explore competing perspectives on a single event or experience. The writing assignment for this segment of the course is to tell the same story from two or three different angles of vision—to embody those perspectives and write from them—and then to step back and analyze how as authors the students invested each perspective with authority. The different angles of vision from which they have to write for this assignment help students to grapple with the idea and the practical implications of bias. When does a writer or scholar need to acknowledge her assumptions? How might a writer accommodate competing interests?

We then shift the focus from personal perspective to disciplinary perspective. Striving to integrate the personal and the academic, and scrutinize our own disciplinary bents, each of us teaches the same lesson—one along the history bias, one along the literary studies bias, and one along the education bias—to each of the three class sections. The subject of the rotating class is Jamaica Kincaid's *The Autobiography of My Mother*.[9] Our lessons emphasize the different assumptions the fields of education, literary study, and history might bring to this text, which yields particularly rich readings along each disciplinary bias. For this segment of the course, students write an essay that includes their reading of Kincaid's novel from each of the three disciplinary perspectives. This assignment requires students to identify specific methods and interests that inform a particular discipline, to explore how a text can be read along the bias of that discipline, and to read critically for what it includes and what it leaves out. Toward the end of the semester, we switch to another medium to explore the notion of bias. We use a collection of photographs,[10] and we ask students to explore how an image tells a story, how the photographer as well as the viewer renders and reads a photograph along particular dimensions. The final assignment of the course is to create a portfolio through which students must look back critically on the semester's work and tell a coherent analytical story of how they developed as readers, writers, thinkers, and speakers.

These assignments and activities unfold within a course structure that is divided among a number of different modes or ways of interacting. There is, of course, reading that students complete individually: texts that all students are assigned and that each reads, most likely, alone. Half the class meetings are devoted to discussions and activities designed to help students to explore these texts. Much time is spent in whole group discussions. In addition, we often have small group discussions during which students prepare informal presentations to give to the rest of the class on specific chapters of books or aspects of texts the students have read. We also engage in creative and critical writing based on reflections on students' own experiences of school, viewing a painting, or rewriting the final scene of a short story.

The other half of the class meetings is devoted to writing workshops. During these class meetings, students bring drafts of papers they have written for the course, and they use the entire class period to meet with two other classmates, exchange papers, and offer one another critical feedback. As instructors, we join writing groups when invited or read over drafts if students have brought extra copies with which they feel they need particular help. Often students meet in their groups outside of class as well to help one another with papers. Dawn Skorczewski suggests that in a classroom in which professors are not the only readers of student work—classrooms in which students are also readers of one another's work—student writing can become what Mary Louise Pratt describes as "safe houses . . . places for healing and mutual recognition . . . [places] in which to construct shared understandings, knowledges, claims on the world."[11] It is from within such safe houses that students can draw the courage to take risks, both emotionally and intellectually. As Paulo Freire emphasizes, to learn one must be "open to risk, to the adventure of the spirit."[12] Students find and achieve this risk-taking in collaboration with their classmates.

The final mode of interacting is individual conferences with their respective instructors, which students schedule after they have drafted a paper and taken it through at least one writing workshop. Thus, over the course of the semester students explore individually and in various collaborative configurations a range of their own and others' biases. Through this process students translate compositions—uses of language and other media to communicate perspectives and insights—and they translate themselves—not only their "cognitive generalizations"[13] about their experiences but also their identities in time and relationship.

The Challenges of Translation

The first semester of the sophomore year is a particularly challenging time for the traditional-aged, all-female, undergraduates at Bryn Mawr College. After their first two semesters of study, then a return home for the summer, many of these students have a difficult time reconciling their original selves, defined primarily by their families and friends in their pre-college years, with the new versions of themselves they are becoming in various relationships and contexts at college. One of the reasons for the difficulty is that the narratives of themselves and the world that have thus far held them in place come under scrutiny, their own and others', as their personal connections expand and their academic careers unfold. Differences in perspective and discrepancies in interpretation thrust these students into what one describes as "a period of self-upheaval." The changes of context, of language spoken, and of stories told and heard prompt crises of identity and meaning in students embarking on their second year of higher education.

The fact that the course in which these students are enrolled is about explorations of selves—the biases selves have, and how those selves interact with others in various contexts according to those biases—not only makes it an ideal context for translation but also throws into relief the need for and the possibilities of translation. The course aims to "open up for students ways of knowing that are too often underrepresented in the curriculum—a willingness to value ambiguity, to invent, to suspend closure, to situate the self in multiple and complex ways through discourse."[14] Deliberately merging the personal and the academic realms, this course aims to counteract the force under which many students have buckled after years of schooling premised on keeping those realms separate. One student, Melissa Holt,[15] eloquently describes this division:

> When I was young, I was a very good writer. I had no spell-check, no deadlines, and so my Fisher-Price desk was covered with half-finished stories scrawled in crayon diligently revised until my five-year-old attentions were drawn elsewhere. But somewhere in the course of my schooling, I forgot how to write. Instead, I learned formulas, and I learned them well. I learned how to use the passive voice, and I clung to it until my writing indeed became passive. It was no longer an extension of my heart, but a mass-produced product that ran tangential to my thoughts. I built a wall of scholarly essays around me, closing in everything that was a spark of personality. It took me 18 years to become truly proficient, but by the time I reached Bryn Mawr, I was a master.[16]

Holt is not the first to suggest that school writing requires an eclipsing of the self through the elimination of personal voice, of bias. As Brodkey laments, students are not taught "what every writer knows, that one writes on the bias or not at all," that a writer's search for a narrative traces that bias that emerges, insistent, from within the self.[17] College reading and writing courses are filled with students like Holt, or like Hope Kaiser, who reflects: "Sometimes I think I'm not cut out for academia because I can't write well in formal language for my life." What reads at first glance as an awkward construction is in fact Kaiser dislocating language into meaning—illustrating in her sentence the disconnect between life lived and formal language used to describe that living.

Such descriptions of how selves are split, silenced, and submerged through their schooling are offered by other writers as well. Adrienne

Rich describes how her schooling to write poetry, which consisted primarily of reading and emulating male writers, clashed with her identity and impulses as a woman. What she calls dissonances—between the images in the poems of male writers that she was expected to mirror and the daily events of her own life and the words that would capture them—demanded from Rich "a constant footwork of imagination, a kind of perpetual translation, and an unconscious fragmentation of identity."[18]

"Finding the Bias: Tracing the Self Across Contexts" strives to work against that division of word from experience and of self from self, that fragmentation of language and identity. The course invites each student to "situate the self in multiple and complex ways through discourse."[19] It offers her the opportunity to move in and out of the "multiple communities against and within which she defines herself."[20] It urges her to engage in writing "as a self-defining activity."[21] By its very nature this course requires acts of translation—drawing connections and distinctions between the ways of living, speaking, understanding that are specific to the students' different communities—communities that often have few values, language, or cultural practices in common. It requires repeated acts of interpretation and repeated renderings. And the course throws into relief the ways in which the self is composed of various representations in text and of self—compositions that must be continually revised if their vitality is to be preserved.[22]

Discerning Language and Context: An Early Phase in Translation

The first contexts that we explore in the course are home and school. We read Jeannette Winterson's *Oranges Are Not the Only Fruit* and selections written by a variety of educators.[23] To evoke each student's self and particular experiences in home and school contexts, we require a number of short writing assignments. The first year we taught the course, we asked students to write a two- to three-page essay in which they defined "self" and "context" in the abstract. Although they produced very interesting papers, this assignment was extremely difficult for students, so in the second and third years we asked them instead to write a two- to three-page family story/myth from their early childhood that defines them—based on a trope Brodkey uses in her essay—which was a topic students found far more accessible and generative. The second assignment is a comparison of that myth to Brodkey's governing myth in her essay. The third is a one-page vignette that captured each student's experience of school. And the fourth is to select three texts—at least one written by a published author and at least one written by a student in the course—and to compare and contrast the three educational experiences represented in the texts.

The first of these early writing assignments strives to evoke students' original selves—the early, consciously constructed narrative of self composed (and likely re-composed) by each of them as soon as she had the cognitive capacity to engage in such composition and be metacognitively aware of the composing process—and to give students the opportunity to analyze how and perhaps why these compositions were constructed as they were. Paul John Eakin claims that "the writing of autobiography emerges as the second acquisition of language, a second coming into being of self, a self-conscious self-consciousness."[24] The essays in which students draw on their own stories and compare and contrast them with others' stories are intended to juxtapose various perspectives. In these early assignments and discussions of them, students begin to see how language is central to the identities they and others have constructed for them as well as how that language can be used to locate selves in different ways.

Reflecting on these initial essays in the portfolios they produce at the end of the semester, students analyze the ways that they used language to complete this assignment and, more generally, to construct and present themselves. One student, Sana Abida, writes: "In writing these [early] pieces, I needed to examine myself closely, consciously dig out details, view myself as a character to unravel."[25] What some students see is "how selectively I used the quotes from texts to support my arguments"[26] with no intention "to provide both sides of the story."[27] Writing early in the semester from a single angle of vision, students focus on single-minded arguments at the cost of excluding the "many biases woven into the fabric of a text"[28] and of a self.

Tracing the ways she used language to construct an argument at the start of the semester and projecting toward how she might use language differently in the future, one student, Dawn Jankov, writes:

> After mapping out my ideas of "self" I realized that the most prominent idea, for me, was uniqueness. Thus, this paper focuses on the "non-existence" of the self—a generic, universal self. For me, this was my first attempt to break free from a norm. I strove to achieve the freedom to write and think freely and stretch my mind beyond the limits. In the past I would have referred solely to the dictionary's definition. . . . Yet, the refutation also shows that I could not break completely free. Even in refuting the idea of "the self," I was relying on the generic definition as a basis for refutation. If I were asked to define the self at this point, I would work on developing a central metaphor, which I would carry throughout the paper, clearly explaining with examples. I would perhaps even write it more poetically.[29]

Jankov's analysis of her desire to break away from the norm—to change the way she uses language to name self—as well as her realization that she did not succeed in doing so illuminates the tension, both generative and frustrating, between norms of discourse practices and the desires of individuals.[30]

Jankov explores this tension further in her story of a learning experience, the third of the early assignments in the course. Her story opens with this sentence: "I learned to write in color, but then the teachers taught me to write in black and white." She proceeds to a vivid and extended description of how, at first, school for her was full of colors, but then the color drained away. She explains in her analysis of this story:

Black and white is synonymous with objectivity . . . . [In this story] I could trace my experience with objectivity and [writing] rules and regulations by focusing on describing my relation with colors . . . . Writing this story taught me a lot about the process of learning. If these rules had not been stressed so greatly in the past, I would not have improved my writing skills to the degree that I did. But now, I have internalized them, so others don't need to impress them upon me, only remind me of them . . . I believe that this is the manner in which many learn. . . . After individuals internalize certain skills, they can make valuable judgments based on understanding of these techniques. . . . Now when I write, I use a combination of the "rules" and my own "technique."[31]

Jankov is describing not only the process of learning to write well but also the process of any formal education. Mary Soliday analyzes "those moments when the self is on the threshold of possible intellectual, social, and emotional development," and she explores literacy narratives as "sites of self-translation where writers can articulate the meanings and the consequences of their passages between language worlds." She suggests that when the students in her class are "able to evaluate their experiences from an interpretive perspective, [they] achieve narrative agency by discovering that their experience is, in fact, interpretable."[32] The students enrolled in "Finding the Bias" also articulate meanings, evaluate their experiences, and achieve agency as they create these compositions early in the semester.

By starting with students' own experiences, our goal is to make explicit what students already know and assume, what has been inscribed in their own experiences and how, what the "original texts" we are working with are. Trusting that meaning is there to be found, we make these compositions legitimate texts for study and analysis. As students begin to compare texts, they open up spaces of interpretation that the juxtaposition of different things can accomplish. Just as metaphor can open up spaces of imagination by bringing together two seemingly unlike terms, by comparing and contrasting seemingly disparate texts, students open up new spaces of imagination.

One significant challenge many students face in completing the assignment in which they compare several perspectives is bringing a critical lens to bear on published writers, classmates' texts, and, in some cases, their own writing (when they choose to use their own stories as one of the three texts they analyze). Analyzing her paper, which focused on turning points in three different students' lives, one student, Serena Matthews, writes:

The main challenge I faced when writing this piece was quoting myself. Since I already knew what I felt, I had trouble referring to how I felt in my rough draft. . . . Despite my challenge, the most important thing I learned when writing this paper is depicted in the quote I used which states, "A man cannot be comfortable without his own approval" by Mark Twain. . . . Before [I wrote this paper] I thought that the actions of others caused people to be happy. Now, when I analyze decisions that people make, I know that they are because this person is trying to reach an optimal goal that they have set for themselves.[33]

Matthews's struggle with gaining enough perspective on her own experience to write about it, and the lesson she learns about people's motivation for action, including her own, teach her important life as well as composition lessons. Another student, Jean McMann, makes explicit this connection between composing a life and composing texts when she writes: "Looking back at my work this semester, it is impossible to see my [academic] progress without simultaneously tracing the progress I've made in my life."[34] The translation of her texts, McMann suggests, is inextricably connected with her translation of herself.

When more than one perspective is brought to bear on something, one of the most powerful realizations that students have is that the search for truth in compositions and in life, the belief that such a thing as truth with a capital "T" even exists, is problematic. Of her attitude and approach to writing early in the course, another student, Marianna Jolie, writes: "I was still in the mode of searching out 'the answer,' pinpointing 'the truth,' and piling up concrete evidence in support of it."[35] Likewise, Mindy Sutton explains: "When I entered [this class], I had hoped for my ideas about and grasp of the truth to change and grow. Instead, I find myself looking for a different perspective on the ideas I already have, a different side of the tiny truths I already know rather than an epiphany of cohesion of all of those bits of reality into The Answer I sought at the beginning."[36]

While this point could be made about intellectual understanding in general, here it is a more precise point about translation: that in compositions—including compositions of the self—only parts of an idea, experience, or message can be captured and made meaningful. Those parts that are captured and rendered are the translation; they are what is selected, integrated, and carried forward. In textual compositions, they constitute the version that is settled on (for a time), submitted in a class, published. In compositions of self, they include "an awareness of self-continuity and enduring, personally meaningful memories."[37]

The Challenges of Translation: Deeper In

As the students enter the now-familiar classroom, they are confronted with a painting on display against the dark background of the green blackboard. It is an oil painting of a market scene in Nepal. One or two students recognize it. To most it is utterly unfamiliar. I ask the students to place themselves somewhere within the painting and to spend five minutes writing a short description of what they see and how they feel from that perspective. I tell them that I will ask them to read these descriptions aloud once they are finished.

Some students move closer, sit on the floor in front of the painting. Some remain in their seats. All look from painting to paper and paper to painting as they move in their minds between what they see and what they write. The room is silent, full of composition—of the translation of image through imagination to text.

After the students finish writing, I ask them to read their descriptions aloud, one at a time, without comment or explanation of any kind. One voice after another fills the room. Some students locate themselves outside the frame of the painting, most position themselves somewhere within it. Some emphasize color and light, some concentrate on the activities of those represented in the painting, and some offer minimal literal detail and focus on what is going on in their minds. With each description those listening discern the location of the speaker, see the painting anew through her words, relocate themselves between the descriptions they have written and each new description they hear.

When we have heard from every student, we discuss what issues these descriptions raise about introducing a setting and locating the self in that setting, as Dorinne Kondo does in her opening chapter of Crafting Selves, *which the students read in preparation for today's class discussion. Kondo uses in her first chapter what Clifford Geertz has called thick description,*[38] *and she evokes through her words the sights and sounds, the smells and images, of the city in Japan in which she lived. The students have engaged in a form of thick description as well, and as Winterson reminds us, "Everyone who tells a story tells it differently, just to remind us that everyone sees it differently."*[39] *The juxtaposition of their different texts throws into relief the fact that there can be as many versions of a story as there are people telling it.*

In the selection that students read from *Crafting Selves*, Kondo offers first standard, anthropological, "thick" description, then she undoes and complicates it. We are doing a version of that here with this activity of describing the painting then analyzing the descriptions. An assignment that follows shortly after this activity is presented in the syllabus this way: "Tell the same story or offer the same (focus of) analysis from two or three perspectives and then write a postscript or afterward (one page) which offers a critique of which perspective carries what kind of authority and why." The first part of this assignment is about taking on and tracing biases. It is essential that students assume those perspectives and write from them, not simply describe them. It is equally important for the second part of the assignment that students then step back and analyze how as authors they invested each perspective with authority—how they followed, or failed to follow, each bias faithfully.

The multiple-perspectives assignment is pivotal for students in terms of re-defining the self and the compositions selves create. Furthermore, the analyses of what they produce in response to the assignment, offered both in the final segment of the assignment and in the portfolios that students compile at the end of the semester, provide particularly vivid illustrations of translation. Through the multiple-perspectives assignment, and in their final reflections on it at the end of the semester, students strive to effect translations of themselves by struggling to translate different perspectives into texts. In attempting to translate their own and others' perspectives and words in a deliberate and self-conscious way in a text, then reflecting on that attempt, students transform their understanding, and thus themselves, through the attempt and the analysis of that attempt. This transformation makes meaning for themselves and for others. It is not simply change; it is change made between people as well as within individual students, and earlier interpretations are contained but repositioned by new ones.

Like the course as a whole, the multiple-perspectives assignment deliberately challenges conventions that separate the personal and the academic. Although the instructions we give to students regarding the assignment do not specify the kind of story students should tell, in my section of the course most students choose to tell very personal stories, and they almost invariably choose to include their own perspectives as one of the multiple versions. In choosing to tell very personal stories, students relive life "events in discourses with others."[40] Furthermore, they "call upon the resources of their personal lives in order to make sense of their subject matter and to negotiate their stances relative to the conventional demands of academic discourse."[41] The subject matter in this case is bias. Their stances relative to conventional demands of academic discourse vary. But the intersection of bias, personal stories, and analysis throws into relief both the disconnect between the personal and the academic and what it might mean to reconnect them.

Many students feel a strong need to re-tell the story they choose to focus on for this assignment, to work it through. Raushan Rakhmetullin's urgency in choosing to write about a moment when she became aware of the loss of a significant family member is representative of this need. Describing her conversation with another family member about the event, and her own subsequent silence regarding it, Rakhmetullin writes about her composing process: "All the words of our telephone conversation still ring in my ears. I had to voice all of my experience."[42] Citing Walter Benjamin, Azade Seyhan reminds us that "a translation emerges not from the life (*Leben*) of the original but from its afterlife—literally its survival or endurance (*Überleben*). In other words, translation grants a second life to the original. If autobiography is seen as a form of self-translation

. . . [a writer can get] a new lease on life" in what she writes.[43] The combination of emotional investment in an event that was, for many students, life-shaping, and the pressure, always present in an elite educational institution, to write well and achieve academic success, make for a highly charged atmosphere around this assignment. Personal desires and academic impulses intersect for students in complex ways.

The unconventional nature of the assignment coupled with students' emotional investment in the stories they tell require that as instructors we must ensure that clear structures and supports are in place for students to keep them from straying into an unexamined confessional mode. Comfort suggests that the reason many student efforts to include the personal in their academic writing fail is that they are "invited to invoke the personal, but not given any explicit rhetorical insight regarding its effective use."[44] The multiple-perspectives assignment requires not only that students write the same story from two or three perspectives; they must also write a postscript, an analysis of the process, the challenges, frustrations, epiphanies, and so on that they experienced while writing the different versions of the stories. This postscript may not simply be descriptive, nor may it simply reiterate what each perspective already revealed. Rather, it must offer a cogent, thoughtful, distanced, but still connected critical analysis of the experience of authoring the different perspectives—an analytical account of the authorial choices students made, the rhetorical effectiveness or ineffectiveness of those choices, and the lessons about reading and writing that students learned through completing the assignment. By offering these guidelines, and reminding students of them throughout the time we spend on this assignment, we strive to provide the structures and supports that facilitate students' successful inclusion of the personal in their academic writing.

The multiple-perspectives assignment integrates three elements Madeleine Grumet identifies as essential: situation, narrative, and interpretation. As she explains: "The first, situation, acknowledges that we tell our story as a speech event that involves the social, cultural and political relations in and to which we speak. Narrative . . . invites all the specificity, presence and power that the symbolic and semiotic registers of our speaking can provide. And interpretation provides another voice, a reflexive and more distant one."[45] The assignment requires that the students take on the first two of these simultaneously, but they begin by writing their own version of the story, writing from the perspective with which most students say they feel the most comfortable, of which they feel the most certain. They evoke narratives, most often from their pre-college lives and almost always involving family, friends, or other intimate relationships, that they "know" from their perspectives but that they want to work through again. These renderings of their own perspectives are, of course, translations, which many students recognize, but they generally experience less difficulty with and express less concern about representing their perspectives and themselves in texts than they express about representing others' perspectives and selves.

Some students come face to face early on, however, with the potential this assignment has to upset their confidence or comfort in their own perspectives and the stories they have told themselves and others about themselves. Of course they know in the abstract that different people have different perspectives on an event, but knowing that in the abstract is not the same as learning it on a deeper level—of thinking through the consequences of that difference, as a deep feature of communication, whether in writing or in conversation.

Katherine Stevenson articulates the necessity of re-grounding herself in her own experience before she can begin to imagine other people's: "It was essential that I wrote my account first to establish myself and my bias." Not only was it essential for her to identify her bias for herself, it was also essential to establish it for a reader. This assertion of her own narrative gave her the confidence to turn to others' versions: "Because I felt confident that my own story was my own personal 'truth,' I was no longer afraid of finding a story that was different than my own interpretation because my story was already strongly established and I believed in its validity."[46] Stevenson's approach proved reassuring to her; she was successful at re-stabilizing herself and accepting her version as one, but not the only valid one.

Melissa Holt had a more unsettling experience. After having drafted her own perspective on the event she planned to write about—the first time she met her boyfriend's mother—she consulted her boyfriend about his recollection of the event. Holt was stunned by how much his recollection differed from hers, and she recognized, with a jolt, that "I expected his memory to support my own." Reflecting on this startling awakening, Holt writes: "Before even writing the perspectives, I had subconsciously centered the story around my experiences, viewing [his] and [his mother's] renditions as supplementary. As the tailor of these pieces, the reconstructor of these events, I inevitably awarded myself more emotional authority, and the other two characters only possess the thoughts and feelings I allow them to have."[47] This statement is a very honest and sophisticated expression of what many students may know on some level but, if pushed, might not wish to admit: they believe that their version is *the* true one, even if they acknowledge that others have other perspectives. Not only does Holt think about the emotional consequences of this realization but also about the cognitive and intellectual ones—how that authority matters in explaining, describing, presenting the event for a reader.

These students' reflections on their assumptions about composition and its relationship to truth offer glimpses into students' rethinking of themselves in relation to others and all selves in relation to composition. As notions such as that there is a true story, and that it is possible to tell one, come under scrutiny, so do the "true stories" that students have told of their own lives. For some this scrutiny results in a reinforcement of the perspective and self that students thought they knew; it resonates. For others it results in a complicating of that self and its previous compositions. But in all cases it results in a reconsideration of the notion of truth. And once "the true story" as a category, as a possibility, comes into question, the necessity of translation becomes clear, because if there is always more than one version of a story or an experience that can be told, there will always be a need to re-interpret and re-render.

After students have settled on their own initial version of the story they tell for the multiple-perspectives assignment, they must move on to attempting to tell one or two other versions. Like translators of a text from one language into another, students approach this assignment with known voices in their heads; the perspectives students attempt to represent belong, for the most part, to people they know—themselves, family, friends—and issue from contexts with which they are familiar. Like translators of texts, students' first concern is with finding or choosing the right words in which to render those familiar voices. They pose and answer questions for themselves such as, "Would he use that word?" and "Is that something she would say?"

Some students do not find this a daunting prospect. Rebecca Jansen states: "I have no problems writing from someone else's perspective. Although I tried to be as accurate as possible, I know there is no way I was completely correct in the choices I made. It does not matter, however, because this is my representation of how I think of these people."[48] Jansen leans toward one pole of what Sherod Santos claims is a necessary balance in translating: on the one hand, "the artistic impulse to take over a text, to overcome its otherness and force its assimilation to one's own language" and on the other, "that scruple which begs to preserve the integrity of that otherness."[49]

Jansen is somewhat of an exception in her comfort with rendering others' perspectives; most students are concerned about preserving the integrity of whatever otherness they are struggling to render. As Linda Evanson explains: "the hardest aspect of this assignment was trying to get inside other people's heads and think as they do . . . I discovered that describing a person and how they think and then thinking like them are very different."[50] Elizabeth Bonner offers a similar explanation of her struggle with this assignment: "It is one thing to inspect and explore my own biases, quite another to try and put myself into the biases of two other individuals. At first it was intimidating to think of telling a serious story through the eyes of my mother and sister. I had a fear of misrepresenting them, or doing little justice to their feelings."[51] Bonner is concerned about what the narrator in A. S. Byatt's *The Biographer's Tale* suggests is true of all writing: that it betrays "our own desire to translate everything, everyone, all reasoning, all irrational hope and fear, into our own Procrustean grid of priorities."[52]

As with the challenge of finding words in a translation from one to another language, a good translator, according to Marjorie Agosín, "translates what is not said." A good translator does not focus on the words, Agosín continues, but on "how to arrange all of these words so that these words will have a meaning, so that these words will have an echo, will have a sound."[53] Students face this challenge if the words are in their own language but need to convey the sense of belonging to others. Brenda Gillman describes the challenge this way: "The most difficult part of writing these two perspectives was always attempting to keep certain ideas out of them; there was so much to say, but not all of it was true to the voice in either perspective."[54] Because the voices Gillman strives to represent belong to real people, and thus have a vocabulary and tone familiar to her in real time, she hears in her head an "echo of the original"[55] but struggles with how to capture and render it.

Every act of naming, listening, or reading, any act of communication at all, is a translation.[56] Rendering someone else's perspective, particularly if it is situated in another language and culture, is a particular form of translation. Sana Abida explains the challenge she faced in rendering her mother's perspective: "I am used to hearing her speak Oriya, and even her English seems to me more like Oriya words translated to English with the tone remaining mostly Oriya."[57] Abida describes her task succinctly: "I had a multiple translation problem: I did not know how to translate my idea of her thoughts into written language." Abida wishes "to preserve the integrity of that otherness"[58] in her mother's words. Her efforts reflect Antoine Berman's claim, quoted in Douglas Robinson's *What Is Translation?*: "Translation that fails to maintain alterity, or succumbs to 'the danger of killing the dimension of the foreign'—translation that . . . erases all trace of foreignness, otherness, alterity—is impure or 'bad translation.'"[59] Abida is striving to produce a good translation.

More than writing their own version of the story they choose to tell, writing someone else's version helps students become aware of the translation in which they are engaged and the ethical as well as linguistic dimensions carried in the choices they make. Translation is never simply a matter of finding for the words already written in one language corresponding words in another. Some words have no counterparts,[60] and meanings are not so easily transferred. A successful translation is more than transliteration; it is the re-articulation of a complex human experience.[61] For these reasons, students are right to struggle with re-rendering the voices and perspectives of others and themselves.

Some students frame the challenge of choosing words so they "will have a sound,"[62] an "echo of the original,"[63] as an issue of loyalty. Abida writes about her struggle to be "loyal" to the people she represents in her story—her mother, her brother, and herself. The process with which Abida struggled is the process in which any translator engages. She explains: "Loyalty could have meant making readers see my family members the way I see them, even though that might have involved deviating from their actual behavior to make the writing fit my readers' context. Or it might mean sticking to the 'truth' as far as I could, or to my true beliefs when I did not know the truth. Or it could mean disclosing as little as possible and thus protecting my family from . . . outsiders."[64] Levy suggests that "translating is a decision process: a series of a certain number of consecutive situations—moves, as in a game—situations imposing on the translator the necessity of choosing among a certain (and very often exactly definable) number of alternatives."[65] As Abida puts it: "Trying to write from others' perspectives . . . always involves a compromise of some sort—I can only have the choice of which direction to compromise in."

Thus composition is about withholding as well as furnishing meaning. It can entail streamlining or narrowing possible avenues of interpretation by selectively shaping a text according to specific interests. The multiple-perspectives assignment throws into relief these qualities of composition and translation required both to compose and to learn through and from the composing process.

Translations of Texts/Translations of Selves

As students become conscious of the choices they must make in composing the different perspectives for this assignment, they begin to gain two different kinds of insights: into the perspectives of the others they are trying to represent and into their own perspectives. It's as though the translation process holds up an interpretive lens in two directions. Raushan Rakhmetullin captures the dual effect in this succinct statement: "Through assuming my mother's bias, not only did I get to understand her better but I also realized that my point of view is also a bias." Rebecca Jansen surprised herself with similar insights that she gained through telling the story of an old family argument from the perspectives of her sister and mother as well as herself: "I have been forced to acknowledge the validity of my sister's point of view and my mother's behavior. The worst part, seeing all these events in retrospect, is that had I realized what I was doing at the time and how damaging it was to my own situation, I would have acted differently."[66] Through completing this assignment, Jansen gained an appreciation for her family's perspectives that she did not have before, and she gained a critical perspective on herself and the repercussions in real life of the stances she has taken.

Prema Nabin explains how her awareness increased in these two directions as well, how she too gained insights about others and herself:

> Being forced to "speak" through my father and my grandfather gave me an opportunity to stand in their shoes, advocate their roles, voice their concerns, and weigh their responsibilities and their priorities. In doing this I came to a clearer understanding of our differences and came to appreciate some of the sacrifices and some of the mistakes we have made. I feel less accusatory towards them now, because I have let myself explain what they felt in a way that makes sense to me. I took from all of our long discussion and arguments the components of what they said that felt most convincing to me and reiterated them so that I could hear them explicitly. I also saw how narrow-minded I had been all along, how badly afflicted with tunnel vision. What I feel I have achieved is a heightened understanding of a situation I was too closely tied to by stepping a little bit out of my own set place and letting other people seep through, exploring the same thing through their eyes, recognizing in a tangible fashion that I'm not the only one involved, that other people have their reasons for what they do too, and that their decisions and judgments are just as valid, even if they aren't agreeable to me.[67]

These recognitions of others' perspectives, and the complementary revision of students' own, parallel one of the effects of translation: Steiner explains that "our own being is modified by each occurrence of comprehensive appropriation."[68] As we take and re-render words, both those of others and our own, we change not only the words but also ourselves. As we translate, we are translated.

Katherine Stevenson offers a comparable epiphany, but she adds another twist: "as impossible as it is in reality, the mere experience of creating biases for [the two other perspectives from which I wrote] was by far the most rewarding risk because it brought to light more aspects of myself that I would never have discovered from my own autobiographical bias alone."[69] Embedded in what is almost a throwaway phrase at the beginning of her reflection, Stevenson identifies one of the essential qualities of translation: its impossibility. She is referring specifically to the impossibility of knowing another's experience from the inside, and the ideal would be that in translating one could achieve such knowledge. As Jose Ortega y Gasset queries, "Isn't the task of translating necessarily a utopian task?"[70] Edwin Gentzler echoes this sentiment: translation is "concerned with the recovery and representation of meaning (or the impossibility thereof)."[71]

Students express this realization in a number of ways. June Novak writes: "I discovered (after much trouble) that I cannot be someone else

or even step outside of myself. . . . Trying to construct two perspectives
. . . does not mean actually accomplishing two different perspectives."
She elaborates: "Being able to actually tell the same story from two perspectives requires separating from yourself, stepping outside of yourself,
letting go of your interpretation of the event. You have to be someone else.
Regardless of what language techniques I used, how hard I tried to let go
of my interpretations, or how different both perspectives seem to an outsider, there is only an ostensible or surface difference. Deep within both
stories, I find myself."[72] Holt came to a related realization about the impossibility of translating someone else's perspective through one's own:
"As a writer I may supply words, but voices can never be duplicated."[73]

Attempting to write as someone else, reflecting on that attempt, and
recognizing the impossibility of the challenge prompts students to call
into question some of the assumptions and beliefs that previously guided
their thinking. Holt writes: "I have come to detest the word 'authority'
because in its traditional definition, it implies right and wrong, good and
bad, model and student. I am beginning to learn that authority is an
extremely subjective term, and is defined by perception."[74] Jansen elaborates on this notion: "We only have authority in relation to others. . . .
Only after writing [this paper did I realize] . . . how much people are
defined by their relationships to others—how much we define ourselves
that way. . . . Without others, authority does not exist."[75] What these students are learning is that "translation is not an abstract equivalence game,
divorced from real people's actions in a social context, but a richly social
process,"[76] an "ongoing negotiation between self and other,"[77] a process
through which not only is the message changed,[78] but so is the messenger.

Re-rendering Selves

Students have studied Defining Eye: Women Photographers of the Twentieth
Century. *Their assignment for class today was to select two or three photographs
from the book that capture and represent for them different moments in their own
learning throughout the course. We begin the discussion with some reviewing and
redefining of terms that this book throws into relief: What does "defining eye"
mean? What is the relationship between "eye" and "I"? How do photographs capture time and space, people and places, as opposed to how words capture them?
How do you "read" a photograph? Are you always "reading into" it?*[79]

*We then talk about the specific vocabulary of photography—composition, qual-
ity of light, frame, focus, angle, perspective, exposure, proportion. Some students
are photographers, and they bring special expertise to this exploration. Some re-see
photography and the relationship between photographer and photographed
through this discussion. We talk about how in* Ways of Seeing, *John Berger
writes about how in most classic painting (most of it done by men) men look at*

women and women look at themselves being looked at,[80] *and we talk about how a collection like the one students have read may (or may not) do or allow for something different.*

The students then begin to explain the photographs to one another; each one captures and conveys different key moments of their learning in the course. The photographs become metaphors for those moments: juxtapositions between unlike things that open up spaces of imagination and interpretation. As she later writes in her portfolio, using a photograph called "Plant Detail" by Sonya Nowkawiak,[81] *Abida explains how early in this course she had to "zoom in on myself, as the camera must have zoomed in on the leaf in the picture."*[82] *Writing about the photograph "Atomic Love,"*[83] *to capture a moment in the course when she found her bias, Holt explains:*

Lives can be centered around events, around memories, and around selves. To me, it seems that the woman in this picture leads such a self-centered life, not even viewing the figures surrounding her as humans, but only as props to her existence. I look at this photograph and think of how much more vibrant it would be if each of the characters could move, if each of them could tell their story, if the reader was not compelled to the see the picture only through the eyes of one person. Learning how to view the world as a patchwork of equally important experiences, rather than through a telescope, was liberating to me. The most important thing I learned about biases is that they wouldn't exist in a world of just one person. They are determined and evaluated by their relationships to other biases. When I realized this, I felt as though my world lost a focal point, but was simultaneously made more rich and beautiful when the props and passersby of my life gained existence in their own right.[84]

June Novak, a photographer herself, presents her own photographs, including "Accomplishment," which is a color self-portrait and which represents Novak's sense that "I have reached within myself to go against the norm . . . I have come to the realization that I am deep within whatever I say and do."[85]

In the postscript to Defining Eye, *Lucy Lippard explains that she uses the metaphor of photography in her writing and daily life to "frame and select," a process of "'bringing to light.'"*[86] *As students read and re-read texts and themselves, they live the metaphor of translation.*

Contrary to what one might expect, students find these realizations of the impossibility of rerendering their own or others' words and the relative and relational nature of bias and authority liberating. They feel released to take further risks of expression and interpretation. They feel propelled toward the translation of themselves. They embrace the possibilities afforded them through learning the double meaning of perspective: to see from a particular, narrow angle and to see as though through a wide angle. As students still in a fairly early phase of their formal higher education, they take up with enthusiasm the possibility of looking at things as if they were otherwise[87] and of translating themselves into new selves.

At the end of the semester, in the portfolios that students compile, they capture the transformations in their sense of composition and self.

The pronouns that students use in their portfolios reflect the different choices of composition students make after a semester of critical analysis and they embody the transformation in understanding of themselves that the students undergo. Mawusi Jones opens her portfolio with these words: "When referring to the self, the individual, Rastafarians use the word I-N-I. It is a complex word that expresses the multiplicity of the individual. It is spelled with two 'I's and an 'N' in between. I like that! To me the 'I's demonstrate many sides of the self and the 'N' consists of everything else that shapes the 'I'/eye."[88] Jones writes her portfolio in the voice of I-N-I.

In the preface to her portfolio, Sana Abida writes to her reader: "I do not yet know who you are. You may be me, or you may be a stranger. In fact, even if you are me, you are a stranger, because you will be a different me from the one who is writing this letter. I hope you rejoice in the difference." Not only does she recognize herself as occupying multiple pronouns, Abida self-consciously uses different spelling conventions to reflect the different aspects of herself. She explains: "You may, perchance, notice some inconsistencies in spelling. I am aware of them. I have two conflicting selves—one conforms to American spelling and the other clings to British spelling. To mark the spirit of freedom and acceptance of bias, I have chosen to spell each word here according to the standard I really wished to follow at each point."[89] As Abida learns, she can render herself and her learning in a hybrid language, and she need not be "split by the difference."[90]

Holt opens her portfolio with a letter to her future self that pushes pronouns to capture the multiplicity of her self: "Before you read this, please remember that we never do things the easy way. We are stubborn, and impetuous, and we would rather climb a thorn-covered mountain than give someone the satisfaction of showing us the shortcut. I tell you this in case you've forgotten why we organized our portfolio this way . . . this collection traces our learning, from the initial work, to finding our bias, to accepting its value. I stitched together the texts we read and the writing that we did, and left the thread of our bias showing." "'A translation that "smacks of translation" is not necessarily bad (whereas, conversely, it might be said that a translation that does not smack at all of translation is necessarily bad.'"[91] Holt's leaving "the thread of our bias showing" lets her text smack of translation. It lets both the literal text and the self that has composed it be good translations.

Holt's use of pronouns not only captures the multiplicity of her self but reflects as well how that self/those selves must be continually translated. This pushing of pronouns, another example of what T. S. Eliot calls dislocating language into meaning, is an approach to composition and a rendering of self that Adrienne Rich uses as well. In one of her poems that we read in the course, "Diving into the Wreck," Rich uses the metaphor of searching a sunken ship to capture her experience, as a woman, of looking for her self in "the book of myths" that is the record, the history, of human experience. She writes:

We circle silently
about the wreck
we dive into the hold.
I am she: I am he

whose drowned face sleeps with open eyes . . .
We are, I am, you are
by cowardice or courage
the one who find our way
back to this scene
carrying a knife, a camera
a book of myths
in which
our names do not appear.[92]

In this poem, an "I" can be both "he" and "she," a "one" can be a "we," a single person and a group of people can work together to critically analyze—and perhaps subsequently re-write—a version of history that excludes them. This individual but also shared project, and the struggle to make language capture its complexities, are processes students enrolled in "Finding the Bias" experience as well. The compositions these students chose to construct constituted efforts to retell more inclusive but not necessarily entirely coherent or complete stories. They brought together two or more things to fashion, to construct, to design in a particular way. They may well have come to certain terms, reconciled, or settled. But they did not see their compositions as complete or final. Rather, they saw them as partial representations, selections, interpretations, renderings at a particular moment in time and in context. Likewise, the selves doing the composing were more inclusive but not necessarily entirely coherent or complete selves. They were also selves that must be perceived as different and rendered differently over time.[93]

Sometimes, the different selves people are at different points in time are apparent in the translations they render; Sherod Santos tells of William Wordsworth's choice of composition: "When Wordsworth in the 1850 Prelude omits from the 1805 version over three hundred lines recounting the story of his affair with Annette Vallon (told through the characters of Vaudracour and Julia), has he not performed an act of translation? Has he not attempted to 'carry across,' to render for posterity, a version of himself as a young man that was more reflective of himself as an old man?"[94] We might expand upon Santos's interpretation of why Wordsworth made this choice, speculating that the latter representation might have been more socially acceptable or more suited to his vision of himself in posterity. This example is especially apt for a discussion of young people translating themselves because the "Prelude" focuses particularly on translation between selves with different cognitive capacities: the child has the experience but doesn't know it or what it means; the adult has lost the experience of experiencing without critical awareness but gained the capacity to know and interpret that experience.

With less time than Wordsworth across which to translate themselves and a more explicit challenge to do so, each of the students quoted in this discussion not only recognized but also embraced her multiplicity— her various selves in relation to other selves over time. Each followed in her own way Dorinne Kondo's lead in learning to speak of "selves in the plural."[95] This learning to speak of selves in the plural was facilitated not only by the way the course writing assignments required taking up and analyzing different biases. It was supported as well by the fact that at every stage of this process of taking up and analyzing biases, students were supported and challenged by others in the course.

This support and challenge can be found through identification. Jean McMann writes of how, through reading a peer's explanation of a particular kind of transformation of self, she realized what she wanted in terms of her own transformation: "In Anna's piece I identified what I wanted to work toward: I wanted to start learning for myself."[96] This support and challenge can be found in direct critique. Penny Miller writes: "The final drafts included in this portfolio have been influenced by not only me but also by those who made suggestions on how to clarify, expand, and refine my papers. Without their influences, I could not have grown as I have."[97] Ellen Barton expands on how this kind of support and challenge can work: "[The members of my writing group] were willing to suggest additions and changes without affecting the degree to which my individuality came through in my writing. If there was a point that didn't work, they told me. I didn't feel offended, because I had the right to accept or reject anything that was said."[98] Some students take this kind of collaboration to a significant extreme. Hope Kaiser included in her portfolio both her own critical reflection on her evolution in "Finding the Bias" and the critical reading one member of her writing group offered of her development throughout the course. She explains: "I am choosing to include Emily's perspective on my writing and growth with my own . . . because that is how we have been working all semester—our thoughts bouncing off each other's."[99]

These students describe a deeply collaborative process that embodies what Sfard calls learning as participation.[100] Engaged in an active, co-construction of meaning and identity, they have learned to read one another and themselves for multiple meanings, and they have learned to speak in new, polyvocal ways.

Gained in Translation

The education that students in "Finding the Bias" effect is at once duplication, revision, and re-creation, with meaning lost, preserved, and created anew. This education is not a single rendering that fixes and defines the student's self. Rather, it is a recursive as well as a progressive process of reading and rendering texts and selves in relationship, with an eye to the multiple interests that come together in that relationship.[101] At the metaphorical level, it is also a reflexive act, and as such it becomes the student's own.

Rabassa's assertion that "a translation is never finished"[102] is echoed by students in "Finding the Bias." Writing in the first personal plural, from and to her present and future selves, Melissa Holt characterizes her rendering of her learning in the course: "The finishing knot is loosely tied, so that you may pick it up in the future. I hope the construction will never be complete."[103] Katherine Stevenson writes about this unfinishedness as something she now sees as an exciting opening, a compelling possibility, rather than a frightening prospect:

What I can take forward from this class is a new sense of confidence, and the knowledge that I am worthy to be heard, to express myself, and to share my energy and passion just as I am right now. I used to be leery of taking risks and exploring new areas alone, even within contexts that I was already comfortable in, a constant little internal monologue playing in my mind: "Omigod! I'm not ready yet! Wait! It won't be perfect, I can't do this right now." I realized I was always waiting for perfect confidence and ability that would never come. By seeing that what I am capable of doing right now is important and worthwhile, I have gained the confidence I always thought would come with future perfection.[104]

Here Stevenson echoes Freire's claim that "education does not make us educable. It is our awareness of being unfinished that makes us educable."[105]

The students I have quoted in this discussion have learned that composition takes many different forms and that there are as many biases to be traced in a text, and a self, as there are threads in a piece of fabric or thoughts in a mind. They have translated themselves, but there is "no identity in detail" between the "original" and the translation.[106] There are, rather, unfinished works and selves that will be translated again and again, with each new reading and writing of a text, in each new context and in each new relationship.

The most powerful translation in education is the translation of the self effected by the self. And the recognition that this process is an unending one. The way that self is conceptualized in "Finding the Bias" and the opportunities the students in the course have to define and redefine self within and across contexts stand in sharp contrast to the tendency in higher education—as in almost all but the earliest levels of education—to establish and fix particular roles, relationships, and responsibilities. The students who complete "Finding the Bias" emerge from this course more aware of, facile with, but also more cautious in their assumptions about words, meaning, authority, and other constituents of texts. They emerge as well with more complex, cautious, and confident notions about selves, both their own and others'.

Chapter 4
Translating Within and Against Institutional Structures

Are we the sage on the stage? Or are we in some sense facilitators? Are we in fact not all that different from our students except that maybe we're a couple of years older and we've done these things [that we are introducing to them]?

—A college professor

After a day of work for some and a day of travel for others, a group of forty professors, students, librarians, and instructional technologists[1] issuing from ten different colleges and universities in the Northeast arrive at Bryn Mawr College. They have come to participate in a workshop called "Talking Toward Techno-Pedagogy: A Collaboration Across Colleges and Constituencies." Relieved to be out of the heat of the June sun, participants and facilitators slowly assemble in Bryn Mawr's alumni building in a long, open room decorated with antique furniture and Persian rugs and windowed all around. Over drinks and hors d'oeuvres participants mingle with colleagues and with potential collaborators they are meeting for the first time.

When the room rings with the sound of comfort and connection among people, we, the four facilitators, formally introduce ourselves and the others who make the workshop run smoothly—our three student interns and the anthropologist who documents the conversations. Two of us have driven down from a college in New England, and the other two work at Bryn Mawr. We reiterate the goals of the workshop that we emphasized as part of each invitation to participate: that the workshop is intended to foster a collaborative exploration of the challenges and possibilities both of integrating technology in a meaningful way into teaching and of working collaboratively with others to do so. We express our hope that the four days that workshop participants will spend with us and with one another will inspire a sharing of perspectives and ideas and that all participants will listen to and learn from one another. We emphasize in particular that each constituency represented at the workshop—professors, students, librarians, and instructional technologists—has expertise and a legitimate perspective in this collaboration.

After these introductions, participants sit down to dinner in the faculty dining room. People are seated neither according to constituency nor according to college. We have attempted to mix participants across both, with a facilitator or one of the student interns or the anthropologist at each table of six or so. When people have finished the main course, we ask them to take a few minutes and write on the cards we have left at each table a few words of definition in response to the question, "What is collaboration?"

Participants begin with basic definitions: "Collaboration is dividing up tasks and designating different people as responsible for each." "Collaboration is learning what you are good at and what others are good at and figuring out how to make those things work together." "Collaboration is working together from day one through the culmination of a project—coming up with ideas, making decisions, and implementing them." Then participants pose questions that follow from these definitions: "What can we expect from each other in terms of cooperation?" "How can instructional technologists collaborate more closely with faculty in the development of their courses and during the semester (in a deeper way than just helping them put up web pages or work the equipment in the classroom)?" "How do we foster good communication between students and faculty on more equal footing?"

After everyone has jotted down their definitions and questions, voices start to refill the room as, table by table, we begin to talk through people's ideas. The definitions that participants articulate constitute their premises and practices of collaboration and will thus inform the work they do at the workshop and after they return to their home institutions. By beginning with an invitation to formulate and articulate these assumptions, we hope to help participants make explicit for themselves, for one another, and for us the guiding principles of their practices.

During each of the three consecutive summers in which "Talking Toward Techno-Pedagogy" took place,[2] four constituency groups participated—college professors, librarians, instructional technologists, and students. In this chapter, I focus primarily on the experiences of the professors. Far to the other end of the continuum of formal education from the college sophomores upon whom I focused in the last chapter, the professors brought with them to the workshop long institutional histories and varying lengths of personal histories in the role of professor—institutional and personal versions of original selves. Furthermore, whereas the sophomores occupied a role from within which they were expected to grow and change, the professors struggled in the face of new languages, new ways of interpreting, and new ways of interacting from within an institutionally defined role not premised on the expectation of growth and change but rather on the importance of maintaining subjects and practices long upheld in higher education—certain notions of original content and behavior. Thus they faced multiple challenges to their sense of self, to their established practices, and to institutional expectations.

The vignette with which I open this chapter highlights the central premises and modes of interaction that guided "Talking Toward Techno-Pedagogy":

conversation, critical reflection on roles and relationships, and collaboration. Each of these challenged the professors to resist impulses toward literal translations of the "originals" many brought with them—particular notions of content, media, and (self-)representation. Traditional or dominant practices in their respective fields as well as criteria for promotion and tenure in their respective colleges created both spoken and unspoken calls to professors to reproduce what they (or others in their place) have always done. Canonical texts and accepted research practices, disciplinary discourses, standard library or lab resources and materials, and autonomous management of courses are examples of sources and practices that many consider fixed, set, or given—originals to be preserved or reproduced. As the professors worked to learn new languages and ways of interacting with others, this compulsion to preserve originals with identity in detail,[3] to replicate methods,[4] or to search for one-to-one correspondences[5] created a tension between old approaches to teaching and what is taught and new possibilities for both. The challenge that "Talking Toward Techno-Pedagogy" posed was to read, respond to, and compose texts and selves and to work toward comprehensible and resonant interpretations that would have different meanings for different people in different contexts.

The Context and the Customs

Since I have been teaching at the college level, I have spent most of my time in undergraduate courses with learners who were formally designated "students." Between 2000 and 2002, with support from a grant from the Andrew W. Mellon Foundation, colleagues and I worked in collaboration to make a place for professors, librarians, and instructional technologists, as well as students, to be "students"—a place called "Talking Toward Techno-Pedagogy."[6] Professors—those assumed to be positioned in the role opposite to student—are sometimes unaccustomed to and often blocked from engaging in particular forms of ongoing education.[7] Because of the institutional structures within which they work, and because to change themselves they must work against many of these structures, the translations these "students" effect are often difficult or incomplete, fraught or problematic, but the process in which they are engaged, when they take it up, is nonetheless a process of translation.

In conceptualizing "Talking Toward Techno-Pedagogy," my colleagues and I deliberately foregrounded "talking." Our goal in doing so reflects our goal for the workshop overall: to encourage and facilitate processes of communication and collaboration that would start with thinking and talking through pedagogical issues at a basic level and then move toward explorations of how technology fits, or sometimes doesn't fit, with teaching.

We also wanted to highlight the possibility of collaboration across college contexts as well as across roles assigned to different members of a college community. We have kept up with people since their participation in the workshop through hosting several reunions and conducting follow-up interviews.[8]

For each iteration of this workshop, we invited teams of four, each team from one of the participating colleges.[9] The teams consisted of a faculty member, a rising junior in that faculty member's discipline, a librarian whose area of expertise is in, when possible, or near the faculty member's discipline, and an instructional technologist. During the workshop these teams were challenged on one level to explore their roles and how they might work together to integrate technology into teaching and learning. On a deeper level they were challenged to unearth, think about, and talk through questions at the very root of education: What is learning? What should be learned? How? On both levels, the workshop was like the course in which the college sophomores enrolled: it focused on the surface on standard fare—integrating technology into teaching—but deeper down it called for a reconceptualization of the very processes and purposes of education—in the terms I use in this book, a rethinking of education as banking or cure and a consideration of education as translation.

The teams spent the four days together planning how they would collaborate to revise one of the professor's courses through or with technology. The days were divided up into the following forums:

- Small, constituency-based, breakout groups, which offered participants an opportunity to talk across colleges with people who share their institutional role.
- Presentations and small group discussions with experts from a range of educational contexts (for example, small liberal arts colleges, large state universities, distance learning programs) who were not members of any of the teams but who had extensive experience with exploring teaching and learning with technology. These presentations and follow-up small group discussions with the experts gave participants insights into and inspiration about working collaboratively to integrate technology into teaching.
- Formal, whole group discussions of all forty participants and the workshop facilitators and informal conversations at lunch and dinner, which gave participants an opportunity to discuss themes and issues that arose.
- College-based breakout groups, which gave teams an opportunity to practice and plan their collaborative revision of one of the professor's courses.

Through these forums participants discovered and created ways in which they themselves and others could contribute to teaching and learning in courses. In revising and acting on their own and others' potential to learn, they engaged in or attempted translations: The various group configurations and processes prompted participants to re-read the original identities, ideas, and practices that they and others brought with them, to reconsider how they might interpret or re-interpret others and themselves, and to begin to compose re-renderings.

Facilitated as it was outside of the regular flow of time—an intense four days as opposed to daily life—and, for most participants, out of the context of the place in which they regularly work, this workshop constituted a liminal space: "an in-between place which bridges the indicative (what is) and the subjunctive (what can or will be)."[10] As Turner explains, in such a space, "the cognitive schemata that give sense and order to everyday life no longer apply but are, as it were, suspended."[11] My colleagues and I hoped that by providing what one instructional technologist characterized as a "total immersion experience separate from the home environment," people could move "beyond the constraints of [their] organizational structure" to begin the process of translation first out of context and then continue it in context when they returned to their home institutions.

Each of the four days of the workshop was configured differently. We began the second day by re-emphasizing that we wanted people to start by thinking about their teaching, learning, and support responsibilities and goals and then to think about how technology interfaces with those. The first activity was designed to give people an opportunity to meet and talk with others in the same role; the small groups in which they worked in the morning were of like constituencies. We are aware that people don't often have a chance to talk with those at other institutions who do what they do. This first conversation was intended to give participants an opportunity to have those conversations and through them to clarify their current responsibilities and to think about their needs and goals as students, as faculty, as librarians, as instructional technologists. To help give some focus to the small group discussions, we distributed guidelines. We asked that people first spend five minutes learning one another's names, colleges, areas of interest, and expertise. We asked that they then revisit what they had written about and sent to us prior to the workshop regarding their approaches to what they teach and/or learn, their uses of and needs for technology, and their hopes for collaboration with the other constituencies represented at this workshop.

After they talked in constituency groups, each group took about ten minutes to explain to the entire group what they talked about and shared the main points that emerged from their discussion. One of the facilitators of the workshop recorded the key points on a flipchart and helped to guide a discussion that looked across groups and mapped what people learned about one another's roles, responsibilities, interests, and hopes.

We then moved to a more potentially volatile conversation: a conversation in which the same constituency groups had to clarify and articulate the challenges they face and the challenges they present in their teaching and/or learning responsibilities and needs. We asked that within their constituency groups they address the following questions: What challenges do you face in working with the other groups represented here? What challenges do you think the other groups face in working with you? Given the challenges you have identified and considering your hopes for collaboration, what goals do you have for this workshop?

We reconvened in a large group and each constituency took ten minutes to explain what their group talked about and shared the main points that emerged from their discussion. In facilitating this sharing of perspectives, we reminded participants that this discussion was not about criticizing but about understanding one another. The groups continued these conversations over dinner.

The third day of the workshop focused on experiences of the experienced—people who could offer some concrete examples of how collaboration among constituencies and uses of technology can look. We invited four or five people who have different kinds of experience with this work first to give a brief overview of their work in the large group, such as integrating music and video into a PowerPoint presentation to represent a history of blues music—a project that, in this case, would have been impossible without the close collaboration of a librarian and an instructional technologist. After these short presentations there was some time for clarification questions. We then asked workshop participants to sign up to participate in small conversations with two of these guests. This day gave participants a wide range of concrete strategies for how they might both work collaboratively with others and integrate technology into teaching.

The fourth day was devoted to meeting in college-based teams to conceptualize an implementation plan. The day alternated between planning sessions among college groups and large group discussions in which people identified issues that had arisen in conversation. By the end of the day, participants had to produce a one-page outline that made clear what they planned to do after they returned to their home institutions. We concluded the workshop with some assessment of how people had experienced the workshop and then a dinner.

The Challenges of Translation

Meaning making, learning, and change are always context-specific. Translations are also context-, time-, and audience-specific. And when one switches contexts, the translations that have been effected or that still need to be effected are most starkly thrown into relief. It is at those moments when we need to be most aware and supportive of others', or our own, efforts at translation. The first of the two contexts that highlight the challenges and possibilities of translation I explore in this chapter is the liminal, four-day time and space of the workshop. The second is the home institutions to which participants returned after spending four days together at Bryn Mawr. Moving between a liminal space that attempted to foster revision of self and a home institution that pressured participants to preserve "the original" self was one significant challenge of translation for the people working within these institutions.

Of all the members of the team, the professors found this experience most challenging. Whether they had two or twenty-five years of experience, these professors had lived within academic worlds that powerfully shape identity. The most prevalent metaphors for teachers at the college level aggregate around the teacher as scholar, and one version of that metaphor is "the sage on the stage." The sage-on-the-stage model of teaching assumes that knowledge is passed on or handed down from one generation to the next, with control safely in the hands of the experts, the professors.[12] This model is a legacy from the days when the college or university was "a microcosm, a miniature world offering the whole of knowledge in a restricted arena"[13]—when original forms of knowledge and representation could simply be re-presented, virtually unchanged, each year. Within this model, the professor is both the embodiment and the vehicle of this whole of knowledge, and the language of the original and the self who renders that language must be preserved in their original states.

This model still dominates in many institutions of higher learning. As one faculty participant in "Talking Toward Techno-Pedagogy" explains, she was taught in graduate school "that I was the expert and I was the one who had to do everything for all of my classes." The purveyors of wisdom, indeed its embodiment, many professors remain fixed in their notions of themselves, their subject matter, and their relationships with students and other members of the college community. This model persists even in an information-rich world, full of multiple languages, in which some argue that the role of the professor should not be "to provide information but to guide and encourage students wading through deep waters of the information flood . . . as mentors."[14]

These metaphors—mentor, sage on the stage—do little to move professors and those with whom they work away from ways of thinking about teaching and learning that keep people in their already inscribed forms—ways of thinking that keep people in their "original" states. They do not question the nature of content, they do not problematize notions of language use, and they do not challenge professors to re-conceptualize the selves they must be to integrate new ways of thinking about, representing, and teaching subject matter. Both the language of disciplines and the languages of technology can pose challenges of communication, interpretation, and expression. Professors are faced with languages different from those that many of their students speak and different from the medium that may come to dominate, or at least inform, the educational process: information technology. Discrepancies of vocabulary, of modes of interpretation, and of representation present themselves at every turn. Professors who take on the role of student face these literal translation issues as well as the challenges of metaphorical translation of self that taking on the linguistic challenges entails.

Discerning Language and Context: An Early Phase in Translation

When professors come to the intersection of new information technologies and pedagogy, their first reaction is often simply to transfer all aspects of their instruction to the new medium without considering whether their role and pedagogical approaches need to be revised.[15] In other words, they translate directly: they preserve with identity in detail,[16] they replicate methods,[17] they search for one-to-one correspondences.[18] At a reunion of workshop participants, one professor who participated in "Talking Toward Techno-Pedagogy" described this tendency on his own part. Explaining the project he and his team had designed, he said: "When you teach English, the basic way of analyzing literature is to take a little piece of it and look at it. And so when I moved to analyzing film, which I knew nothing about, I started from the same principle—that you should take little pieces of film and look at them and break them down into their parts." As this professor later explained, this approach did not work the same way with film as it does with written text. But because he did not speak this new language—the language of film—he sought at first a kind of literal and direct translation of his subject matter and his approach to it.

An art history professor who felt more comfortable with a new medium in which she was working did not encounter the same kind of translation issue. She was able to use the new medium that a new form of information technology provided to extend an already successful pedagogical practice. She explains how she uses the note function of Luna Insight (a kind of virtual Post-It note within a software program) both to model a particular kind of interpretation and to ask students to engage in it: "So in some cases I will over-interpret images for [students], or I will ask them to over-interpret, and have them select out which things don't belong and then present to us some arguments about what that is. The stickies become a site for practicing a mode of written interpretation and then speaking about why you interpret that way." In this instance, the professor successfully integrated an existing language of interpretation with a new medium for that interpretation. The effect of juxtaposing a new language and a new medium is quite different from an approach through which the representation and the interpretation exist in separate realms—images in one and text in another. The bringing together of these two previously differentiated modes and media—like the bringing together of two terms of a metaphor—have the potential to fuse and foster new forms of expression and new understanding.

As the English professor I mentioned above also learned through working with the new medium of film and in collaboration with his team, one needs to consider the relationship between the content of a course and the medium through which it is conveyed; one needs to consider how the latter may profoundly change the former or how the latter is or becomes an integral part of the former. After working with his team through the new medium of film, this English professor noted that the medium itself changes what can be perceived and therefore what can be interpreted when watching clips of a film as opposed to reading a single "original"—in this case written—text. This professor's grappling with a new medium, film, in conjunction with a more familiar one, written texts, afforded students opportunities to ponder questions of reading and rendering as well. One student posed the following question at a "Talking Toward Techno-Pedagogy" reunion: "Are films interpretations or adaptations?" Like the art history professor's use of stickies to re-locate students' interpretations of images, this professor's use of film helped him and his students rethink old questions and consider new questions of literary interpretation.

The multiplicity of translations that a medium such as film can render of a single original written text throws into relief what is always true regarding reading and rendering of a text but that presents itself here in a new way: that there are as many possible interpretations as there are readers. As I have already mentioned in reference to translation, the reason for this, as poet and translator David Constantine explains, is that every reader and every translator brings to every text "*etwas . . . aus der eigenen Erfahrung, aus dem totalen Leben bis zu dem Punkt hin . . . nicht beim Interpretieren, sondern beim Lesen, beim Fühlen . . . ob man das merkt oder nicht*" (something . . . out of one's own experience, out of one's entire life up to that point . . . not through interpretation, but rather through reading, through feeling . . . whether one is cognizant of it or not).[19] Although this statement is always true, regardless of the medium, new technologies make it possible to see simultaneously several different versions of a film based on an original written text. In other words, one can view simultaneously several different interpretations, several different translations. One achieves something close to this effect by listening to and juxtaposing musical texts, such as I did in "Finding the Bias" with "Tangled Up in Blue"—first reading the written text, then listening to Bob Dylan's version, then listening to The Indigo Girls' version. But the capacity to view clips from different movies immediately juxtaposed to one another takes this idea one step further. It's as though one could read or hear a text rendered in several different languages at once. But to be able to do this oneself and facilitate it for students, professors must first learn the language of this new medium and then re-think how that language re-renders not just components but the whole of a text. As Constantine has argued, a successful translation emphasizes "the total workings of a text, not just the words," because translation is more than transliteration; it is the re-articulation of a complex human experience.[20]

Students articulate clearly the need for professors to allow for and engage in translation when they encounter discrepancies between language systems and the ways that these different systems can convey understanding. During a workshop, one student spoke specifically about the differences between the language he uses and the language he believes his professors use: "I think there's a gap between the student and the professor . . . I believe that I can express an idea adequately through both pictures and text. It seems that maybe it's a different [way of being], maybe we grew up on it, maybe the technology has changed [the way we think and can express what we think]." This student explained that for a recent class, he created a series of computer animations to accompany his text: "it was a paper as well as expressing the things that I wanted to express through moving images and through images that were, at least I thought, [presented] in an appropriate manner." Although he felt that his professor had not recognized this approach as legitimate, creating this mixed-media form was important for this student because the two forms of expression could "play off of each other" and allowed him "to express things that I didn't think I could express through a paper."

The combination of image and text constituted for this student a language that he needed to capture and convey his understanding. His insistence on mixing different media reiterates the mixing of "media" I mentioned in regard to Cisneros's mixture of Spanish and English in *House on Mango Street*: "The transportation of Spanish words and phrases into English and their seamless integration into the text allow her 'to say things in English that have never been said before.'"[21] This student who used both images and text in his course project had an experience, a perspective, and an understanding for which he needed this new language he forged for himself. This example throws into relief the fact that not only ways of using language to interpret but also language itself are always evolving. And as language itself evolves, what can and can't be said changes. Hence the need for ongoing translation.

This student's sense of the relationship between form and content stands in sharp contrast to the notion that content can remain the same regardless of the medium through which it is presented. As this student articulates, not only did he choose particular media for their capacities to express certain ideas, he also wanted to achieve an expression of his ideas that only the combination of media could effect. His comment at the outset that "there's a gap between the student and the professor" because students have grown up playing with, working with, and thinking to varying degrees through technology highlights the differences between the ways that some students and faculty think and express those thoughts.

This difference can exist as well among other differently positioned members of the college community. Particularly with the advent of the role of instructional technologist, the potential exists for members of the academic community to speak different languages and to live, in fact, in different cultures, different worlds. After students met during one session of a Techno-Pedagogy workshop, one student reported back to the whole group that "I think the general idea about the [instructional technologists] is we have no idea what they do. We just don't know, we don't know who they are, we don't know where their offices are, we don't know what questions to ask, we don't speak the same language." One of the reasons such differences exist is that people are at different points in the process of integrating the culture of technology into the culture of college. At one of our reunions, a student said about the challenges of working in new technological media: "I think it's part of the culture of difference in general and technology in specific, 'cause it isn't conferred the same amount of seriousness [in academic courses], if it's on the computer, it's not intellectual, the content can't be good, anyone can publish [on the Web]." This student's comment points to the difficulty of changing cultural values and norms: a difficulty that is thrown into relief by the discrepancies that emerge in language use, in media of expression, illustrated by the example of the professor's shift from text to film and the student's use of image and text together. Thus one of the challenges that members of the higher education community must grapple with is how to re-think what counts as valid in academic contexts—how to re-think which languages, which forms of expression, can be accepted, understood, and, perhaps most important, co-created. This change is a high stakes one for professors, whose review for promotion and tenure depends on their making choices that will be recognized as legitimate within the existing structures of the academy.

A comment made by a librarian illuminates this problem from another angle. Discussing the challenge of reaching some of the more experienced faculty members, she states: "their definition of instruction hasn't perhaps changed whereas the instruction has and we need to find out ways to reach that group on our campuses in order to help them realize

what it is that we do." This statement echoes another librarian's explanation of the need for librarians to redefine what they do and how they
do it: "for years the librarian was the portal to information; now the computer is the portal"; therefore, librarians "need to help people to find ways
to discriminate between the sources of information and find the best
ways to search." Yet another librarian illuminates how librarians themselves might pose a challenge to such a revision: "librarians are service
oriented"; to work with people in new ways through new languages
"requires lowering lots of barriers and [uncovering] assumptions." After
a session in which they had discussed among themselves the kinds of
challenges they both face and present when working with others in the
college community, the librarians reported that "we need to do a better
job of articulating what it is that we do." They suggested that many of
their difficulties and differences with other constituencies "stem from of
a lack of communication about what it is that we do bring to the table
and how we don't necessarily clarify as well as we could that we are teachers and what are our contribution to teaching is and could be."

These librarians' comments bear out Steiner's claim that all communication, even within the same language —in this case, English—is translation. They highlight the need both for a translation of languages used
in teaching and learning and a translation of the selves that use and need
to learn those languages. Their comments suggest as well that they want
to help professors to translate the languages they use and need for the
practices the students need in order to learn in a contemporary world.
This challenge is a particularly thorny one because a widespread lack of
awareness of the role of librarians contributes to the common phenomenon of librarians being neither considered nor included as integral to
the pedagogical planning process.[21] The original identity of librarians,
like the original identity of professors, can impede the kinds of new versions of self that translation aims to render.

As these examples from a professor's perspective, a student's perspective, and several librarians' perspectives illustrate, one challenge facing
faculty is learning languages that will allow them to communicate with
students and other members of the college community. For a professor to
learn a new language, such as the language of film and the language of
new technologies that render it newly, and particularly a language in which
a student or a librarian, such as those quoted above, feels more fluent,
that professor would need to learn new modes of expression and interaction that, by their very nature, alter the power dynamics that underlie
traditional relationships in institutions of higher education.

Learning a new language means learning to listen to others as well as
to express oneself, and professors need to trust that there is meaning to
be found in the new texts and languages before them and also to listen

to others already using them. Lisa Delpit suggests that "we do not really see through our eyes or hear through our ears, but through our beliefs" and that to really hear one another calls for "a very special kind of listening, listening that requires not only open eyes and ears but also open hearts and minds."[23] One student captures her experience both in general and, in contrast, during this workshop as she perceived professors learning to listen: "Sometimes you're talking to a professor and maybe it's registering but sometimes it's in one ear. [But here] maybe they thought they could actually benefit from this . . . that they were going to be better teachers or more fun in the classroom . . . I think there were many moments when [professors realized that talking with a] student ahead of time saves you the anxiety of planning a course that may or may not work. To realize that is a really liberating thing and I think that happened for a couple of people and I don't think they [had] imagined that as a possibility."

Oldfather points out that "learning from student voices . . . requires major shifts . . . in ways of thinking and feeling about the issues of knowledge, language, power, and self."[24] One of the problems in higher education, as in education at every level, is that it is the professors who define the terms of the conversation as well as when the conversation takes place. Unless professors initiate dialogue about their courses outside of the formal structures required by colleges, moments for students to speak to professors about the content and processes of a course tend to be limited to end-of-the-semester evaluations and sometimes mid-course feedback, and student perspectives almost always constitute advice offered for professors to act on, not participation in actual revision. As one student who participated in "Talking Toward Techno-Pedagogy" explained: "I am usually encouraged to give feedback about what's working [in a class] and what isn't and to develop ideas about what would work better, not to participate directly in making changes."

Not only is how professors and students speak often quite different, but what each has the authority to talk about also varies greatly. As another student participant in "Talking Toward Techno-Pedagogy" put it: "it's very difficult to have an argument with a professor along structural lines . . . their class structure is sacred and it's their way of doing things and if it's not done their way then it's not right. It's very difficult for a lot of students to give input on how a class is structured because of that and they don't necessarily feel comfortable." This student's summary of students' fears is inflected with his awareness that he and his peers have experienced years of not only not being heard but also not being asked to articulate their perspectives on pedagogical issues. For professors to learn to trust that there is meaning to be found in what others have to say, particularly to listen to those with less official power than they—such as librarians, instructional technologists, and students, but particularly students—is a significant challenge facing faculty who want to translate themselves. The institutionally inscribed power hierarchies and their attendant long histories of being played out in practice make it not only hard to listen when these less powerful people speak but, even prior to that, also difficult to imagine that they might even have something to say worth hearing. This issue is a challenge of translation: "All understanding, and the demonstrative statement of understanding which is translation, starts with an act of trust . . . we grant . . . that there is 'something there' to be understood."[25]

The Challenges of Translation: Deeper In

It is the last day of a Techno-Pedagogy workshop, and two faculty members, a librarian, an instructional technologist, and a student sit around a long brown table. The team members are reading over their notes from the preceding three days of the conference, preparing to begin a discussion about how they might integrate some of what they have heard and thought about into their plans for a course the faculty members team-teach with two other department members. One of the faculty members says, "I want to return to the professional development goals of each of the members of the group." This statement is her opening invitation at this stage of course planning, and the responses she receives throw into relief the different perspective each member of the team brings to this collaboration.

The other faculty member says: "I want to find other ways to help students learn to think in this experimental way." Later in the conversation, the student says: "The solution I am suggesting [to this dilemma of students having access to more than one data source simultaneously] is to keep two windows [on the computer] open at once in two different programs." In response to this and as an extension of another question team members raised, the instructional technologist says: "That would work, and you could also have a number of specific answers to questions that students would need to get correct before they could move on with the program." And the librarian says: "I realize this is a simple point, but I never thought of it before: we need to put this software on all the computers the students use, not just the ones in the lab."

Throughout this conversation, the faculty members say: "I was thinking as you were talking" or "Do you think this would work for students?" or "Are there technology pieces that would be interesting and fun for you?" Contrast this approach to course planning with the traditional image of a faculty member working alone on her syllabus, making decisions without the input of these other constituencies, building a course from a single perspective.

The faculty members described in the vignette above did more listening than talking as they planned with their team members. Learning to listen to people one might be accustomed to telling what to do requires a re-tuning of one's ears, a re-consideration of what is before one, a willingness to re-render what one knows and encounters anew. Focusing still on the text of the course, recognizing that students might have invaluable insights early in the process of planning a course, rather than merely in reflection on its efficacy after it is finished, is a first step. During one session of a workshop, for instance, a faculty member commented that "the student participation . . . was really invaluable to me as a faculty member because even though you have [course] evaluations, here we are talking about this stuff and thinking about it and right there you've got this sense of, well, no, that's not going to work at all."

In another case a professor genuinely began to relinquish control, and his student teammate assumed more authority to address structural issues in courses. This faculty member described what a good experience it was for him to work with a student "tearing apart one of my courses." For some professors, it is easier to embrace the notion of sharing authority on a course if it is being designed for the first time, before the professor feels too invested in it. As one group explained during a session of a workshop: "One of the things that has allowed us a lot of this freedom in flexibility is [that the professor] hasn't taught this course before so we're not having to deal with taking an already designed course and trying to re-tool it to add technology to it." And another student, in a conversation at one of our reunions, talked about how the team, and the faculty member in particular, had invested her with significant authority, let her "do grownup things," and really made her feel a significant part of the collaborative process.

These examples highlight moments in which students managed to find a way into the existing structures of education and to make themselves heard by the faculty. There were also moments when other members of the college community made it clear that they want to play a different role in the conceptualizing and teaching of courses; they want to be translators of the text of the course and they want to translate themselves. One instructional technologist explained at dinner on the first night of the workshop that many instructional technologists feel they should be unwavering advocates of technology and its integration into teaching. And yet some, including herself, would feel more comfortable if they could find a balance between the roles of advocate and critic. In the same spirit, inspired to move beyond the parameters prescribed by the way his institution constructs his role, another instructional technologist explained:

As a member of computing services it becomes so easy to function solely within the confines of our day-to-day maintenance of the critical college functions that I find I do not focus on the components of technology that really enhance the curricular mission of our institution. What has inspired me most over the past few days is the understanding that viewing the faculty/library/IT/student groups as a team, we can work together to create opportunities to use technology in a more integral fashion in a way that empowers all the players, and ultimately enriches the student experience.

During a different year in which we facilitated the workshop, an instructional technologist explained to the whole group that members of his constituency feel they are not assigned "authority to contribute anything to the teaching and learning process because the concept of an [instructional technologist] is not necessarily associated with those things." The goal of many of the instructional technologists who participated in "Talking Toward Techno-Pedagogy" was "an evolved role on our campuses . . . over time, whether it's through our own actions or by changing other people's perceptions of us, that we could have more sophisticated involvement with teaching and learning issues."

Some faculty members heard this call and acknowledged that the texts of the courses they are teaching need to be co-constructed or co-translated. In another report from the faculty to the large group, one professor stated: "One of the things I thought I heard very clearly from both the librarians and from IT people was, 'We're teachers, too. And we want to be recognized as teachers, we want our teaching to be understood as teaching.' And we heard that and we agree that that's something that needs to be done. So one of the things that we want to do is to negotiate for ourselves, for you, in what sense we're all teachers and in what sense our authority as being our responsibility for a given course can accommodate the teaching of others." In hearing that the instructional technologists wanted to be recognized as teachers, the faculty began to think about how they might need to translate themselves to make that possible.

Once faculty members accept the possibility that power and authority can be re-conceptualized and redistributed, they can begin to think about how to engage in those processes. After a discussion among faculty members during one session of a workshop, the faculty members reported the following to the whole group:

> When we talked about questions of responsibility and authority we focused, necessarily, on the faculty's sense of being the expert people about the content of the course. Then the question that we asked—to which we had varying answers, quite varying answers—was whether technology has the potential for redefining what the content of the course is and therefore for redefining the issues of authority and responsibility for the course. If we're redefining the nature of the subject matter of the course, then does the relationship between faculty, student, librarian, technologist become a different kind of relationship?

This is a stunning set of reflections and questions when one considers the long history of the sage-on-the-stage model of teaching. Having heard what the students had to say about the changing languages and ways of being in higher education, and having heard what librarians and instructional technologists had to say about their desire to participate more actively in co-constructing courses, this group of professors was willing to question the most basic premise of traditional education: that content and control of courses belong exclusively to professors. These professors took several steps in a process of translating themselves: they moved from conceiving of themselves as the sole experts on content to the question of whether technology can redefine content to the question of whether allowing technology to redefine content means that everybody has to redefine relationships and responsibilities.

Not only hearing what the students, the instructional technologists, and the librarians had to say but also opening the conversation to significant interpretive revisions was inspiring to faculty members. One professor exclaimed: "I have never had such a wonderful opportunity to collaborate with other people on making these judgments. And the things we talked about instead of just thinking about them on my own and making my best judgment, but really bouncing my ideas off of other very well-informed people so that I really think this is going to be wonderful." Others echoed this sense of enthusiasm and possibility. Another professor explained: "Most of [the] initiative of the course came from me, but the ideas were bounced off the IT person and librarian for feasibility." Going a step further than bouncing ideas, another faculty talked about how the "librarian's expertise really changed the notions of what could be taught and how to conduct better research" in the course. Another faculty member commented on how she was repositioned within her course—as a learner. Referring to the projects that students completed for the course, she explained: "It was terrific for me because it meant that I never knew what was coming up, and most of it was really interesting, and I learned stuff that I would not otherwise have learned."

As the members of college communities highest in the hierarchy and with the primary, or at least official, responsibility in the pedagogical realm, faculty need to engage in their own processes of education, their own translations. The kinds of rethinking in which many faculty engaged during "Talking Toward Techno-Pedagogy" suggest that they are open to such a process. Yet when faculty carried their newfound enthusiasm back to their home institutions, many of their efforts at translation were thwarted.

Back at the Home Institutions: The Necessary Conditions for Translation

For translation to be effected, certain conditions must exist within and between individuals and in institutions. As those traditionally assigned the greatest authority in the pedagogical realm, professors must allow space for others in the higher education community to contribute to pedagogy.

One instructional technologist explains first how such efforts can be impeded, and then she explains how they can be promoted: "[Faculty] kind of come and say they want to use technology in class, you know that doesn't really leave you with anything to work with. We need to know a lot more about what that class is about and what they're looking to do and how the technology might be helpful, if at all—it might not always be helpful." In the same vein another instructional technologist explains: "We are really much more interested in hearing about others' needs first before we start contributing a lot of what we have to offer."

Those who work with professors in higher education need to contribute to the creation of an environment conducive to learning, just like a good teacher in any class. One instructional technologist explains some of the ways she has rethought her approaches to teaching: "A couple of things I use over and over: when folks talk to me about being hesitant to use technology, I now ask questions about where they think it will fit. I am working harder at getting hesitant people to just become aware of what technology can do, and opening up a dialogue. When folks express discomfort, I don't pooh pooh it, I'm not nonchalant, I acknowledge the time it takes. I am much more comfortable talking to faculty about using technology." Learning to learn from students and learning to treat faculty as real learners are two significant differences from common practices in higher education.

A librarian similarly describes her approach to establishing a relationship with a faculty member with whom she had not previously worked: "I . . . really had to consciously say to myself, 'OK, you need to approach this with the same kind of mind you did over a year ago, before you went to [the Techno-Pedagogy workshop at] Bryn Mawr,' not just saying, 'OK, here's what we've got lined up, this is what we've done for this course.' As much as I was enthusiastic and proud about that, I really had to consciously tell myself, 'Go to this meeting and say, "What would you like to do?" and "What would you like to see?"'" This librarian had to remember to start where the learner is and to create or allow a space for her to be an active agent. Striving for a balance between saying, "Here's what we've already done," and offering an invitation that allows people to say, "This is what we want," is what professors must do if each class is to be something new and something co-constructed with students. A balance must always exist between "starting over" and bringing what one has already done. This balance is certainly as much of a challenge to professors as it is to those who work with them. Explaining how the Techno-Pedagogy workshop challenged him to listen to student input rather than just deliver what he had prepared, one professor says: "I think I've been able to hide from [hearing the student perspective] before this process because it's been very easy to think about designing a course and say, well, 'This is what I have to offer you, and you're free to take from it or not, as the case may be.'"

Another librarian talked about how she and a faculty member had both significantly revised their sense of themselves and one another through their collaboration. Moving away from what she called the typical, one-time, "canned" library speech, this librarian talked about how she visited the classroom of the professor with whom she worked at the workshop to present multiple, tailored sessions. Another librarian explained that what evolved through the collaboration was an attempt to step out of the library and to offer training on information literacy in the professor's class during class time. In addition, she talked about how, when she was in the class, she "moved away from the podium and the laptop" when she gave presentations. It felt to her like a more "vital and vibrant" discussion about what a scholarly source is. Reflecting on why this experience felt so different than when students come to the library, she mused: "Was it meeting students on their own turf? Was it being more collaborative with a faculty member [both she and the faculty member were part of the discussion]?" These changes in thinking and practice prompted by the workshop throw into relief the limits of some of the ways some faculty and librarians have traditionally been positioned in relation to one another and point to more generative possibilities.

When members of the higher education community are successful in translating themselves in these ways, the results can be not only rewarding but also revolutionary. The very way we conceptualize and enact education can change. One professor explains: "It was very clear right from the beginning that we were a team—[the other people on the team] didn't wait for me to tell them what to do . . . it has been lots of fun and very effective. . . . Among the ideas that we want to disseminate is that you can get much further by starting a project together at the level of, 'This is the problem we are trying to solve' rather by walking in and saying, 'Please set up the following software for me.'"

This revised process of negotiation is an important component of translation of self, but there may well be other members of the higher education community who are not yet actively contributing to or supporting such a process. One professor elaborates:

It's very difficult at some of these institutions to put together teams that include all the key players. We have administrators who are not hostile to the project, but not part of the team. We have a GIS [Geographical Information System] person who is not part of the team. We have a dean who is not against this but is also not part of the team. So there is a lot that happens outside the purview of the team's responsibilities and projects, and that's one place to think about support for actually developing projects that include more than the four of us [faculty, student, librarian, instructional technologist].

Reflecting on the challenges he saw to making the kinds of changes advocated in "Talking Toward Techno-Pedagogy," another faculty member said: "I really think it's important that we don't underestimate the institutional barriers and that if we're going to make progress we have to think very creatively about how to work across those or undermine them." The kind of education in which these professors engaged, the kind of re-reading and re-renderings of texts and selves, required a bridging or bringing together of realms, of words, ways of being, and worlds that are often deliberately kept apart or that fall apart. When the bringing together was successful, it worked like metaphor itself: bringing together unlike sets of terms and realms to more fully illuminate and then re-render both. This process both produces new meaning and opens up possibilities for further meaning-making.

Among the barriers to such bringing together and re-rendering are the recognition, reward, and promotion structures of many colleges. One faculty member talked about how everybody's reputation was enhanced by the collaboration on integrating technology into his course, but he has no idea of the relation between this project and promotion and tenure. Will it count as research rather than teaching? The old categories kept him from being able to do interesting new work. In his words: "I won't get points that will relieve me from other areas in which I am expected to excel." In other words, expectations about the preservation of original ways of working and representing that work kept some faculty members from further translating themselves. Such hindrances have implications as well for other members of the college community. One professor reflects: "With teams of different kinds of professionals—students are professionals in one way, librarians another way—we don't all look for or need the same kinds of returns to keep going. . . . There is a long-term issue of what makes people keep going, keep doing this, and how to create a reward or encouragement system that is equally good for a faculty member or a librarian or an [instructional technologist] as well as a series of students." These comments are about the context one needs if one is going to engage in translation.

Like professors, librarians and instructional technology staff are hesitant about pursuing the kind of learning they believe would be most useful because the institution is not set up to recognize them for those innovations. One librarian explains: "There is no real support" in terms of release time for this type of collaboration. She talked about how her institution is pressing for technology, but she and others at the college do not know how that push relates to policies of the institution: "How does it fit in the overall mission of the college?" Another librarian explained how he developed a database for a professor's course, and the database became a feather in the faculty member's cap, not the librarian's.

Another challenge of this kind of translation is that, as one faculty member put it, "when it finally comes down to it, the person who will take the primary responsibility for the course is always going to be the faculty member. If it goes wrong, who is the one person who is going to have evaluations turned into the administration, it's going to be the faculty member who is going to bear the brunt of that." This professor articulates clearly how the distribution of power and responsibility can work against certain kinds of translations of self.

One faculty member explains what she thinks might be the root of the problem; it is not so much an institutional set of barriers as a cultural expectation: "The real issue is fear to look stupid and take risks of not appearing to know. . . . A real unwillingness to learn." The result of this unwillingness is that faculty members have difficulty translating both the languages they use and the selves they are. It is always a risk to translate—to try to bridge new spaces and ways of being with new words. To take this kind of risk, certain kinds of relationships must exist between an institution and the people trying to work together within it.

Translation of Texts/Translations of Selves

A small group of professors, students, librarians, and instructional technologists gather in Bryn Mawr College's Rare Book Room. For some it is almost two years since they participated in "Talking Toward Techno-Pedagogy," for some it is almost a year, and for some it is before their courses have yet run, because the professor member of the team has been on leave. The two of us Bryn Mawr–based "Talking Toward Techno-Pedagogy" facilitators are present to host this reunion, and we welcome participants back to the campus. We explain that we want to hear from them in an informal way about what they have been up to, what has worked well, and what has proven challenging or problematic about the work they have been trying to do.

One professor volunteers to explain what her team has done. "We taught, I taught the course that we worked on [during the Techno-Pedagogy workshop] last fall." She reminds us what the course was, and using the Web site that the student member of the team constructed, she focuses on the final project required for the course. Referring to the planning the team had done during the previous spring, she explains: "We wanted to incorporate a research project, which had not been a part of the course before. We worked on several different aspects of this. [The librarian] helped put together a really nice list of resources . . . and also ran a session at the library . . . [students] were excited and encouraged and did come to talk to [the librarian] about various aspects of their projects." The librarian adds that this was a change for her: "I was glad to have so much involvement in the class, and then to have quite a few of [the students] come to me, either through email or just to walk up to the reference desk. . . . For most classes, the best I can really hope for is a forty-minute class session, that's all, not to have the Web presence as well and to have the individual consultations."

The professor continues: "So one of the components of the course, and this was something that we had talked about last spring when we were designing it, which [the student] was particularly in favor of, was the idea that the final project should be a research project, but that it could take any form, a creative project or . . . a formal essay." About this aspect of the course, the student explains: "I helped two people with their projects, and they were really excited about it, and I was excited about it too, so it was fun to work together like that. It's more interactive than what a lot of other people are doing."

The team continues to explain the details of their collaboration and to take us through the Web site, which includes a number of final projects completed by students. After this presentation we hear from members of the other teams, each at a different point of reflection on or preparation to teach their class.

A shift in language use, whether it is conscious or unconscious, can signal a shift in ways of thinking and being. One of the shifts we hear in the ways that people talked about their work as teams after the Techno-Pedagogy workshop echoes the shift in the college sophomores' use of pronouns as they found themselves engaged in translation. As professors, librarians, instructional technologists, and students talked about their experiences of collaborating on revising courses, they used "we" rather than or in addition to the more typical "I." In the vignette above, excerpted from a larger conversation, the professor uses "we" five times.

Talking about the work she had done with a professor, a student also uses "we"—eight times. She explains:

Because [the professor I worked with was on leave the year after we participated in Techno-Pedagogy] we spent a whole year reconstructing the course, and then I had taken the course two years before, and I attended every class [this year]. I was very involved with the students, talking with the students about how the class was going, and also doing a lot of work keeping Blackboard up and running . . . and we were doing a lot of discussion-board work . . . we chose to do that rather than have people email each other because people lose emails and that way all the information was on the Web and . . . we could drop in and see how they were doing and not be monitoring but have them aware that we could tell who was contributing to groups . . . we really wanted the small group work because of the kinds of understandings we wanted them to be coming to, we thought that would help.

Phrases such as "we chose to do that" and "we really wanted the small group work because of the kinds of understandings we wanted [the students] to be coming to" reflect the profound ways in which this student was involved in the thinking through and deciding upon pedagogical issues in the class. Moving from "I" to "we" requires a major revision of one's own identity as well as they identity of others and the relationship one has to those others. In a world and an educational system that values individuality, it is a significant shift, and one with many implications.

The translations of self in which the student participants in the workshop engaged affected their sense of their identity as students as well as their relationship to the courses they helped revise and teach. Pushed on whether she would call the course on which her team worked "my course," one student said: "I don't think it's my course, but I think that class is my class. I mean, it's his material, it's his idea, it's his brainstorm, but I helped *that* class run better." She explains one of her roles during class time:

Because they spent a lot of time in small groups, that meant that two people could be wandering around and talking with people, and catching problems earlier. They're not willing to raise their hands in a small group . . . I was a lot less intimidating, in asking me a question they weren't admitting to the professor, because they had the questions before they came to class and they didn't have the answer yet, and also it made dropping in on and listening to a discussion a lot more possible with two people in the room. And one of the things that we found was really surprising was that students would come up to me outside of class and talk to me about how the class was going and ask me to tell them things anonymously and we set up an anonymous drop-box, but nobody ever used it; they just walked up and talked to me . . . maybe they saw me and thought about it; it wasn't something that they were so deliberate about that they were going to sit down and write an email.

I suggest that students had this response because this student was a real, live person who had lived through the class, understood it, and would respond right away. Students didn't need to write a message, drop it in a box, and wait for an answer; they could have a real dialogue. Another student added: "I think it's having that extra link between the professor and the student; it just makes everything more active. 'Cause they can tell you something and know that you'll have some sort of authority, some sort of knowledge, but you're not going to be like, 'Hmm, I'm not going to give him a good grade.'" The student who works with a professor in this way is, in a way, "safe" to the students taking the course—because he doesn't have a judging role, but he has knowledge. A student positioned in such a way in a course—not simply a TA but a collaborator—helps effect translations not only of her professor and of herself but also of the other students enrolled in the course. The kind of mediation in which this student was engaged was itself a form of translation.

For a professor to translate herself in a way that allows and fosters this kind of participation on the part of other members of the college community requires a profound revision of the notion that the professor must be central to all pedagogical processes in the classroom. Demonstrating how he had embraced such a revision, one professor asked students in his course to work in teams and use a relatively simple form of technology—the editing function in Microsoft Word—to critique one another's papers. Another member of the team explained this approach, which she helped to orchestrate: "[The professor] did not want to be involved in the draft stage . . . because he wanted [the students] to be focusing on each other's comments. If he had put his comments on the drafts, they wouldn't look at anyone else's, they would look at his, and write to his. He wanted them to focus on each other's and the writing mentor's comments." This professor translated himself from sole authority to one, albeit the ultimate, among several. This professor embraced this revision believing it would improve student writing and found that it did; his goal was to create a space for students "to exchange drafts of their papers and comments on those drafts both with other students in a writing group and with their writing mentor and to use those comments as a way of improving their own papers so that the version of it that I saw and eventually graded and commented on in the old fashioned way, would be better than it otherwise would have been." To create this space this professor had to dis-place and then re-place himself in both the actual texts students composed and in the relationships he had with his students and the course.

Gained in Translation

When professors acquired new languages or deepened and complicated their sense of a language they already knew, and when they translated themselves in the ways I have discussed, they built more complex, nuanced, and reciprocal relationships across traditional boundaries of role and relationship. They gained as well a deeper and richer understanding of the context(s) in which they and others work. Finally, they developed an openness to continuing to look for more than a single individual or cultural perspective.

Like the college sophomores who took "Finding the Bias," the professors who took up the challenges of "Talking Toward Techno-Pedagogy" developed a greater facility with language and with interactions as well as a willingness to risk more varied and various interpretations of content and of selves. Whereas the process in which the sophomores engaged was certainly social but focused on individual compositions and selves, the translations the professors effected unfolded as a social process in which many people—a plurality of voices and perspectives—sought to disrupt and replace hierarchy.

The profound challenges to their assumptions about meaning, authority, and truth prompted the students in "Finding the Bias" to re-examine their perspectives on compositions and selves within and beyond the course itself, but at stake for many of the professors were not only their personal perspectives but also their professional identities and careers. More institutional structures were both supporting and restraining them, and thus the "success" of their translations was more varied. Their experiences reinforce the need continually to challenge the idea that translations are either failed or successful. The process of attempting translations matters as much as the product of any given attempt. As the sophomores learned to read and compose more critically, to analyze as well as narrate, so too the professors learned to listen better to more variously positioned people, to reconsider as well as reproduce. For both groups the process was one of generative struggle to create as well as to find meaning and to integrate that process of creation into the sense of self they carried forward.

Chapter 5
Translating Between Student and Teacher

> I must translate myself . . . by the motions of understanding and sympathy . . . by slow increments, sentence by sentence, phrase by phrase.
>
> —Eva Hoffman, *Lost in Translation*

One by one fifteen college seniors enter the classroom at Bryn Mawr College in which I teach "Curriculum and Pedagogy," a course for preservice middle and high school teachers offered in the semester prior to their student teaching experience. Each preservice teacher takes a seat around the long tables that form a square in the center of the classroom. Some of them know one another and some don't; I know many of them from having worked with them in previous education courses, but some of them are new to me, and all of them are new to the prospect of assuming responsibility in the following semester for classrooms full of middle or high school students. I begin the class with a welcome, explain the guiding ideas and expectations for the course, and ask each person sitting around the table to articulate his hopes and expectations.

After this preliminary discussion, I explain that we are going to get started with a three-part activity, that this activity will be typical of the kind of thing we will do throughout the semester, and that it will raise issues we will address over the course of the class. The first part of the activity is this: I ask the preservice teachers to write a story of a time they learned something. It can be in school or out of school. It doesn't matter what they learned. I want them simply to write about what comes to mind: any powerful learning experience.

In the silence of the classroom, they write about all varieties of things: learning to tie their shoes, learning to ride a bicycle, learning to drive a car, learning to write a research paper, learning to communicate better with a sibling. Their stories range across contexts, characters, and critical incidents, but all are deeply felt experiences that stand out in these preservice teachers' minds as particularly memorable moments of learning.

After they spend about fifteen minutes writing silently, I ask the preservice teachers to step back from the story they have written, to read it over, and to look at it through a critical lens. I ask them, What does your story tell you about yourself as a learner? This part of the assignment asks preservice teachers to shift frames: from a narrative retelling of a lived experience, which was for many quite emotionally charged and which re-evokes those feelings, to a cognitive and analytical frame through which they assess their own experiences from a critical distance. They write silently for another five minutes. "I need someone to show me how to do something first, then I need to try it myself, and I need a lot of pushing as well as support." "I am often afraid to try something new. I'm more comfortable sticking with what I know. So when I have to learn something new, I can get very disoriented; it's like I forget everything I already know. So I need someone to help me make connections between what I already understand and the thing I am supposed to learn." "I am most comfortable figuring things out on my own and I don't like it when someone looms over my shoulder or keeps offering advice." These are among the lessons these preservice teachers derive from their own stories.

Finally, I ask the preservice teachers to read both the story and what they have written about what they learn about themselves from it and to spend another five minutes writing about how they could become the teacher who could create a classroom in which students could learn in the way they describe. With this part of the assignment I ask them to shift frames yet again, this time to focus on the role of the teacher, to begin to imagine what is required of them to facilitate, not simply experience, education. "I need a teacher who will constantly monitor my work." "I need a teacher who will leave me alone." "I need a teacher who is very well-organized and a class that is tightly run." "I need teachers who are tough on me." "I need teachers who are gentle and ease me into things."

I break this activity down in this way for a variety of reasons. In response to the first challenge—to write a story about a time that they learned something—I want preservice teachers to listen to what comes first to mind. Thinking creatively, unconsciously even, simply concentrating on the experience they had, they get at their most basic needs and preferences as learners. If I were to ask them to complete all three parts of this assignment at once, their analytical minds might obscure their more creative and profound insights. But after they have composed their stories, asking them then to step back and engage in analysis of those stories accomplishes a number of things as well. It helps them shift from the emotional/experiential to the analytical, it validates their stories as texts worthy of study, and it is a version of the shift they will need to make as they translate themselves into teachers. The final phase of the activity makes the need for this translation concrete: they must imagine themselves moving from someone positioned primarily as a student to someone positioned primarily as a teacher.

After the preservice teachers have completed all three parts of this assignment, I divide the blackboard into three big columns and we map each of the three aspects of the assignment. We start with the preservice teachers, one at a time, sharing the essence of the narratives of their learning experiences and the insights they gained into themselves as learners. After each student tells her story and shares an analysis of it, I ask others in the class to add any insights they have: anything they heard in the story that suggests something about the kind of learner the particular preservice teacher is. Then we fill in the final column—what kind of teacher would one have to be to meet the needs of each of these students? The differences in learning styles and needs that emerge just within this simple exercise, and the attendant variety of challenges that any teacher faces in a classroom with up to three times as many students per class as are in a small liberal arts college seminar, are at first daunting for the preservice teachers. But we spend the semester studying and talking together about ways to become the teachers they describe at this first class meeting.

The three phases of this first assignment in "Curriculum and Pedagogy" encapsulate the translations of language and self that the students enrolled in this course are challenged to effect. In these students' experiences we find the accustomedness to engaging with new languages and ways of thinking, because they are still formally students, combined with the vertigo of having to change themselves that professors in the last chapter faced, because they are preparing to be teachers. They are at a particular moment of necessity in translation—a moment one faces when one moves from one culture or country to another—when one must not only learn to speak in new languages but must become a new person.

Students at this point in their formal education look back to their own high school experiences as well as forward to the experiences they want to provide for their future students. They prepare to encounter a familiar context (high schools) and group of people who are foreign (current high school students). And they struggle to develop—in collaboration with high school students like those they are preparing to teach—ways of speaking and interacting that are comprehensible and meaningful to both groups. Their generative struggle is how to redefine the central relationship in education—that between teachers and students—and thus on a more profound level how to conceptualize and practice education.

The Context and the Customs

Working against the training model of teacher education, which "presents a distorted image of the beginning teacher as passive, isolated, and rightfully dependent on the expertise and experience of others,"[1] my goal in "Curriculum and Pedagogy" is for preservice teachers to be active in forging their new identities as well as aware of that process. Sumara and Luce-Kapler describe learning to teach as a negotiation of the dissonances between preservice teachers' preteaching lives and their lives as experienced teachers.[2] Allender tells the prospective teachers with whom he works of the value of achieving "a momentary awareness of both your teacher self and your student self at the same time" because he feels that this awareness is "unusually helpful for learning how to become an effective teacher."[3] Britzman argues that "[l]earning to teach—like teaching itself—is always the process of becoming: a time of formation and transformation."[4]

The metaphor of translation follows in the spirit of these dynamic ways of conceptualizing learning to teach, and it illuminates the educational experience of preservice teachers as they develop discursive forms through which they can both understand and be understood by high school students and as they forge dynamic and integrated identities for themselves. This approach to education does not require these preservice teachers to divide themselves and replace one designated language and prescribed set of practices with others; rather, it allows them to move between languages and cultures "without being split by the difference[s]."[5]

The people I write about in this chapter are students in the first semester of their senior year, but they are looking toward assuming the role of teacher. "Marginally situated in two worlds,"[6] they are cast in the dual role of student-teacher, and they are expected to transition from the former role into the latter as they prepare to move from the college culture (back) to the high school. At this point in their formal education, many preservice teachers have trouble reconciling the different contexts, languages, and identities that are intersecting before and within them. To support them as they prepare to translate discourse practices and themselves, I have designed a course and a specific project within it in collaboration with school-based educators. The course, "Curriculum and Pedagogy," is divided into three parts. During the first part of the course, called Exploring Students' Perspectives/Needs, the preservice teachers reflect on their own schooling experiences and work to uncover some of their assumptions about education, teaching, and learning. They also read a variety of published texts and transcripts of discussions of pedagogical issues among high school students. In addition, the preservice teachers begin an exchange of letters with high school students (I explain the role of high school students in the course more fully below), meet regularly and exchange emails with experienced teachers, and begin as well to visit the classroom in which they will be completing student teaching the following semester. At the end of this section of the course, students draft the first section of their portfolios, which focuses on themselves and others as learners.

During the second segment of the course, called Analyzing Standards, Models of Curriculum, and Forms of Assessment and Evaluation, we explore different notions and models of curriculum and different sets of standards (national, district, and so on). Preservice teachers continue their correspondence with their high school student partners and their collaboration with experienced teachers as well as their visits to class-rooms. At the end of this segment of the course, preservice teachers draft another section of their portfolios, which includes a statement of what they believe high school students need to know and be able to do in the subject area for which the preservice teachers are preparing to teach and relevant standards and curricular models that the preservice teachers plan to use.

The final phase of the course, called Developing Pedagogical Approaches, focuses on putting into plans for practice what the preservice teachers have thought about all semester and over the course of their preparation to teach. We read and discuss texts on different pedagogical approaches, classroom management, lesson planning, and assessment and evaluation. This segment of the course culminates in preservice teachers producing an analysis of their exchange with the high school students as well as a draft of the third section of their portfolio, which must include an idea/metaphor for themselves as a teacher, lessons they have been developing, and examples of forms of assessment and evaluation they plan to use.

Within this course my school-based collaborators and I facilitate a project called Teaching and Learning Together.[7] This project was designed by me and a practicing English teacher at a local high school. We designed it to address what we saw as a significant problem: that in almost all formal conversations that shape educational policies and practices in the United States, students' voices are not among those with the authority to define what prospective teachers should know and be able to do.[8] In designing Teaching and Learning Together, we wanted to disrupt the hierarchy according to which theorists and researchers generate pedagogical knowledge and pass it down to teachers, who labor under perpetual pressure to implement every new or recycled reform, with students simply waiting on the receiving end of this transfer. We also wanted to bring into direct dialogue those preparing to teach with those who are taught, and we wanted to alter the power dynamics that usually inform that teacher-student relationship. Finally, we wanted to bring into conversation high school students separated by the tracking systems, both acknowledged and implicit, that designate their daily schedules and thus in large measure their trajectories throughout their schooling lives.

We decided to position a diverse group of high school students as teacher educators both in conversation with preservice teachers and in conversation with one another. As I discuss elsewhere,[9] our idea was that this radical project would allow us to enact and model an approach to teacher preparation that could disrupt the one-way transfer of pedagogical knowledge, the assumptions that adults only teach and young people only learn, and the stereotypes and assumptions students with diverse identities have in one another's and society's eyes. We hoped that this repositioning of high school students would challenge how most teacher educators think about teacher preparation, how most preservice teachers think about and interact with students, and how most students think about and act themselves.

The central component of this project is a weekly exchange of letters between preservice teachers enrolled in "Curriculum and Pedagogy" and selected students who attend a local public high school. The dialogue is a private exchange between the preservice teachers and the high school students focused on issues my collaborator and I recommend as well as those that the pairs believe are relevant to teaching and learning. This written dialogue is complemented and informed by weekly conversations between the preservice teachers and me in the college classroom and weekly conversations between the high school students and my collaborator at the high school. Both sets of conversations have the same focus: topics listed on the course syllabus, such as creating a classroom environment conducive to learning, designing engaging lessons, creating effective tests, and so on. The conversations held among the high school students are audiotaped, transcribed, and given to the preservice teachers as part of their required reading for the course. At the end of the semester, the preservice teachers draw on their letter exchange, course readings, and these transcripts to write formal analyses of what they have learned from participating in this project.

Thus in "Curriculum and Pedagogy," preservice teachers are required to collaborate with those they are preparing to be—high-school teachers—and those they are preparing to teach—high school students. I focus in this discussion on the dialogue that they have with high school students, but it should be kept in mind that this dialogue unfolds within the larger context of multiple conversations and collaborations. Within these multiple contexts and relationships, the preservice teachers must bridge several languages and cultures.

The Challenges of Translation

The preservice teachers enrolled in "Curriculum and Pedagogy" are preparing to re-enter what is, from one angle, a familiar context. When one re-enters a context, one may think that one knows that context and how those who populate it speak and behave. Because every preservice teacher has spent seventeen years in classrooms as a student, she may assume that she is fluent in the language of schooling and understands the ways of interacting appropriate to that educational context. Over the course of a lifetime spent in school, preservice teachers have developed deeply ingrained assumptions about and images of students,[10] and they typically have derived some "well-worn and commonsensical images of the teacher's work."[11] As Bullough and Gitlin argue, "the beginning teacher brings to teacher education a plethora of often unarticulated and unexamined beliefs about schooling, teaching, and learning, and the self that require scrutiny."[12] The assumptions and images many preservice teachers bring to their preparation to teach have much in common because, as hooks points out, "most of us were taught in classrooms where styles of teaching reflected the notion of a single norm of thought and experience, which we were encouraged to believe was universal."[13]

Although they bring with them a set of images of and assumptions about pre-college educational contexts and modes of participation appropriate to them, the four years preservice teachers spend in college can contribute to the pre-college classroom's becoming a strange place. This alienation is due, in part, to the distance between K–12 classrooms and college teacher-preparation programs; in most models of secondary preservice teacher education for undergraduates, conversations about teaching and learning are carried on at a significant remove from the places and people they concern—high school classrooms and high school students. Framed primarily in theoretical terms, conducted almost exclusively in college classrooms, and generally limited to exchanges among preservice teachers and teacher educators, these discussions remain abstract explorations of ideas rather than grounded professional preparation. Within such forums, preservice teachers develop pedagogical beliefs and approaches with little or no input from those they are preparing to teach. This situation is analogous to attempting to render a translation of a text for a context and audience for which one has outdated, vague, or no understanding and yet, perhaps, one believes one knows and understands. Like the predefined and fixed roles many metaphors offer teachers, the perspective, understanding, language, and sense of self a preservice teacher brings to her teacher preparation can remain fixed in a place and time in the past that no longer exists. Forged in what might have been a similar context—a high-school classroom—they have been reshaped through college and are in need of further re-rendering before they can make sense.

The context revisited after years of distance is not all that is new and strange; so too is the necessity of speaking in new voices and creating new identities. To learn these new languages and something about the context in which they are spoken, preservice teachers need to listen to and talk with high school students.[14] The amplification of the high school students' voices challenges preservice teachers to attend to the language of a constituency that has values and perspectives that might not initially make sense to the preservice teachers. They need exposure and time to re-learn or in some cases to learn for the first time languages they need to communicate with middle or high school students and to express ever-evolving understandings. They bring with them languages forged in other times and places, and now they need to learn and forge new languages together with students. This process is not a matter of developing a simplified language or way of thinking with which to communicate with high school students; it is, rather, a matter of developing *with* high school students ways of thinking and talking that work for both groups.

One of the reasons that this learning is particularly challenging for preservice teachers in their senior year of college is that for three years they have been steeped in a very different way of thinking, speaking, and writing. Bartholomae describes how, when students embark upon their higher education, they must "learn to speak as we do, to try on the peculiar ways of knowing, selecting, evaluating, reporting, concluding, and arguing that define the discourse of our community." Students must engage in this process, Bartholomae suggests, before they feel the authority or have the fluency to succeed, since participation in the discourse community of higher education is required before the skills to do so are learned.[15] In other words, when students enter the culture of higher education, in order to be accepted in that culture, they must speak a foreign language before they know it. I had to speak German before I knew it. Anyone who enters a new culture or context must do the same.

Like all college students, preservice teachers seeking certification at the undergraduate level have just undergone this process. With their nascent fluency in the language of the academy, they still recall what it felt like not to be able to find words. In an effort to bridge these worlds, the preservice teachers in my course work simultaneously on their translations of language and on their translations of themselves through reading, talking about, and composing within the following forums that constitute the Teaching and Learning Together project: the letters that they write to the high school students, the conversations in the college class among themselves and with me, the conversations among the high school students, which are transcribed and assigned to the preservice teachers as required reading, and the formal analyses they write at the end of the experience.

Each of these forums serves as what Mary Soliday calls a site of self-translation;[16] the preservice teachers have the opportunity within each to try out and to reflect on the language they use and develop as well as to interpret the translations of themselves that they produce in the various forums. They find that their experiences are interpretable, and their interpretations prepare them for subsequent readings and translations.

The idea behind having this project in the semester prior to the practicing teaching semester is to give preservice teachers the opportunity to learn and re-learn languages and ways of interacting with high school students before they take on the formal role of teacher in a classroom. In other words, it gives each preservice teacher an opportunity to experiment with the languages of learning and teaching as well as render and re-render herself in ways that resonate both for her and for students or in ways that clearly need to be revised before she re-enters the high school context. This process is a challenging and potentially daunting one that can, however, invigorate learning. When she first re-encounters high school students and schools, a preservice teacher might feel uncertain about how to read and respond to them. Rather than embrace a prescribed set of discourse practices and a prescribed role, she can try out a variety of interpretations and modes of expression. Some of these attempts may work to capture her meaning and student attention and some may be flat, ineffective, or otherwise unpleasurable. After a number of attempts at creating a language that bridges herself and her high school student partner, a preservice teacher can begin to develop some confidence in her ability to express herself and to interpret others, even if the language sounds at first strange to her ears. Through much practice and reflection, she develops greater comfort and fluency. After extensive practice, she may come to see that the process of becoming a teacher is an ongoing process of interpretation and a continuous changing of condition and form.

Discerning Language and Context: An Early Phase in Translation

Becoming successful students in college moves preservice teachers away from the dominant discourse practices of high schools. When they turn to conversing with high school students, preservice teachers are disoriented by the ways that the high school students express themselves. The high school students' language sounds odd, unfamiliar, and foreign, and it refers to life experiences that the preservice teachers may not share. Confronted with surprising words and the often unfamiliar experiences to which those words refer, preservice teachers must look for ways to make meaning. Their first responses to the high school students' words reflect their first efforts to interpret both texts and the people who composed them. Some preservice teachers are like their students and some are not, and how similar or different they perceive themselves to be shifts the challenges of translation.

Upon receiving a first letter from her high school student partner, one preservice teacher, Lisa Grant, states: "[My partner's letter] was very informal. Really honest. Very negative about things he was negative about and positive about things he's positive about. This one comment was very blunt. A name he called one of his teachers. I wasn't sure how to respond."[17] Another preservice teacher, Mary McClean, describes her very negative initial reactions to her high school student partner's early letters, which were written in simple sentences and referred to the student's personal interests: "The simple sentences irritated me. I took them as indications of either stupidity, insincerity or both [and I thought that] if this was the level we were going to communicate on, then I was certainly not going to get anything out of the project."[18]

It is not that these preservice teachers do not understand the literal meaning of the words they read in the high school students' letters; it is, rather, that these words are offensive or carry negative meaning for the preservice teachers. In the first instance, Grant is taken off-guard by the blunt and direct language her high school partner uses. She finds this use of language inappropriate, and her uncertainty temporarily brings her up short. In the second instance, McClean reads the words of her partner as repugnant and irrelevant. Her interpretation of these words makes it unlikely that she will embark on any kind of translation process because "all understanding, and the demonstrative statement of understanding which is translation, starts with an act of trust . . . we grant . . . that there is 'something there' to be understood."[19] Connected to the necessity of trust is the necessity of desire: we must want to understand and be understood.

This challenge is not a one-way translation issue; the language that the preservice teachers use also makes little sense to the high school students. One preservice teacher, Pia Rao, learned how her use of particular words provoked a response from her high school partner that she had not anticipated and that made her aware of a need to revise her use of language. Rao explains that the first time her high school student partner wrote back to her, she said: "By the way, what does 'eloquent' and 'aloof' mean? I'm a retard and don't understand them." Rao was horrified to realize that she "had been trying to be responsive and supportive [of her high school student partner] . . . but instead unknowingly made her feel belittled." Realizing her mistake, Rao took note "not to use 'vocab' words in order that we might have clear communication." She continued, "it's fruitless to try to explain a new concept to students or to engage them in a discussion if they cannot understand what you are trying to say." Elaborating on this point further, she states: "teachers must make sure that their avenues of communication are clear with students. Seemingly insignificant things like word choice and tones of voice are important to how the student perceives you."[20] This statement not only evidences translation but is also about translation.

Another preservice teacher, Nicki Weaver, had a similar experience after her first exchange of letters with her high school student partner. She explains: "He's really expressive about his ideas [but] I think I scared him a little bit. I just jumped right in to talking about pedagogy, and he wrote, 'Whoa, I barely know what that means.' So . . . that really helped me just kind of step back and think about how I am going to communicate with him in the future."[21] Realizing that this was not simply a language issue but a perspective issue as well, Weaver continued: "I need to start from where he is, see what he brings up, and then sort of build on that, rather than asking him to build on one of my ideas."[22] Weaver realizes that she cannot simply use words that are familiar and meaningful to her; rather, she must learn the language her high school partner uses to express his perceptions. Like Rao's recognition of the potential for language to impede as well as facilitate communication, Weaver's realization highlights as well her profound insight into what learning is. Here, as elsewhere in this book, Jerome Bruner's words are particularly apt: "One starts somewhere—where the learner *is*."[23] Of course, with the translation of a text a translator begins with the "original" she has before her. The notion of beginning with the *person* that one has before one is less common. When this process of interpretation is understood within the conceptual framework of translation, however, then what it means to "read" and interpret what is before one—a text or a person—changes dramatically.

As these examples illustrate, the worlds that these high school students' letters open up, and the language that the students use to describe their lives in these worlds, are at first disorienting to preservice teachers. Many simply don't like the words and worlds; others pass initial judgments that there is no meaning in them to be had. But something else is happening to these preservice teachers as well—something else that contributes to their unease. The strangeness of the high school students' language and ways of thinking calls into question the preservice teachers' own language and ways of thinking. As when one first begins to learn any different language, it is common to feel confused by all the new words and structures that characterize that language. But more than that one also begins to question what one thinks one knows about one's own language and ways of thinking. Any significant encounter with the unfamiliar can evoke a feeling of alienation that causes one to re-evaluate all that one thinks one already knows.

At this stage of the project I try to reassure the preservice teachers that there need not be a single correct interpretation of and response to any given interaction and that they will not lose in any permanent way their grip on meaning. Part of what Teaching and Learning Together affords the preservice teachers is the opportunity to try out multiple possible forms of expressions—a range of translations. Their questions and uncertainties are valid and can be educative. They must compose and re-compose, embracing the notion that this rendering and re-rendering is part of an ongoing process.

Although unease and uncertainty characterize the early moments of the letter exchange, the initial translations that the preservice teachers hazard are thoughtful because of their awareness of the need to understand and be understood—a need made immediate by the presence of the high school students. At this early phase of translation, vocabulary, tone, and other syntactical choices are foregrounded as preservice teachers attempt initial interpretations and renderings. One preservice teacher, Linda Russell, explains, "it took me a long time to decide if I was going to type or hand-write the [first] letter."[24] Some preservice teachers mirror or match in their responses the tone of the letter they received. Jessye Patterson explains, "My partner was really formal so I wrote back formally."[25] Others want to set a different tone. In her response to her high school student partner, whose language she had found blunt and inappropriate, Grant explains: "[T]he best response seemed to be one that would lead by example. I wanted to *show* him elaboration and detail; I wanted to *show* him that I cared more about explaining a personality than about insulting a person."[26] No matter what choices of interpretation and expression they make, all of the preservice teachers want to move the translation process forward so that communication and learning can take place.

Talking with one another and with me in the college class, preservice teachers work through their own interpretive and composing processes as they articulate how they respond to their high school students. Russell explains that she took things her high school partner "had written about in a personal narrative about herself and [tried] to formulate some of those into questions in my letter so that she could directly respond to them."[27] Like Weaver, Russell started "where the student is"; she started with the text and person before her. Another preservice teacher, Eileen Dormand, adopted a similar approach, choosing "to make the questions interesting so [my partner] could write a letter back."[28] Dormand elaborates that she "tried not to overwhelm her [partner] with questions, I only asked a few questions in the first [letter], and I knew I had to ask them in a way she could respond to." Russell clarified her understanding of this negotiation—"So almost like reframing it"—and Dormand reiterated her approach—"Trying to make it real personal."[29]

Choices about form and tone are choices about translation. Every decision about the way a text looks and every decision about self-representation affects the reader's experience and interpretation, and the preservice teachers must weigh possible meanings, consider audience and context, and make choices about renderings. Interpreting the words of their high school partners and striving to compose responses that will be comprehensible and compelling, these preservice teachers are attending to the voices of the high school students and experimenting with their own. As they interpret the language of their dialogue partners and teach themselves a language through which to communicate with those high school students, these preservice teachers engage in "a transformative rather than an additive process."[30] Each exchange changes the meaning a preservice teacher makes of the dialogue. These exchanges are early drafts of translations. They seek to preserve an echo of the original, a spirit, a sense—one that is pleasurable to read in one's own language[31]—but they also seek to create new versions. All are produced in the spirit of trying to better communicate—to connect.

In my role as supporter of the preservice teachers' translations, my goal in the early part of the semester is to raise the preservice teachers' awareness of the need for translation while not making them overly self-conscious. When one is faced with new or seemingly unfamiliar languages, practices, ways of understanding, and ways of being, a danger exists of becoming overly sensitized, self-critical, and even paralyzed. One can quickly move from initial uncertainty—"I wasn't sure how to respond"[32]—to feeling unable to make a choice of interpretation or expression. By highlighting the need for translation, and by encouraging and supporting the preservice teachers as they make initial attempts at translation, I convey to them that I believe that they can, in fact, translate what they read and what they want to express in meaningful ways.

The initial renderings preservice teachers compose can sound strange to them. In a discussion of how her "voice" is changing, Nancy Chadwick expresses the strangeness of this change:

One thing I notice is that [my partner will] be asking me questions, and I'll be asking about things like workload or what a good class is like. And then I'll re-read what I've written and I'll think, "I sound like such a geek." It sounds like, "Yeah, it's good to have a teacher that pushes you" and stuff like that. But if I'm out with a friend and we're talking about teaching, we just bitch about it, you know what I mean? And it's just interesting to see that when I'm talking to someone who's younger, that I see as the kind of person I would be teaching, I'm already picking up this mindset that is not my mindset, you know what I mean? You know it's like, "Courses are a really good way to study things you want to study." And on the one hand I feel that way, but I don't usually articulate it that way.[33]

Chadwick recognizes that she is changing not only her language but also her position in relation to an educational context and those within it. She is neither falsely taking up a position nor speaking falsely; she believes what she is saying—"on the one hand I feel that way"—but what startles her is how she is saying it—"I don't usually articulate it that way". Her appeal to be understood—marked by her repetition of the question "you know what I mean?"—suggests that she wants her own process of translation to be recognized and legitimated.

This stage of education is a strange and disquieting one. The preservice teachers hear themselves speaking and don't recognize their own voices. The medium they are using to express themselves is still relatively strange to them. Their responses range from reflecting tone and content, to reacting against it, to trying to find some meeting place in between.

The Challenges of Translation: Deeper In

In late September, "Curriculum and Pedagogy" begins, as usual, with a discussion of how the exchange of letters with the high school students is going. Jessica starts the conversation: "I've had to think of new approaches because my student writes very little. I try to couch it very personally . . . I think I have to draw him out . . . talk more about his life."[34] Other preservice teachers discuss ways they have attempted to do the same thing. Karen explains: "What I do is I bring up something and talk about my experience, and then I ask him how he felt in the same situation."

Not all preservice teachers are initially willing to try to draw students out; some do not yet trust "that there is 'something there' to be understood."[35] A month into the project, Mary is still extremely frustrated. Angry and disappointed, she tells us that she has not written a letter to her high school partner this week, and that she doesn't think she can. An uncomfortable silence follows this assertion. I wait.

Then Mary's classmates step in to try to guide her. One of her peers, Julie, careful to respond not only to what Mary has said but also to the feelings behind the words, says, "I keep thinking about this in the context of, if this were one of your students, and my first reaction is that you can't give up and not write back." Another peer, Justine, suggests approaching the interaction from a different angle: "Is there maybe a non-confrontational approach you could try? Like, 'Here's my phone number'?" Michael poses a question to clarify his and Mary's understanding of the tone of the relationship: "She's not antagonistic toward you, right?" Building on this point, Jeffrey confirms the possibility of successful communication: "I think you can send her a message that's very clear without necessarily being angry."[36]

The message that all of her classmates send is that with students one cannot quantify and judge their participation. Rather, it is the teacher's responsibility to continue to try to make the relationship with a student work. Inspired by this support, Mary leaves class to write to her high school student partner. But it takes her until the end of the semester to fully realize that she needed to take responsibility for interpreting her high school partner in a different way and for constructing a different self with which to interact with high school students. In her dialogue analysis paper, she writes:

In becoming aware of how assumptions I made set the stage for the unfolding relationship between [my high school partner] and me, I realized that I was judging her according to my interests and strengths; I was defining intelligence solely in reference to myself. I made the mistake of interpreting her different (from mine) writing style and her level of comfort with written self-expression as lack of intelligence. . . . Now I see that I had abdicated my responsibility in our conversations and in the relationship as a whole. I had felt uncomfortable . . . and my result was to retreat into my own skeptical perspective. Essentially, my failure to assume responsibility for the early steps of our relationship left her floundering.[37]

    Mary is able to come to a better understanding of her high school student partner and of herself, as she explains, through "a process of self-examination that I not only want to continue, but will have to continue to be the kind of teacher I want to be."[38]

The preservice teahers who participate in the project struggle in different ways and to different degrees. Many possible layers of meaning exist in every text and interaction, and the words one chooses to use and the words one chooses to emphasize shape what is conveyed or perceived. These choices are based on unconscious assumptions as well as deliberation. Explaining how she learned both to make meaning of what was there and create a new version, one preservice teacher, Jessica Barnett, tells how she struggled with how to discern in her high school partner's stories implications for teaching practice and how to compose her own theoretically grounded ideas in a language accessible to her dialogue partner. She explains: "When I first undertook the dialogue project with Arthur . . . I expected that I would share ideas about education with a person representing those whom I would eventually be teaching. However, his introductory letter listed the types of music he liked, some career possibilities, his after-school job. He did not mention any specific thoughts about education. By the third week, I realized that Arthur was not terribly interested in educational issues, at least not as I had presented them."[39]

Because she brought an expectation about the form in which Arthur would share ideas about education, Barnett finds herself disappointed. Her initial response is to "give up" on what she had hoped to get out of the project: a sophisticated dialogue about how to be a good teacher. So, instead of focusing on issues clearly connected to pedagogy, Barnett explains that she "strayed from the texts and issues we were covering in 'Curriculum and Pedagogy' and discussed instead a wide range of topics based primarily on interests or thoughts that seemed pertinent at the time." In other words, she turned to starting where the learner is.

As their correspondence continued, Barnett found that it was effective to share stories from her own experience as a way to invite Arthur to address important issues. She explains that "it was through examples from my personal life that I asked him about such topics as motivation, block scheduling, career choices, community service, and school policies regarding dress codes." Barnett shared the same perspective in one discussion in "Curriculum and Pedagogy": "My partner wrote a lot [this week], 'cause he responded to a situation I gave him with my sister. I used that as a way in, saying, 'This happened to my sister. What do you think of this?' And he said, 'Oh, wow, that happened to me too.'"[40]

Barnett found she could elicit responses from Arthur that "embedded his opinion within situations he had experienced or witnessed." As she put it: "His interests and needs came not through a discussion of Freire's pedagogy, but instead from his own personal experience." Although at first Barnett expected Arthur to tell her directly what he liked, how he learned, what worked, and what did not, in a language she was accustomed to at college, upon reflection she realized that she needed to co-construct with Arthur a language that integrated his narratives and her theories. Reflecting on this experience at the end of the semester, Barnett writes: "I remained mildly frustrated until I realized that I was expecting [Arthur] to speak in my language. Amid our discussions of student voice and its value, I had neglected to realize that his learning, his method of articulation, was through experience and concrete examples. I had sought to give him voice while failing to hear the sound of his individual words."

Barnett learned to attend to the words before her, to trust that there is something there to be understood.[41] The realization that she had led Barnett to recognize that not only did she need to learn to listen differently but that she also needed to adjust her discourse practices, although not necessarily her ideas and expectations, when conversing with high-school students. She recognized that she must be careful of her "tendency to use academic jargon and academic approaches" and to avoid alienating students with a strange vocabulary. She concludes her dialogue analysis paper with these insights: "Although many students may be capable of thinking abstractly, they may not have practice doing so or be comfortable with it. Therefore, if I come into a classroom assuming they can, I may immediately alienate them. I must instead associate concrete examples with what I am teaching. Arthur offered quite a few insights, drawing on his own experience and projecting accompanying conclusions to global significance. Nonetheless, I failed to recognize them because I viewed them only as narratives of experience."

Barnett might well have persisted in seeking to elicit certain contributions from Arthur—to "give him a voice"—and, in conjunction, to dismiss Arthur's insights because they were not clothed in the discourse privileged in the academy—the abstract. Instead, she realized that she needed to find a language that bridges and integrates her academic discourse and Arthur's experience-based expressions. She realized that the translation must be a mutually informing, ongoing negotiation that leads to the creation of a shared language. She recognized in her analysis

of her interaction with Arthur what Constantine asserts about the translation of poetry: "a language is a living language only in so far as it can
move and change."[42]

Although it is more often the case that preservice teachers misread a
high school student's use of language and self-presentation as wanting in
sophistication and lacking substance, the reverse can also happen: a preservice teacher can misread a student as more sophisticated than he
might be. Preservice teachers can be brought up short by the discrepancies they experience—between ways of speaking and understanding the
world. Sometimes, however, they are brought up short by the realization
that they had mistakenly believed that there were no gaps in understanding—and thus no need for translation. One preservice teacher,
Michael Wilder, did not realize that he had been misreading his student
partner until the end of the semester when he reflected back on the
exchange of letters.

In a class discussion, Wilder explained why he was so impressed with
his high school partner, Jim: "[It was like] talking to Holden Caulfield
because he was so perceptive and aware of his perceptiveness."[43] Wilder
elaborates in his dialogue analysis paper:

I was genuinely amazed to read some of these phrases from the hand of a sixteen-
year-old. This is not to suggest that I underestimate teenagers, but Jim struck me
as truly remarkable. While it is not uncommon for a student to be aware of what
(s)he is learning, it does indeed seem rare for a student to be aware of his awareness. And this double awareness shaped my conversation with Jim throughout the
eleven weeks, and it led me to possibly overestimate Jim's ability to deeply engage
himself in his ideas, and, even more importantly, led me to underestimate my
role in helping him to further explain his ideas.[44]

Jim's sophistication allowed Wilder to avoid focusing on what he must do
as a teacher to offer scaffolding to help Jim deepen his ongoing analyses
and efforts toward self-expression. Throughout the semester, the conversation had seemed so fluid. There was no wrestling with definitions, no
disagreement about meaning, no obvious discrepancies in interpretation.
Because they seemed to be speaking the same language and making the
same meanings within it, there was, apparently, no need for translation.

In retrospect, however, Wilder had a different reading. He explains:

throughout this dialogue project it seemed as if we were always on the same page,
but to the extent that a struggle within the dialogue appeared absent, my lack of
communication with Jim as to what I wanted him to do put us on very different
pages. I am not even sure if Jim was capable of really explaining his responses to
the degree I hoped for. His talents, which were so obvious through his writing,
hid from me that fact that he was not my peer, but rather a sixteen-year-old boy
who was not going to (or could not) simply answer my questions about why he

feels this way or what made him feel this way. He is not a college senior who is used to the difficult task of continuous reflection.

Wilder's analysis adds an interesting dimension to the question of what kinds of translation are necessary. Even though two people can seem to make the same meaning out of the same words, what Wilder learned is that understanding surface meanings—decoding or literal comprehension— is not enough. Their seeming congruence of expression and interpretation masked what could have been deeper meanings or interpretations. A deeper, more ongoing analysis is necessary to discern the subtle and perhaps not so subtle nuances and complexities of a text and a person. As Constantine argues about translating poetry, one must consider "the total workings of a text, not just the words."[45] Wilder's realization that Jim's sophistication "led me to underestimate my role in helping [Jim] to further explain his ideas" is an important realization about a teacher's responsibility as a facilitator of the translations in which students are perpetually engaged.

Like Wilder, Melanie Jones also came close to profoundly misreading and misinterpreting a student, but she caught herself. After half a semester of very productive dialogue, Jones explains in her dialogue analysis:

[My high school partner] Sally wrote to me, "Sometimes teachers treat me differently because I am in special education. Would you treat a student differently if they came up to you and you knew they were in special education?" I was shocked. This bright, well-spoken girl I had been enjoying dialogue with for a few weeks was a special education student. I didn't know what that meant, for me or the project. I wondered if I should have been asking her different questions. Should I be treating her differently? I was amazed. I did not even guess that she had any learning difficulties at all.[46]

At Jones's high school, she explained in her dialogue analysis, one third of the students were "kids who had been diagnosed with ADD [attention deficit disorder] or ADHD [attention deficit hyperactivity disorder], who had poor SAT and other test scores, and more importantly had significant problems reading and writing. These students, if they went to college at all, almost always went to community colleges, and often had behavioral problems in school." Based on her own high school experiences, Jones had developed an interpretation of students labeled with learning disabilities. And, as she explained, "Even though we spoke often in 'Curriculum and Pedagogy' about integrating learning disabled students into classrooms, I admit I hoped I would never have to try to teach this type of student."

Given the interpretation that she had assimilated from her own high school experience, Jones had no basis or cause for comparison between the students who had been labeled learning disabled in her high school and Sally. And yet as soon as she learned that Sally was labeled as a learning disabled student, the "original" text that Jones held in her mind resurfaced and caused her to call into question the present experience she was having with Sally. Earlier forms of language use and interpretation that we have developed inform all subsequent translations. For Jones, the meaning of this original interpretation and earlier iterations of it were so deeply ingrained that they overshadowed the evidence she had before her that Sally was functioning perfectly well in their dialogue.

Fortunately, Jones kept her focus on what Sally had to say: "I asked her why she was considered a special education student. She replied, 'because I can't take tests and I have a hard time understanding things and the teachers sometimes have to explain things over and over for me to understand.'" Instead of reverting to her older interpretation, Jones chose to re-read the text before her. Doing so allowed her to find new meaning not only in Sally's experience but in her own as well. Reflecting on Sally's explanation of why she was deemed a special education student, Jones writes: "Actually, I thought, that's really not all that different from me, or most other students I know."

Jones learned a very important lesson through her dialogue with Sally, her reflection on it, and her willingness to critically analyze and revise her response to Sally's learning disabled status:

I thought about [Sally's] question and realized I would have treated her differently had I known. I would have acted on my assumptions about learning disabled students and never would have gotten very far in the dialogue. She made me realize that my conceptions about students with learning disabilities were incorrect. By sharing herself with me and helping me to destroy an unfounded assumption, [Sally] helped me to realize that teaching learning disabled students is not something to be viewed with apprehension. I actually now hope to have the opportunity to teach students like Sally who have enormous potential but just need some extra help and a good teacher.

Thus Jones not only re-interpreted the original image she had in her head of a learning disabled student; she revised her own sense of her self as a future teacher—as someone not only open to but interested in working with students so labeled.

Another preservice teacher, Jeffrey Livingston, also realized through initial mis-readings and subsequent revisions what his responsibility as a teacher must be. Initially Livingston read his high school student partner as disaffected and disengaged from school. When he met Don, he thought he was "a really bright student . . . who made the choice to rebel against the system, and damn whatever future he was destroying."[47] Throughout their initial conversation, Livingston perceived that Don "was less than enthusiastic about getting involved" and "muttering under his breath was his only seemingly bitter and disgusted means of communication." To Livingston's eye, Don fit a certain stereotype, developed while Livingston was himself a student, which dominated his reading of Don: "even his dress reminded me of those students I thought were slackers at my own [high] school."

This initial reading might have kept Livingston from trying out other interpretations. Instead, he worked to get to know Don. By their fourth exchange, Livingston had learned that Don had had an accident, the effects of which included short-term memory loss and fine motor skill impairment. With this new information, Livingston began to re-interpret some of Don's behaviors. As he explained, "Don's initial low grades may not have been a sign of apathy, but rather a circumstance of his ADHD, and his preference for verbal expression over written." Similarly, after corresponding with Don about the lack of support he had received after his injury, Livingston surmised that perhaps Don was muttering "to reinforce his short-term memory, or because of insecurity. Maybe he was disgruntled or upset, but it certainly seems justified considering how little help he's had." Through their dialogue, a more complex image of Don emerged, which helped Livingston identify ways in which he as a future teacher could better understand and more effectively connect with students like Don. Thus, this realization was not limited to his experience with Don; it made Livingston realize as well that he needs to continually read and re-read students.

Livingston's rethinking of his view of Don led him to a profound realization. In his own words: "It is frighteningly easy [for a teacher] to misframe student struggle as apathy. Apathy is a [teacher's] quick fix, and it removes our responsibility as teachers to do something. . . . Such a denial of assistance is an inexcusable course of action, and one I am much more conscious of after learning about Don's struggle." Livingston recognized that taking the time to read all of his students as carefully as he did Don would make his role as teacher more challenging: "This realization has, in many ways, made teaching harder for me. I see now that if I want to help all of my students achieve, I need to know them, to work with their skills and their abilities, and I need to somehow do this all in the framework provided by a particular educational system."

Don's assessment of Livingston as a future teacher is testimony to the efficacy of Livingston's attitude and approach. In the final meeting of the high school students and the preservice teachers, Don said that his dialogue with Livingston "made me respect teachers more. I never really thought that they wondered about some of the things that [Livingston] asked me. And just to think that they actually wondered about that or cared about that made me respect them a little more."[48]

Each of these preservice teachers is in a process not just of learning to be better readers, better interpreters; they are also learning to translate themselves. These retrospective accounts tell the stories of how these preservice teachers realized what kinds of translations of student texts and selves they had been rendering, how they must re-read their exchanges and re-write their interpretations, and that to do so requires a translation of self.

Translation of Texts/Translation of Selves

In a reflection on a relatively early moment in her exchange of letters with her high school student partner, Eileen Dormand's words capture the relationship between translating words and translating selves: "The interaction between Cynthia and me was teaching me how to listen to a student, to analyze her thoughts, to apply them to the formation of my own teaching persona. . . . The relationship we were building brought my reflections back to my own goals of being an effective teacher and interacting with future students."[49]

The preservice teachers are particularly attuned to the process of translating themselves precisely because they are between formal roles. Not yet responsible for a classroom full of students, yet in dialogue with a high school student, the preservice teachers who participate in Teaching and Learning Together are in an undefined, in-between position. As one preservice teacher, Nicki Weaver explains: "My role was ambiguous . . . I was not a teacher or a student or an adult or a teenager. Here I was, trying to be myself, but not sure how much and what parts of myself to share."[50] The "in-between place"[51] or liminal space between student and teacher that Weaver describes can be conceptualized as that between one kind of "confinement"[52] and another—a fixed definition of student and a fixed definition of teacher. Alternatively, it can accommodate the kind of un-fixed understanding that both language and social roles tend to work against. In an effort to keep this space open, I discourage the pursuit of fixed, unambiguous roles. Instead, I encourage Weaver and other preservice teachers to try out various ways of rendering themselves. Many preservice teachers feel, as Chadwick did, that the letter exchange in Teaching and Learning Together "allow[s] for a great deal of role flexibility. Within each paragraph [in the letters] the dynamic of who was teaching and who was learning changed. We were both students, experiencing teachers, at the same time as I was preparing to become one."[53]

During the mid- and latter part of the semester, when preservice teachers are no longer struggling with word-level interpretation, each new exchange of letters is a part of a larger exchange that takes place on grounds already established. The preservice teachers have forged a working vocabulary; they can communicate with the high school students, even if they find upon reflection, as Wilder did, that the communication was not as clear as they had thought. This process parallels my own when I began to focus more on discerning and conveying larger meanings when I was learning German and became a different self through that process. It parallels as well the experience of the sophomores as they became new selves by writing through a variety of perspectives. And it parallels the experience of the college professors in that as they became different selves by shifting their notions of authority in teaching, these preservice teachers produced new versions of themselves. The preservice teachers see this as a process of co-composition. As one preservice teacher, Sharita Watkins, puts it: "I have come to realize that . . . my students will provide me with new ideas and my incorporation of those experiences into my identity as a teacher exemplifies the flexibility and constant changing of myself."[54]

Not only do these preservice teachers recognize that the roles of student and teacher can be fluid and dynamic, they also realize that they have the option and the responsibility to create that fluidity. As one preservice teacher, Lynne Castle, explains: "People can choose to close themselves into a role, or they can step in and out of many. Roles and knowledge are on a continuum, a spectrum of choices and expectations. [My high school partner] Vanessa and I built our knowledge [together], rather than giving it to one another, and neither one of us was ever only a teacher or student in the traditional sense."[55] In the late 1970s, Rorty criticized narrow categories of learning and teaching that dichotomize the roles of student and teacher.[56] Although the pressure to choose between the two persists, Castle refuses to accept the dichotomy. Projecting into her future as a teacher, she writes: "I want to always be thinking, interpreting, exchanging. I realize that the school system will force me into a role that is more closed than I would like it to be, but there is no reason why I cannot interpret it as I like. There need not be a dichotomy between teacher and learner. I can indeed be both."[57] Castle realizes that being a teacher-student is not being "a living oxymoron"[58] but is rather the first of many renderings of a complex role, a complex self.

These preservice teachers' initial attempts to recompose their identities yield translations that resonate, and the preservice teachers indicate that they will continue to translate themselves. Other preservice teachers have the equally educative experience of producing initial interpretations of themselves that call for re-interpretation and re-rendering. One preservice teacher, Tina Spinelli, used the following questions to frame her analysis of her dialogue with her high-school partner Anub: "How much of myself [do] I want to reveal when I teach[?] Do I want to take on a persona that differs from the one I really have, and if I do, how much different? Is it possible to be someone other than who I really am; won't my true personality just come through anyway?"[59] Read within the conceptual framework of translation, with Spinelli understood as both "text" and translator, these are profound questions about meaning, representation, and interpretation. What is the essence, the "spirit,"[60] the "echo"[61] of the original that must be preserved as it is re-rendered in a translation? Spinelli ponders the tension between "faithful" representation and alternative images. "[T]he ideal model for translation becomes that which creates the simultaneous experience of both proximity and separateness, intimacy and alterity."[62]

In trying to decide how much of her self to include in her interactions with students, in her representations of herself to students, Spinelli reflects on an exchange she and her high school student partner Anub had about religion. A very devout Christian, Anub raised questions with Spinelli about controversial topics such as abortion and the death penalty. Reading this exchange retrospectively, Spinelli felt that she had gone too far in expressing her own opinions, possibly shutting down, confusing, or upsetting Anub because she, as an authority figure of sorts, expressed beliefs contrary to his. Looking ahead to her future, she explains: "as a teacher I will have even more authority, so my opinion will matter to my students even more. I plan to push my students to question the beliefs that they hold, but without making them feel threatened. I think in this case I went too far, and I will be wary of doing so [again] in the future."

Reflecting on her struggle over the course of the semester to render versions of herself with she felt comfortable, Spinelli explains that "some of my decisions concerning how I represented myself have been ones I would make again, while others have resulted in situations where I have not been comfortable." Although Spinelli experienced some discomfort in some renderings of herself, she turned this discomfort into an important lesson. She explains that there is no "defined formula" for being a teacher; "I will have to struggle with this issue throughout the rest of my teaching career." Spinelli recognized that she will have to translate herself anew in each teaching situation.

The words and phrases these preservice teachers use—dynamic, interpreting, exchanging, constant changing of myself, struggle with this issue throughout the rest of my teaching career—are words that reflect the ongoing work of becoming a teacher. Weaver's choice to make rather than accept her identity, Watkins's explanation of how her students' input will prompt her constantly to redefine herself, Castle's insistence that she can define and redefine her role for herself, and Spinelli's struggle to render herself in ways that are comfortable to her and leave spaces for students—all of these prefigure the kinds of ongoing translation of self these preservice teachers will engage in when they enter their own classrooms.

A practicing teacher must make herself "comprehensible to others in a new sphere" many times across her career and many times within a day—in classroom interaction, in individual conferences with students, in interactions with colleagues, in interactions with parents. In each case, her role or the version of herself that she composes is different, but it is nonetheless a rendering of herself.

On the Brink of Practice: The Necessary Conditions for Translation

The semester is drawing to a close. The preservice teachers have discussed with their high school partners how to end their correspondence—or maintain it, as some choose to do—and all the preservice teachers and high school students are gathered together for one final meeting and celebration. Boxes of pizza, assorted bottles of soda, and piles of napkins are scattered across the desks in the classroom at the high school where we meet.

After everyone has had some time just to munch and chat, we invite preservice teachers and high school students alike to comment on their experience of the project. One preservice teacher, Jessica, says: "I think what this project taught me was that students at the high school level think about these issues just as much as we do, except we've been studying them in textbooks so we have all these names for the things, but Reggie would say something in one way, and I would say it in another way, and we would be saying the exact same thing."[63] Another preservice teacher, Julie, explains: "My whole life I've been a big talker, I've never really been that great of a listener, so, it took me a little while to realize that I wasn't listening very well and that I needed to start doing that. I'm glad that this project was here so that you can learn to do that kind of listening in a different kind of way than you ever have before."

High school students offer their reflections. Maria explains: "I came from South America about four years ago, to this country, and still, up to this date, I found myself at a lower level than I wish I would be in being a student, intellectual-wise. So this project, just having discussions and meetings after school every Wednesday has helped me in my thinking process and my thinking skills. I think they've developed a lot."[64] Another student, Sarah, explains: "it kind of made me think about how to be a better student almost 'cause it makes you think that . . . a teacher is up there and they [sic] worked hard to come up with this lesson plan, and if you're not going to put in a hundred percent then you're letting them [sic] down in a way."

Both the preservice teachers' and the high school students' comments reflect ways in which they are translating or thinking about translating themselves: into people who can understand one another even though they speak different languages; into people who know how to listen; into better students. Their evolving ability to listen and integrate what they hear will make their interpretations of themselves and others as well as their rendering of themselves more vivid, compelling, and communicative.

For preservice teachers to be able to effect translation, certain conditions must be in place to support them. The forums provided in "Curriculum and Pedagogy" both facilitate and throw into relief the translation processes in which these preservice teachers will engage as teachers, but a hundredfold (with a full roster of high school students) and without the benefit of time, support, and feedback from others. Teaching and Learning Together legitimates and facilitates a process that might otherwise feel like a perpetual crisis of identity and an inability to make meaning. It does so through its consistent challenge to maintain and to analyze a reciprocal interaction; the ongoing rendering and re-rendering of the self that participation in Teaching and Learning requires offers a unique and generative opportunity to engage in the process of learning to teach. A critical aspect of this process is discerning where gaps in communication and understanding are, what it takes to bridge these gaps, and what selves can be produced through an ongoing process of reading, discussing, revising, and re-rendering.

Through the exchange of texts, the ongoing oral analysis of them, and the culminating written reflections on them, the preservice teachers both maintain a sense of who they are and forge new identities. Looking back from the final moment of the semester, the preservice teachers perceive this process of identity formation and what it means. In her dialogue analysis paper, Julie Arribas writes about her process of becoming a teacher as "affirming the identity I have created for myself"[65]—an identity that makes connections between her former self and the self she is becoming. Barnett describes this connecting in terms of different realms: she explains that she can be both "practitioner in the real world and scholar from the academic world."[66] To avoid a "return to my former, disconnected way of thinking,"[67] a preservice teacher can instead learn to integrate and weave words, worlds, and perspectives. The complement to this affirmation is affirmation of high school students. Not only must the preservice teachers learn to interpret student language, they must also take the responsibility for creating with students a shared language—a language that integrates two worlds and maintains the integrity of both parties.

Teacher education is never ending,[68] just like translation. Learning to teach is a complex, ongoing, and recursive process—the work of a lifetime. Understanding that learning to teach is the work of a lifetime suggests that the translating process must begin right away, prior to student teaching, and it must be a dynamic process that prepares preservice teachers for the kind of interactions, interpretations, and expressions that will be required of them as practitioners. Without the opportunity for such education prior to entering classrooms, preservice teachers run the risk of finding themselves unable to communicate and uncertain about how to position themselves in classrooms. If they do not learn to translate themselves, they run the risk of speaking their own language only and not communicating with students, as too often happens in schools.

Although learning to teach must be begun during the preservice phase of teacher preparation, it cannot be completed during that phase. It should begin while preservice teachers have the time, the support structures, and the explicit challenge to develop ways of thinking, speaking, reading, and writing that will serve them well in their classroom practice. But until they are immersed in the culture of the classroom, they can only progress so far in the process of translating themselves. If they begin early and maintain their processes of translation, rather than be daunted by new and often unanticipated differences, teachers can embrace each new group of students as offering invitations to produce intriguing variations on selves and interactions. Such an attitude makes them more open to possible new meanings, less willing to settle or interested in settling for fixed and final definitions and interpretations. Such teachers are perpetually learners—analyzing, revising, and re-rendering themselves in context after context in ways that both preserve what is vital in the former self and create what is vital to the self one strives to become.

Gained in Translation

Preservice teachers must be prepared for "coping with ambiguities, negotiating conflicting demands, managing inevitable dilemmas, and picking a path through the minefield of power relations that constitute the working environment for teachers."[69] These capacities require a particular kind of support and attention. It is essential that a prospective teacher learn as early as possible how to support and sustain this kind of development herself. The framework of translation provides that structure and fosters that attention because it creates space for a preservice teacher to be "the author of the teacher she is becoming."[70]

Education that is translation can foster a more "reciprocal and holistic connection between teachers and learners."[71] In Constantine's words: "Translation . . . is, like teaching, an intrinsically humane activity . . . translating is the practice and the proof of that statement by Terence in the second century BC: 'I am a human being. I count nothing human foreign to me.'"[72] This sense of connectedness to other human beings, the willingness to find words and ways of being with people, makes translating and teaching vital activities.

Translation can, however, prompt fear of losing one's permanent grip on meaning. As I learned German, I sometimes felt as though I was "losing my mind." As college sophomores reconceptualized their ideas and practices of composition, they often felt the impossibility of, but also the pull toward, imagining others' biases. As college professors struggled to redefine their relationships to teaching, to technology, and to those with whom they work, they felt the danger of letting both institutionally and personally defined meanings change. And as the preservice teachers redefined their relationships and identities, they too felt the old and familiar questioned and often replaced or reconceptualized.

George Herbert Palmer suggests that "a finished teacher is a contradiction in terms."[73] A teacher, like a student, is always learning, and it is the very "awareness of being unfinished that makes us educable."[74] Likewise, "a translation is never finished."[75] As the metaphor *education is translation* teaches and re-teaches me, a finished student, a finished teacher—indeed, a finished person—is also a contradiction in terms. Redefining what it means to compose and be composed as a student, redefining what it means to be a professor working collaboratively with others, and redefining what it means to be a student/teacher are all unending processes.

Chapter 6
"Desiring the Exhilarations of Changes"

> A text lives on only if it is at once translatable and
> untranslatable. . . . Totally translatable it disappears as a text, as
> writing, as a body of language. Totally untranslatable, even within
> what is believed to be one language, it dies immediately.
> —Jacques Derrida, *Writing and Difference*

> My objective was . . . to maintain myself in this gap, carrying it
> into a listening where all opposition between dead language and
> living language would be forbidden, where everything that unites
> through separation and everything that separates by continually
> translating itself would be affirmed.
> —Abdelkebir Khatibi, *Love in Two Languages*

> If perfect fits were achievable between social relations and
> psychic reality, between self and language, our subjectivities and
> our societies would be closed. Completed. Finished. Dead.
> Nothing to do. No difference. There would be no education.
> No learning.
> —Elizabeth Ellsworth, *Teaching Positions*

These three writers are referring to different realms: the realm of texts, the realm of relationships, and the realm of education. And yet these realms overlap with and inform one another in complex ways, and they assert some of the same ideas from different angles: that one-to-one correspondences or "perfect fits," even if possible, are undesirable; that for a text, a relationship, or a learning experience to be meaningful, it must be "alive"; that a language, human interaction, or learning is living "only in so far as it can move and change."[1] This last point is the same one that Wallace Stevens makes in the poem, "The Motive for Metaphor," a line from which I use as this chapter's title.[2] All of these authors point to the spaces that exist and that should be preserved between words, ideas, texts, interpretations, and people, and all celebrate rather than lament the unending process of striving to connect across those spaces in which we must all engage to make meaning.

To make of the educational experiences I have related in this book some (provisionally) final meaning, I apply one last time the framework that translation provides to analyze the following: the spaces of imagination and action that were opened within "Finding the Bias," "Talking Toward Techno-Pedagogy," and "Curriculum and Pedagogy," the transformation of language and self each aimed to support, the deeply collaborative nature of all of them, and the requirement of reflection during and at the end of each one. Each of these foci represents a revision and an extension of the pedagogical convictions I discussed in Chapter 1. There I emphasized how my experience as a student learning German threw into relief my convictions that educational opportunities must be based on constructivist and critical pedagogical principles, recognize the centrality of power and risk to educational processes, acknowledge that one brings one's entire self to any educational endeavor, provide time for reflection and analysis, and place students at the center. There is no one-to-one correspondence between those initial convictions and the categories of analysis I use in this chapter. Rather, with this final, provisional look, both are re-composed and re-rendered as part of my ongoing efforts to make meaningful educational experiences. I understand the challenges and process of education both more deeply and differently as a result of looking at them as translation. To bring my analysis full circle, I conclude this chapter with one last look at my own educational experience as I see it now and as it continues to unfold. While this chapter is the last in this book, it is not the last version of my analysis of education or of myself that I will render.

Creating Spaces of Imagination and Action

Throughout my analyses I focused on the spaces of imagination that metaphor has the potential to open up. If, as I discussed in Chapter 2, our minds do indeed "organize our perceptualized experiences by reference to their relative distances from each other on some prelinguistic quality space," and if this tendency "arises out of the very nature of life in a world defined by gravitational forces,"[3] then this understanding of why metaphor is ubiquitous in human thought can be applied not only to our deliberate re-thinking of which metaphors are generative and can usefully guide action in general but also specifically to the kinds of educational opportunities we create for students. If in designing and facilitating formal education we create spaces, both literal spaces and "spaces" for thought, we reiterate in practice the way metaphor works in the mind to carry meaning—a process of change to a new place of understanding and action. The different contexts I explore in this book all strove to be and to open up spaces of imagination and action.

The spaces of imagination that "Finding the Bias" aimed to open up were spaces between and among disciplines as well as spaces between what is considered personal and what is considered academic. The course drew upon but also complicated traditional disciplinary distinctions, each of which constitutes a "culture"—a collection of values, ways of thinking, writing, and speaking, and practices. It also invited students to think critically about their own lived—personal—experiences. Within these sets of spaces students discovered and reconsidered various "pulls"—ways that they defined and were defined by their relationships to people, places, times, and ideas.

"Talking Toward Techno-Pedagogy" created different kinds of spaces of imagination and action. Facilitated as it was outside of the spaces and the flow of time to which participants were accustomed, this workshop constituted a literal liminal space and inspired participants to create new spaces of imagination and action between and among themselves. The "total immersion experience separate from the home environment" that one instructional technologist described the workshop to be allowed participants to move "beyond the constraints of [their] organizational structure"—to begin the process of translation first out of context and then continue it in context when they returned to their home institutions. Participants were challenged as well by the differences of language that constituted and opened up spaces between and among them. The bringing together of previously differentiated modes and media—such as film and text, images and text, or a particular software program and text—like the bringing together of two terms of a metaphor or trying to translate from one language to another, fused and fostered new forms of expression and new understandings.

The Teaching and Learning Together project created spaces of imagination and action in yet a third way: by highlighting juxtapositions both within the preservice teachers' selves and between those selves and high school students. By explicitly juxtaposing the preservice teachers' student selves and their teacher-to-be selves, the course created a space of imagination between their past selves and their future selves. By bridging the chasm that generally exists between those preparing to teach and those they are preparing to teach, this project made that chasm palpable and supported the preservice teachers as they worked through ways of bridging it. "Marginally situated in two worlds,"[4] these "students" occupied a liminal space between this "practice" and the actual performance in classrooms, and the ways that they read, re-read, and re-rendered their understandings of high school students and of themselves pointed the way to future actions in actual classrooms.

In all three of these contexts students had the opportunity to "reorient consciousness" and "move from a kind of confinement to something wider."[5] The spaces within and between which they made these movements constituted and created "moments when the self is on the threshold of possible intellectual, social, and emotional development," and the "texts" that these learners produced—whether written texts, courses and practices created through techno-pedagogy workshops, or modes of interacting with students—were "sites of self-translation."[6] Like the space that German juxtaposed to English, and the country of Germany juxtaposed to the United States, opened up for me, the new places, cultures, languages, and practices in and through which learners in these contexts worked fused various "separated realms of experience" to provide "new perspectives"[7] or to express "significant and surprising truths."[8]

Facilitating the Transformation of Language and Self

Within the spaces of imagination and action the courses and workshop opened, participants were challenged to transform both language and selves and to take action based on those transformations. Kenneth Burke has argued that "language itself is action," that words are "purposive, in all the motivational and 'creative' complexity of that term."[9] Thus the language of translation, through its various definitions and associations, has inscribed within it the purposes—both the explicit ideas and the implied actions—of translation. Similarly, the definitions and associations of terms more commonly associated with education, such as "teach" and "learn," also have purposes and actions inscribed within them. These root definitions illuminate the purposes of the courses and workshop I have explored in this book and how they facilitated the transformation of language and self.

As I discussed in the opening chapters, the several ways that "translate" builds on the Latin *translatio,* meaning "to carry over or to transfer," include making a new version of something by rendering it in one's own or another's language; bearing, removing, or changing something from one place or condition to another; changing the form, expression, or mode of expression of, so as to interpret or make tangible, and thus to carry over from one medium or sphere into another; and transforming.[10] The roots of the words "teach" and "learn"—*tæcean* and *læran,* respectively—mean to lead or show the way; both have inscribed within them movement from one "place" to another through guidance and through self-directed action.

Although my colleagues and I did not articulate our purposes in these terms when we conceptualized the educational contexts I discuss in this book, looking at them again within the conceptual framework of translation illuminates for me their shared and respective purposes. Juxtaposing the purposes as they were originally articulated and the re-visions as seen through the metaphor of translation animates both the originals and the revisions. The explicit purpose of the course designed for college sophomores, "Finding the Bias: Tracing the Self Across Contexts," was not to find fixed definitions of biases, selves, or contexts, but rather it was to challenge everyone in the course to improve their abilities to read, think, talk, and write about, as well as to live, these things—to engage in ongoing interpretation and re-interpretation of compositions and of selves with the goal of having those interpretations inform participation in college and life. The explicit purpose of "Talking Toward Techno-Pedagogy," the workshop designed for professors and their librarian, student, and instructional technologist teammates, was to foster a collaborative exploration of the challenges and possibilities both of integrating technology in a meaningful way into teaching and learning and of working collaboratively with others to do so. And finally, the explicit purpose of Teaching and Learning Together, the project based in "Curriculum and Pedagogy," in which preservice teachers enrolled during their senior year of college, was to give those preservice teachers an opportunity to interact with those they were preparing to teach before they entered classrooms of their own and, specifically, to foster in preservice teachers a belief in and openness to high school student perspectives as a legitimate source of authority on approaches to teaching and learning.

One way of understanding these purposes as different aspects of the same purpose is to see them as aiming to facilitate forms of carrying meaning from one language to another or from one form of the same language into another. That could mean the learning of one or more new languages, it could mean the re-learning of one or more languages that one thinks one already knows, and it could mean rethinking and changing one's use of language. Within the conceptual framework that translation offers, we can see the purpose of both courses and workshop as challenging those who enrolled in them to engage in various kinds of reading, interpretation, and composition as they moved from one language to another or re-thought a language with which they were already familiar. Because every act of language use both constitutes and leads to action, by focusing on what we wanted students to carry over into new spheres of communication and action we can see the purpose of these educational contexts as aiming to provide spaces within which students could engage in translation.

Speaking in new ways and sensing oneself as a new self can be vertiginous experiences, born of the "vertigo of language"[11] itself as well as the vertigo prompted by the juxtaposition of selves.[12] Changing one's condition, making oneself comprehensible to others in a new sphere, making a new version of oneself, and transforming oneself can be as deeply unsettling as it is exciting because of what is preserved, what is lost, and what is gained in the translation process. Translation must always be "the re-creation of the original into something profoundly different,"[13] an equivalent and "not a replica,"[14] a re-articulation of a complex human experience[15] with no identity in detail[16] yet with something of the essence preserved, some "echo of the original."[17] In each of the contexts I have explored, within the spaces of imagination and action the contexts opened up, I aimed to facilitate a transformation in participants' sense of language and of self.

In "Finding the Bias," students had a difficult time reconciling their "original selves," defined primarily by their families and friends in their pre-college years, with the selves they were becoming in various relationships and contexts at college. The compositions that had defined them came under their own and others' scrutiny and prompted in many of these students crises of identity and meaning. Students struggled with the eclipsing of self required by most school writing. They struggled with the challenges of achieving the right distance from and proximity to self—the "simultaneous experience of both proximity and separateness, intimacy and alterity"[18]—that, when achieved, allowed them to gain perspective and insight. And they struggled with issues of power in discourse and relationships; they struggled to find a balance between the acquisition of knowledge, which "has the permanent quality that makes the privileged position of its owner equally permanent,"[19] and the "process of becoming a member of a certain community . . . [which] implies that the identity of an individual, like an identity of a living organ, is a function of his or her being (or becoming) a part of a greater entity."[20] The processes in which students engaged as they struggled with these various challenges adhered to the premise that the self is constituted by compositions that must be continually re-composed if their vitality is to be preserved.[21]

The participants in "Talking Toward Techno-Pedagogy" faced the challenges of learning new languages, of deeply reconceptualizing ways of perceiving and interacting with other members of the college community, and of trying to achieve these processes of change within contexts that are at base conservative. All participants in the workshop articulated the sense they had that people in the different positions of professor, librarian, instructional technologist, and student "don't speak the same languages." The education in which participants engaged required that they learn to communicate across existing different languages as well as learn new ones. Regarding the reconceptualization of ways of perceiving and interacting with other members of the college community, long-established and inherited notions of what a professor is supposed to be create a certain kind of pressure to preserve this "original." Finally, while the workshop fostered and supported translations of language and of self, when participants returned to their home institutions, they had to confront structures and practices intent on keeping things as they have always been.

In "Curriculum and Pedagogy," the preservice teachers' greatest challenge was to grant that in the texts and the high school students before them there was "'something there' to be understood." This act of trust is a prerequisite for "the demonstrative statement of understanding which is translation."[22] First misreading or devaluing words and producing versions of texts and selves that were sometimes satisfying and sometimes not, then learning to re-read and re-assess others' texts as well as revise and refine their own, and finally integrating what they read and produced into new understandings of themselves and new plans for practice, the preservice teachers slowly worked their way into what will be an ongoing process of translation.

The issue of authority was central to the translation that participants attempted and effected in all three contexts. Some students in "Finding the Bias" wrote about how "authority is an extremely subjective term, and is defined by perception";[23] that "we only have authority in relation to others. . . . Without others, authority does not exist."[24] The professors who participated in "Talking Toward Techno-Pedagogy" also struggled with issues of authority. Rethinking their roles and responsibilities in teaching and learning, some professors raised "questions of responsibility and authority," starting with the inherited assumption that faculty are the "expert people about the content of the course" but then moving to the question of "whether technology has the potential for redefining what the content of the course is and therefore for redefining the issues of authority and responsibility for the course." The preservice teachers struggled with the issue of authority as well, many of them starting by resisting high school students' perspectives but just as many ending up realizing that they had "learned so MUCH from [my partner]" and focusing on ways in which, throughout the dialogue, they had failed to attend to what the high school students had to say to and teach them. As one preservice teacher put it: "'I'm not listening. I'm not listening, I'm just saying things to her, and not listening.' She was listening to me and I was not listening to her. You need to hear the student's voice; that's the reason for teaching." If one is an authority, one has power derived from opinion, respect, and esteem.[25] An author can originate—make or compose—something. At the root of the terms "authority" and "author" is power: "the ability to take one's place in whatever discourse is essential to action and the right to have one's part matter."[26] Questions of whose words counted, made sense, or carried weight, of who could take what places in the discourses essential to action, were central to both processes and challenges of translation.

Struggling with profound issues of identity, meaning, and authority, and attempting to negotiate all of them in ways that would lead to informed action, participants in all three contexts transformed the languages they used and the selves they were. Because language learning is a transformative process,[27] in the same way that I had to re-learn English after starting to learn German, and re-learn or learn anew a new self, each of the students and professors whose experiences I have explored engaged not only in translations, he was also translated through those processes of translation because "our own being is modified by each occurrence of comprehensive appropriation."[28] Thus language learnings and re-learnings facilitated translations of self—metaphorical and reflexive embodiments of the definitions and purposes of translation.

Collaboration

As one student enrolled in "Finding the Bias" pointed out, "we only have authority in relation to others."[29] This insight is central to the mode through which many of the individual translations explored in the chapters of this book were facilitated—indeed, made possible: collaboration. To collaborate—literally, to labor together—means bringing more than one perspective, more than one way of seeing and acting, together to work toward a new vision and set of practices. The courses and workshop I have explored in the previous chapters were designed and facilitated collaboratively, and those who participated in them worked collaboratively. The generative work of meaning making unfolded in the spaces between people and ideas.

"Finding the Bias" was collaboratively designed by three professors who issued from three different academic disciplines. "Talking Toward Techno-Pedagogy" was collaboratively designed and facilitated by two directors of education programs and two directors of libraries. Teaching and Learning Together was co-designed and co-facilitated by a college-based teacher educator and school-based educators. Each of these collaborations spanned fields or realms, literal as well as semantic spaces, cultures and contexts that are often kept separate. Working to communicate across our differences and to co-construct generative educational opportunities for participants, we engaged in the process that Freire claims constitutes education: dialogue. He explains: "Without dialogue there is no communication, and without communication there can be no true education."[30]

Within each course or workshop, collaboration was the modus operandi as well. In "Finding the Bias" students worked in various collaborative configurations—small group conversations, whole group discussions, writing workshops—all of which became spaces "in which to construct shared understandings, knowledges, claims on the world."[31] These students identified with one another's assertions,[32] revised their writing and their selves in direct response to one another's critiques and encouragement,[33] and even included each other's voices in their own narratives of their development in the class because "that is how we have been working all semester—our thoughts bouncing off each other's."[34] This kind of collaborative process is an active, co-construction of meaning and identity.

The entire premise of "Talking Toward Techno-Pedagogy" was collaboration. Our invitation to participants stated explicitly that each constituency represented at the workshop—professors, students, librarians, and instructional technologists—had expertise and a legitimate perspective, and that participation in the workshop was to be collaborative. The realization on one professor's part that "all of these wonderful ideas can come to fruition without me doing and being everything"[35] and the ways that participants switched from using "I" to using "we" capture the powerful potential of collaboration to transform ways of thinking and interacting.

Within "Curriculum and Pedagogy," Teaching and Learning Together was also premised on collaboration. In the exchange of letters between each preservice teacher and high school student, in the class conversations among preservice teachers and me, in the analyses of what they learned from the project completed by each preservice teacher at the end of the semester, these teachers-to-be came to see that "[my high school partner] and I built our knowledge [together]"[36] throughout the dialogue and that when these preservice teachers become teachers, "students will provide [them] with new ideas and [their] incorporation of those experiences into [their] identity as a teacher exemplifies the flexibility and constant changing of [themselves]."[37]

The kind of collaboration that both underpinned and unfolded within the three educational contexts is a version what Sfard calls learning as participation, which stresses "the evolving bonds between the individual and others . . . [and] implies that the identity of an individual, like an identity of a living organ, is a function of his or her being (or becoming) a part of a greater entity."[38] It complicates the notion that we are "self-authoring" by highlighting the ways in which we always translate ourselves in relationship and context.[39] It is only through collaboration—through working together—that we can both generate and re-generate life.

Reflection

Reflection is a prerequisite as well as part of the process of translation. Genuinely engaging in a process of translation—genuinely engaging in education—requires and prompts reflection. This engagement is both automatic and deliberate: it is automatic in that when one is confronted with something new, particularly something that challenges established perspectives or practices, all that one already knows is called into question, and one looks back, even if only briefly, over the already known; it is deliberate in that once the known is called into question by the new, one can choose to learn from the juxtaposition, use it to provide different angles of vision, and use it to deepen understanding of both the known and the new. When one resists reflection, or when one refuses to let the new challenge the known and when one chooses not to revise or deepen understanding, then one is refusing to engage in education.

The metaphor of reflection is ubiquitous in education, popularized in the early 1980s by Donald Schön in *The Reflective Practitioner* and taken up subsequently by many educators as essential to good teaching practice. Reflection as generally applied to pedagogical practice refers to the process through which an individual seeks to refine her professional capacities (skills, knowledge, and self-awareness) through coaching by more experienced, successful professionals.[40] Advocates of fostering the development of reflective practitioners[41] argue that in the absence of reflection, "one runs the risk of relying on routinized teaching and . . . not developing as a teacher or as a person."[42] The ongoing interplay of reflection and action, or what Freire calls praxis,[43] although not generally built into the "structure of teaching,"[44] is essential to good pedagogical practice. As Zehm points out, reflection on the human dimensions of teaching is a useful tool for self-exploration as well as for professional development.[45] Furthermore, not only does becoming a reflective practitioner mean developing the disposition to reflect on practice; it also means "finding the words to express those reflections to others—through collaboration, building a shared language and a shared knowledge of practice."[46]

I fully concur with the importance of critical reflection for students, for teachers, and for people in general. Like some other educators, however, I am concerned with the potential of the metaphor to be too flat. The association many people have of reflection is based on a mirror: a flat surface that reflects back only what is immediately in front of it. But to return to the root of the word, we find that "reflect" comes from "re" and "flect," and "flect" means to bend or to turn and is the root also of "flexible" and "reflex." Therefore, although what has generally emerged is a notion of mirroring still images back, the "original" meaning of reflect is not the simple mirror-image idea, but the flexing of the mind and body as it turns again, bends again, in a new direction. Thus motion, animation, and movement are at the root of the word.

Carol Rodgers animates the metaphor and emphasizes just such flexibility and movement in her discussion of "the reflective cycle"—the process through which teachers alternately slow down their thinking enough to allow a shift of attention from their own action to student learning and then a shift in focus back to acting on what they attend to.[47] Rodgers's model of the reflective cycle is particularly relevant to the argument I make in this book not only because it emphasizes a rigorous and systematic process that when engaged in over time, allows for more thoughtful action in the moment, but also because it puts students and student learning at the center of practice.

Arguing for the revision of reflection from another angle, Alice Lesnick suggests that the concept of reflective practice needs to be revised "in light of the unfinishedness (Freire, 1998), contingency, complexity, and even unknowability (Ellsworth, 1992) of the reflecting agent and the context reflected upon." Working to complicate the metaphor of reflective practice, Lesnick offers "catching sight of one's reflection in the window of a passing car, in a remembered home movie, or in the shadow play of figures against a sunlit wall." She suggests that even these revisions of the reflection metaphor are "only partially successful in representing the dynamic processes of and under reflection, highlight movement, the interplay of various figures, and the impossibility of complete or final clarity."[48] Understanding the kind of dynamic reflection Rodgers and Lesnick call for as a prerequisite for as well as a result of translation, I revisit here how participants across contexts in this book engaged in reflection in thought, in speech, and in writing throughout and at the conclusion of their educational experiences.

In "Finding the Bias," students were required to reflect in numerous ways. Early in the semester, they were required to reflect on their own experiences of school and use these reflections as texts the entire class analyzed. Throughout the semester, they were asked to reflect critically on their own and others' uses of language to compose texts and selves. Specifically, they reflected on their assumptions about composition and its relationship to truth, and they reflected on their attempts to write as someone else. At the end of the semester, they reflected on all of their thinking and writing—on their experiences, their assumptions, their own and others' composing processes, the relationship between representations and realities, and questions of authority and agency in all of these. Reflection was essential to these students' translation process; students strove to effect translations of themselves by struggling to translate different perspectives into texts. In attempting to translate their own and others' perspectives and words in a deliberate and self-conscious way in a text and then reflecting on those attempts, students transformed their understanding, and thus themselves, through the attempt and the analysis of that attempt.

In "Talking Toward Techno-Pedagogy," professors were challenged to critically reflect on their roles and relationships, their identities as the purveyors of knowledge, and their assumptions about who has what kind of knowledge and what kind of knowledge and participation can contribute to designing or redesigning a course. They were asked to reflect before they undertook a particular pedagogical project; in other words, they had to consider ahead of time—before they taught or re-taught a course—what might make sense and what might not. They reflected on individual and institutional barriers to translation, such as a lack of clear articulations of roles and responsibilities, lack of communication, and outmoded criteria for promotion and tenure. They reflected as well on new possible configurations for collaboration and on how they might become the kinds of selves that could carry that form of collaboration back to their home contexts.

The preservice teachers who participated in Teaching and Learning Together, like the students in "Finding the Bias," reflected on their educational experiences, but they did so within the frame of imagining themselves as teachers. They reflected on their assumptions about students, about learning, and about the relationship between language and meaning. They reflected on the language they and high school students use and how meaning was and was not carried in those uses of language. The dialogue with the high school students prompted particularly deep reflections on the relationship between the selves the preservice teachers were at the moment they took the course and the selves they wanted to become as teachers.

The lesson all participants learned through their engagement in these various, formal, educational contexts is that "self-reflection and critical consideration can be as liberating as they are educative,"[49] and they qualify as educative because they are liberating.

Gained in Translation

Revisiting concepts and practices that are familiar to the world of education, such as collaboration and reflection, but seeing them anew through translation, helps to reanimate them, perhaps expand their possibilities, building upon what is already useful in them. It throws into starker relief what is wrong with the current educational system. Recognizing the fundamentally social nature of education and culture, and thus the need for collaboration in educational contexts and in life, calls into question the focus on individual achievement in much of U.S. education. Likewise, insisting on reflection as an integral part of the educational process calls into question the emphasis on speed and efficiency embodied in the root metaphor *education is production* and in the various ways that educational practices are standardized.

Evoking concepts and practices that are less familiar or explicit in the world of education has a different, and perhaps even greater, potential to expand possibilities of educational theory and practice. To think of classrooms and schools as spaces of imagination and action calls into question traditional images of classrooms as spaces of containment for production or quarantine. Likewise, thinking of education as facilitating transformations of language and self means thinking of education as an ongoing process of change rather than the transmission of a fixed body of knowledge and set of practices.

Thinking of education as translation not only supports existing critiques of education and offers further critique, it also provides an alternative in both thought and action. I am calling for education that is translation, but I do not mean to imply that undertaking a formal educational experience means to be constantly changing, constantly moving, constantly carrying meaning forward. As I discussed in Chapter 3, the word "composed" means to come to terms, to reconcile, to settle as well as to labor to fashion or to construct. Each satisfactorily finished or final version of a text or self that we compose is to be celebrated and enjoyed, but then it must be built on and moved forward from. Thus what is gained in translation is not only a new version of words and selves but also new energy to create subsequent versions.

What Does This Mean for Educators?

David Hawkins writes: "The most basic gift is not love but respect, respect for others as ends in themselves, as actual and potential artisans of their own learnings and doings, of their own lives; and as thus uniquely contributing, in turn, to the learnings and doings of others."[50] Whether through embracing the metaphor of translation or creating other metaphors more resonant for particular people in particular educational contexts, what I call for in this book is a profound rethinking of how we conceptualize and practice education with those in the role of student not only as the focus but also as the agents of their own education. Moving beyond the existing commitment constructivists share—that students need to be authors of their own understanding and assessors of their own learning—educators need to put more power in the hands of students as they compose not only their understanding but also themselves. This change requires trust. As my experiences as a student and as a teacher have taught me, and as my own and others' research supports,[51] when students feel trusted, they trust themselves and their teachers more, and when this is the case, education is more efficacious. I wrote in Chapter 1 about the role of trust in my own learning of German, and in each of the chapters in which I analyze others' educational experiences, trust was both a prerequisite for and a result of the educational experiences students had: trust that there is meaning to be discovered in a text or person; trust that the honest risks and chances learners take will be supported and will lead to further learning; trust that, although education can never be finished, it is worth engaging in the process.

Trusting that there is meaning to be found, that the search is worthwhile, requires willingness to accept partiality. It requires what Welch calls a feminist ethic of risk: "an ethic that begins with the recognition that we cannot guarantee decisive changes in the near future or even in our lifetime . . . [and that] [r]esponsible action does not mean the certain achievement of desired ends but the creation of a matrix in which further actions are possible, the creation of the conditions of possibility for desired changes."[52] As teachers constructing educational contexts, we can create conditions within which a student changes her condition, makes herself comprehensible to others in a new sphere, makes a new version of herself, is transformed. These processes are never finished; they are always open to further revision and always lead to further re-renderings. Many students in "Finding the Bias" experienced the recognition that their education is never finished as an exciting opening, a compelling possibility, rather than as a frightening prospect. They recognized the truth of Paulo Freire's claim that "it is our awareness of being unfinished that makes us educable."[53] The professors who participated in "Talking Toward Techno-Pedagogy" also recognized the nature of their work as ongoing and unfinishable. And as I discussed in analyzing the experiences of preservice teachers, "a finished teacher is a contradiction in terms."[54] One preservice teacher put it this way: "I have come to realize that . . . my students will provide me with new ideas and my incorporation of those experiences into my identity as a teacher exemplifies the flexibility and constant changing of myself."[55]

One of the results of conceptualizing education as production or education as cure is a focus on—even an obsession with—finishedness as an outcome of that education: finished products and cured patients. It is essential that the idea of finishedness not continue to dominate thinking about and practices of education in the United States. Standardized curricula and standardized testing are premised on the idea that education can be finished and tested within a prescribed time frame. Success is evaluated in terms of finishedness, and educational contexts are structured toward achieving finishedness. But as the educational experiences I have analyzed here illustrate, what is important is unfinishedness. I return to Gregory Rabassa's words one last time to emphasize how translation can be a reminder of this important lesson: "a translation is never finished . . . it is open and could go on to infinity. . . . This matter of choice in translation always leaves the door open to that other possibility. . . . The translator can never be sure of himself, he must never be."[56]

Related to the idea that education is unfinishable is the idea that it is impossible. By "impossible" I mean that what we intend and attempt in educational experiences for others—and even sometimes for ourselves— is rarely what actually happens. Ellsworth discusses this point extensively in *Teaching Positions*, both in regard to teaching and in terms of the fit between social relations and psychic reality, between self and language. But to say that something is impossible is not to say that we shouldn't try to do it. The unending process of change in which we strive to connect, temporarily succeed or fail, and then seek to establish new connections is the process of education.

Metaphors are among the most generative resources we have to help us think about and enact change in both thought and action. Davidson suggests that "there is no limit to what a metaphor calls to our attention."[57] Metaphors have the power to define the ways of thinking and acting on cultural as well as individual levels, and as cultures and individuals evolve, so must the metaphors that emerge to define and create them. Indeed, revolutions in thought may be "no more than the mutational replacement, at certain critical points in history, of one foundation-metaphor by another in man's contemplation of universe, society, and self."[58] We should deliberately take up this inevitability in order to more thoughtfully guide the development of educational theory and the enactment of that theory in practice; as Borges argues, it is given to us "to invent metaphors that do not belong, or that do not yet belong, to accepted patterns."[59]

Since it is the intersection between the metaphor itself and how it is used that determines its generative or destructive power, we must always remember that we are using metaphors; we must not lose ourselves inside them but rather keep our critical faculties attentive to their workings. Furthermore, we must not stop with one metaphor or another but rather keep moving as new metaphors open up new spaces of imagination—spaces that may well re-animate old metaphors as well as lead us into unfamiliar spaces. The metaphor that I have developed emerged out of the need I felt for a way of understanding and enacting education that was not inspired by the metaphors that already exist. It is a response and a critique of prevailing metaphors as well as a product of my own experience and my own time. As such it is part of the territory of other metaphors— history. I might have imagined a different metaphor had I been responding to different historical or personal needs. Given where education in the United States is now, translation offers an alternative to current pedagogical theories and practices that is both critical and generative.

Turner suggests that in a liminal space "the possibility exists of standing aside not only from one's own social position but from all social positions and of formulating a potentially unlimited series of alternative social arrangements."[60] In evoking metaphor in general, I am opening up such a liminal space, because metaphor is itself a liminal space. And in proposing a particular metaphor—*education is translation*—and specifically designating the person assuming the role of student not only as the thing translated but also as the translator, I am suggesting that we let this metaphor be a liminal space in which we redefine social arrangements within education and that we carry those changes back into the actual world in which we live. This inclination toward change may be more "natural" than we think. Martinez suggests that "what's natural to us is the desire to change, rather than stay the same."[61] This desire to change is at the root of metaphor, of translation, and of education.

While no single metaphor can "capture all of the nuances, intricacies and complexities of human interaction and experience,"[62] metaphors evoked and re-evoked can help us in such endeavors. If we remember that it is a metaphor and do not take it literally, the metaphor of translation as applied to education may help us to support the "survival of the human."[63] The poet Archibald MacLeish claims that "A world ends when a metaphor has died."[64] Thus we must think carefully about the "life-sustaining or life-generating power"[65] of metaphor. As Greene reminds us, "imagination is the capacity to posit alternative realities. It makes possible the creation of 'as-if' perspectives."[66] By opening up spaces of imagination, people can "break with what they simply assume or take for granted as given and unchangeable."[67] Thus we must think about the worlds we want to create with the creation of a new metaphor. I do not suggest that translation is the ultimate metaphor for education; it is, rather, an impetus to continue to move toward generative metaphors. With changes of the times, technologies, and human relationships, we will need and generate new metaphors.

Citing E. L. Doctorow, who claimed that the development of civilization is essentially a procession of metaphors, Booth argues that "the quality of any culture will be in part measured . . . by the quality of the metaphors it induces or allows."[68] At this point in history, Ellsworth contends, we must address the question of whether those of us concerned with education can think and perceive differently than we have thus far "if we are going to go on looking and thinking at all."[69] If, as Freire suggests, "our teaching space is a text that must be constantly read, interpreted, written, and rewritten,"[70] we need to learn to see in ways that provide not only for ourselves in the present but also for other selves in the future. We must be continually "reaching out for meanings."[71] If, as Morgan suggests, we live in a world that is becoming increasingly complex, the metaphors we evoke and create for education ought to accommodate complexity and constant change.

In his poem "The Motive for Metaphor," Stevens writes of a figure in different times and places in which light from an "obscure moon" illuminates "an obscure world / Of things that would never be quite expressed, / Where you yourself were never quite yourself."[72] The desire for language to illuminate, for metaphor to carry us out of ourselves, is not a desire to fix understandings and ways of being. The motive for metaphor is the desire for change, Stevens argues—a language always striving beyond itself, a self always striving beyond itself. Such a striving for ongoing transformation is the desired, the only viable understanding of education, of relationships, of selves. In considering provisions that we might want to make for the educations of all kinds that lie ahead, the journey or experience (*Erfahrung*)[73] we might want to make, we need to keep seeing anew, keep opening up the spaces within which we can gain perspective and revise our ideas and practices in learning and in life. The purpose of education, like life itself, must be re-understood as change: change of understanding, change of expression, change of relationship.

Translation is the metaphor that, at this point, I find most useful for engaging in and facilitating change. It is my hope that readers will find the metaphor of translation useful in rethinking their own experiences and practices of education and of daily life, but I hope as well that people will push beyond the realms of formal education that I explore here and apply the metaphor to other formal and personal contexts. Like any generative metaphor, translation helps to open spaces of "freedom— spaces where people make choices [of interpretation]."[74] These choices are neither free from history nor free from consequences. My hope is that people will continue to try to find new metaphors that animate education and life.

Returning to My Own Educational Experience

Looking again at the various educational experiences I explore in this book and reflecting on what my argument means for educators prompt me to look one last time at my own educational experience as a student. The contexts evoked, the dynamics within those, and the ways that participants translated their words and selves both echo and influence my analysis of my own experience. The first chapter of this book told the story of my traveling to another context, taking on roles and relationships within that context that put me at a different angle to myself and others, and undertaking a formal educational experience that complicated and deepened both the personal and the academic realms of my life. In this last section of this last chapter I come full circle to tell the story of returning to that context and, shortly thereafter, returning to the ongoing process of revising my analysis of it and the metaphor *education is translation.*

In the summer of 2002, I returned to Göttingen with Moritz, Lisa, and their parents, and spent two weeks revisiting the people and places I had gotten to know during the previous fall and winter. The experience of returning was another double experience, both like and unlike the double experience of being a teacher and a student when I had taken courses at the Goethe Institute. I assumed neither one of these formal roles during the summer. Rather, with versions of both those selves in abeyance, present but not foregrounded, I revisited what and who was still there in Göttingen, and I observed myself—or rather selves—revisiting. I retraced my steps through the parks and along the streets of the town, passing under the green leaves and among the peopled café tables of the summer, and I remembered my walks through the first turning, then bare trees and along the almost empty ice- or snow-covered streets of fall and winter. I returned to the *Spielplätze* (playgrounds) with Moritz and Lisa, who could play in different parts of the playground, on swings and slides that had before been too big for them, and who could now describe in their own words the changes that had taken place since we were last on those playgrounds, ask me if I remembered, and know that I could answer. I revisited the classrooms of the Goethe Institute, the same intersections of old wood and new technologies, world maps on the walls and open windows, now filled with new students learning what I had learned from the teachers I had come to know. In each case my memories of the previous fall and winter were strong enough still to be with me, but they coexisted with the visceral and intellectual sense I had of time having passed, seasons having changed, people having come and gone, my own self having evolved. The landscape, the familiar places, the classes, and the people were both the same and not the same: they were translations of themselves.

I felt this complex sense of preservation and transformation first as I walked through the town. The language, the places, and the ways of being I had learned I knew still and could navigate with even greater ease than I had managed previously. This ease was partly due to the fact that I had continued learning in the meantime—continued developing my language, continued analyzing metaphors and the educational experiences they named, and continued building the relationships that inspired and supported my learning as an integral part of my life. I knew the ways fairly well—to walk, to talk, to function and move forward—and yet still they felt as new as they felt familiar, as different as they felt the same. The quality of light as well as the eyes through which I was perceiving it held both what had been and what now was.

Returning to familiar places with Lisa and Moritz had the same quality. Wearing sandals rather than snow boots, we revisited people and places they had encountered six months before. They remembered and asked to return to these people and places; they recounted in great detail stories of what we had done the first time we were there; they commented on who was still there and who was not and how the playground equipment had changed or remained the same. Lisa and Moritz, their parents, and I returned as well to the Harz Mountains, the origin of one branch of my family, this time on one of the hottest days of the year as opposed to in winter, when we had traveled on one of the coldest. The contrasts were striking, but they also highlighted the connections: the familiarity of the buildings, contours of the land, the history both still held.

What had been preserved and what had been transformed were perhaps most powerful for me at the Goethe Institute. None of the students with whom I had studied remained, but all three teachers were still there. I know this experience myself as a teacher: the sense of cycling through new iterations of the same courses while students move forward in a steady, ever-changing stream. But only rarely have I had the experience of returning as a student to a place of previous learning and living. Sitting in the same classrooms, listening to the same lessons, I already "knew" what the teachers were teaching, but I had the opportunity simply to observe and to re-learn both the content and the processes in which the teachers and students were engaged. What struck me most forcefully is how open and vulnerable students must be to learn and how attentive to them teachers must be to facilitate and support that learning. This realization was also not new but rather newly felt as I watched and remembered how hard it is to learn, how long it takes, how patient and passionate everyone has to be to work their way together toward meaning.

While I was returning and turning anew to Göttingen, a group of friends and colleagues were reading a draft of the manuscript that has become this book. This group of readers included some of my collaborators in designing and teaching the courses, projects, and workshops; it included students who had participated in these educational forums; it included teachers who work in other educational contexts; and it included theorists in a variety of academic disciplines. When I returned once again to the United States, I met with these people to listen to their critiques of the manuscript, to gather their impressions, their questions, and their recommendations. In groups of three or four, or in individual email exchanges, we discussed together what this book is about and how to organize and present its various aspects in a way that readers would find compelling.

Everyone had different ideas. People spoke from disciplines as various as biology, history, literary studies, folklore, and language studies and from educational contexts including college, high school, and middle school. Listening I heard under- and overtones of each person's own experiences, her own beliefs, her stories of experiences being told or revised. I was moved by how each reader brought his entire self to the text—his ways of thinking, speaking, and interacting—to his interpretation of and hopes for the book. I remembered Constantine's claim: that every reader brings to every text "*etwas . . . aus der eigenen Erfahrung, aus dem totalen Leben bis zu dem Punkt hin . . . nicht beim Interpretieren, sondern beim Lesen, beim Fühlen . . . ob man das merkt oder nicht*" (something . . . out of one's own experience, out of one's entire life up to that point . . . not through interpretation, but rather through reading, through feeling . . . whether one is cognizant of it or not).[75]

Listening to each reader argue for a revision or a greater or lesser emphasis of a point, I heard, one after the other, the translations each person had made of the text and the translations each person had made of herself in reading the text. They had each "made" an experience out of their reading that reproduced, revised, and created new meaning. As I listened I was struck anew by the phrase that Verena Stefan had used so many times in her talk—"I made an interesting experience"—the German construction she had brought to an English utterance because, consciously or unconsciously, she felt that it captured for her what she had done and the sense she had made of it. I heard my text translated back to me both in ways that I had anticipated and ways that I hadn't. I was struck by the ways I felt deeply understood as well as by the ways I felt misunderstood. As I listened and talked, I recognized that we were all engaged in yet another form of translation: we were living on yet another level the metaphor about which I had been writing. To understand that both the understandings and the misunderstandings were born not of careless writing or reading or of any form of inattention but rather of the very careful readings each person had undertaken and the very intimate and individual processes in which each person had engaged was to understand anew how education is translation. These discussions were part of my ongoing education—a learning process as well as a composing and revising process—just as they were part of my friends' and colleagues' education processes: all ongoing processes of translation.

As a writer and a teacher, and as a person, this was an important experience for me. It reminded me that when we write and teach, and when we simply talk with one another, what we are trying to convey is rarely what people actually comprehend. And yet when they can, people make sense of what they encounter—both within themselves and between themselves and other people. Ellsworth suggests that if both participants in an interaction do not realize and accept that they are both always representing and making meaning, they end up with "an untranslatable dialogue in two languages."[76] If they do realize it, however, they can move forward in their efforts to make connections and meaning. What inspired me most about these conversations with such a varied group of friends and colleagues, outside of the good suggestions for revision that people offered, was the hope that those who read this book will engage in just such acts of translation—of interpretation and re-rendering through the medium of their own experiences, relationships, and languages—that they will know that this translation is the process in which they are engaged, and that they will embrace it as a powerful form of education: one they choose, one they enact. What I relearned through this process is that as a writer and a teacher, I can only try to create a conversation in which others can undertake that process of making meaning. That "only" is as fraught as Forster's in his "only connect." But perhaps that is the most important lesson of all.

Appendix
A Sampling of Educational Metaphors

Of the metaphors for schools, education, learning, and teaching that I found, those for schools can be most easily linked with particular time periods in or phases of U.S. history. I indicate those within the brief discussions I offer below. In my discussions of metaphors for education, learning, and teaching, I indicate time periods in which the metaphor emerged or held sway, but many are idiosyncratic (unique to a single teacher, for instance) and do not clearly or obviously reflect larger social or cultural tendencies or shifts.

Metaphors for Schools

Schools are melting pots.

The term "melting pot" first appeared in 1908 as the title and theme of a play written by Israel Zangwill in which a great alchemist "'melts and fuses' America's varied immigrant population 'with his purging flames.'"[1] This metaphor of the melting pot shaped the evolution of public schools from the early 1900s through the 1970s. Within this metaphorical framework, the job of the school was to "educate students from many cultures through a common language, a common history, and common goals, principles, and values."[2] This approach assumed a "predetermined standard of desirability"[3] and asserted "that the American experience molds all into modern-day clones of the (mainly) white, Protestant Anglo-Saxons who founded the Republic and established cultural hegemony here."[4] In the early 1970s, a spate of critiques of the metaphor filled journals and book pages with the contention that the melting pot metaphor—and myth, according to the critics—needed to be replaced with cultural pluralism or multicultural education.[5] Although the melting pot metaphor was called into question in the 1970s, some argue that its power remains in how schooling is conceptualized.[6]

Schools are educational wastelands.

In the early 1950s, Arthur Eugene Bestor contended that schools were promoting the degeneration of the American mind. He argued for the rejuvenation of U.S. public schools and lamented the vanishing sense of purpose in education. He asserted that until educational leaders and practitioners based their educational theories and practices on the same assumptions, there could not be anything that we could call an educational system but rather only a hodgepodge of schools.[7] The set of common assumptions Bestor sought was to find its manifestation in a single body of knowledge taught—"what every American needs to know" to heal himself and contribute to a healthy body politic.[8] This work paved the way for the writings of Allan Bloom, E. D. Hirsch, and others concerned about "the closing of the American mind"[9]—what they suggest is the intellectual atrophy and decay of the collective U.S. brain.

Schools are shopping malls.

During a phase of relative prosperity and complacency in the United States, after the turbulent, alternative, and powerful movements of the 1960s and 1970s, Powell, Fararr, and Cohen wrote: "If Americans want to understand their high schools at work, they should imagine them as shopping malls." They describe secondary education as a "consumption experience." The consumers vary greatly: some know what they want and "efficiently make their purchases"; others "come simply to browse"; and still others do neither: "they just hang out." Within the shopping mall high school are "specialty shops" for students with particular preferences, "product labeling" for the array of course options available, and special and "unspecial" students to select, or be selected by, those options. The shopping mall high school offers accommodations "to maximize holding power, graduation percentages, and customer satisfaction."[10]

Metaphors for Education

Education is growth.

Informed by thinkers such as Rousseau in late eighteenth century France and Herbart in early twentieth-century Germany, this metaphor argues that students should be nurtured and let to learn in their own ways at their own pace, and, if properly nurtured, will act morally according to their own free will.[11] In the early twentieth century in the United States, Dewey built on these premises, arguing that continuity of life means continual re-adaptation of the environment to the needs of living organisms.[12] Proponents of progressive education have continued to argue that we must start "where the learner is"[13] and design educational experiences, such as those in Waldorf and Montessori schools and in pockets of progressivism in all school systems, in which students can build their own knowledge[14]—in which students can grow themselves.

Education is banking.

Freire explains this metaphor he coined in 1990: when the teacher is assumed to know all and the students nothing, education "becomes an act of depositing, in which the students are the depositories and the teacher is the depositor." The student's role within this model is limited to "receiving, filing, and storing the deposits." As passive recipients of others' knowledge, students are, according to Freire, denied the opportunity to "be truly human"—the ability to engage in inquiry and praxis, to create, not simply receive, knowledge, which "emerges only through invention and re-invention, through the restless, impatient, continuing, hopeful inquiry men pursue in the world, with the world, and with each other."[15]

Metaphors for Learning

Learning is acquisition.

Writing in the late 1990s, Sfard argued that the metaphor of learning as acquisition reflects the basically materialistic culture of the Western world. Nowhere is this materialism more fully embraced than in the United States, established as it was in the wide, open space of what was considered free but was in fact acquired land rich in resources. Explicating the metaphor, Sfard explains that concepts are "basic units of knowledge that can be accumulated, gradually refined, and combined to form ever richer cognitive structures." The lexicon of the acquisition metaphor includes words like "fact," "material," "sense," "idea," and "notion," and underlying these words is the impulse toward accumulation of material wealth, signaled by Sfard's use of words such as "accumulated," "refined," and "richer." The actions according to which one makes the commodities of facts and ideas one's own include "construction," "appropriation," "transmission," "attainment," and "accumulation." Within this metaphor, "[l]ike material goods, knowledge has the permanent quality that makes the privileged position of its owner equally permanent."[16]

Learning is participation.

Comparing this to the learning-as-acquisition metaphor, Sfard explains: "the terms that imply the existence of some permanent entities have been replaced with the noun 'knowing,' which indicates action." She argues that this linguistic shift signals a profound conceptual shift: "[t]he talk about states has been replaced with attention to activities . . . the permanence of *having* gives way to the constant flux of *doing.*" The vocabulary of this conceptual framework includes words such as "situatedness," "contextuality," "cultural embeddedness," and "social mediation." Learning is "conceived as a process of becoming a member of a certain community. This entails, above all, the ability to communicate in the language of this community and act according to its particular norms." This metaphor for learning stresses "the evolving bonds between the individual and others...[it] implies that the identity of an individual, like an identity of a living organ, is a function of his or her being (or becoming) a part of a greater entity."[17]

Metaphors for Teachers

A teacher is a scholar.

In a survey of the roles, images, and metaphors used to represent teachers and teaching in textbooks published in the United States before the 1940s, Pamela Joseph discusses a number of "ideal images," including this one: a teacher is a scholar.[18] The notion of the teacher as an intellectual sharply contrasts the teacher as technician or as clinician. This "open-minded scholar" must engage in the same intellectual pursuits in which he asks his students to engage, because "'[s]cholarship [can] bring delight to the teacher who [grows] intellectually along with his students'"[19] and also because "there must be a thinking teacher before there can be a thinking child."[20] The metaphor of the teacher as scholar positions teachers alongside other serious investigators into the nature and workings of things of the mind. It runs the risk, however, of privileging the realms of scholarship into which adults who have already been through the educational system make forays over the realms within which students still in their formal process of education explore.

A teacher is a reflective practitioner.

The phrase "the reflective practitioner" was coined by Schön in the early 1980s. Advocates of fostering the development of reflective practitioners[21] argue that, in the absence of reflection, "one runs the risk of relying on routinized teaching and . . . not developing as a teacher or as a person."[22] The ongoing interplay of reflection and action, or what Freire calls praxis,[23] although not generally built into the "structure of teaching,"[24] is essential to good pedagogical practice. As Zehm points out, reflection on the human dimensions of teaching is a useful tool for self-exploration as well as professional development.[25] Furthermore, not only does becoming a reflective practitioner mean developing the disposition to reflect on practice, it also means "finding the words to express those reflections to others—through collaboration, building a shared language and a shared knowledge of practice."[26] Thus the metaphor of teacher as reflective practitioner would appear to strive for more of a balance between calling for dwelling in the world of scholarship, like the teacher as scholar, and dwelling in the world that that teacher creates in the classroom.

A teacher is a researcher.

In the mid-1990s, a movement began to legitimate the systematic, intentional inquiry in which practicing teachers engage. Aiming to disrupt the one-way flow of educational knowledge from university-based researchers to curriculum and policy specialists to teachers, the teacher research movement argued that teachers can and should generate legitimate knowledge about educational practice. Teacher researchers use the sites of their own educational practice as subjects of inquiry with the more far-reaching goal of developing, assessing, and revising theories that inform practice.[27] Teacher research positions "the classroom teacher as 'practitioner-inquirer' rather than perpetuating the exclusive claim of the university professor as the 'scientist-theorist' of the educational research past."[28]

A teacher is a sculptor.

Writing in the early 1990s, Scheffler suggested that the child "is clay, and the teacher imposes a fixed mold on this clay, shaping it to the specification of the mold." He continues: "The sculptor's statue does not grow of itself out of the rock, requiring only the artist's nurture; the artist exercises real choice in its production, yet his initial block of marble is not wholly receptive to any idea he may wish to impose on it." This metaphor, in Scheffler's discussion, throws into relief the power and control of the teacher, but it does not take into consideration those aspects of teaching and learning that are not within the teacher's control. It casts the student as something inanimate—clay—yet something that can take shape. The consistency of the clay, of the student, and the properties it brings to the creative process, help shape what is created.[29]

A teacher is an artist.

Like education as growth, the teacher as artist has surfaced at various points in history. The artist knows what it takes "to fashion works whose form and structure are holistic and unified."[30] An artist is someone who sees the "all-overness" of her process and who knows how, through that process, to create a new image.[31] Gage writes of teaching as a "practical art" which calls for "intuition, creativity, improvisation, and expressiveness—a process that leaves room for what is implied by rules, formulas, and algorithms."[32] Art embraces both sensory and intellectual dimensions of the human mind. One teacher who sees herself as an artist states that in her classroom, "the air is full of possibilities"; within such a classroom, a teacher must be comfortable with ambiguity and flexibility.[33] Teaching, writes another teacher, "is an art full of subtle nuance."[34] Words such as "holistic," "all-overness," "intuition," and "possibilities" highlight the indeterminate nature of this metaphor. An artist "disturbs, upsets, enlightens, and he opens ways for better understanding."[35] The technique an artist uses must be "evoked by the spirit of the things she wish[es] to express."[36] To create a work of art, or to inspire others to create a work of art, teachers must both be guided by their own internal and individual visions and also "go to kindred spirits—others who have wanted [to create a particular] thing—and study their ways and means, learn from their successes and failures."[37]

A teacher is a coach.

Teachers who are coaches share the responsibility of making sure that students achieve excellence with other members of the school community, parents, and the students themselves. Coaches understand, explains Ladson-Billings, that "the goal is team success." Although they operate "behind the scenes" and "on the sidelines," coaches are always present to "players" through their expectations.[38]

A teacher is a director.

Allender explains: "I think of teaching as if I were directing a play—an improvised play in which there are no lines for the players to read or only a few at most . . . The script is a set of notes, and at every juncture, detailed directions on how to proceed are given. What unfolds, in contrast, is undetermined and can be surprising."[39] In analyzing his own teaching practice, Allender narrates instances of role-playing and rehearsing—opportunities he offers his students to explore their roles, critique their own and others' performances, and co-construct the ultimate production of the course.

A teacher is a savior.

In his critique of cinematic depictions of teachers between the mid-1950s and the mid-1990s, William Ayers explains that many teaching movies represent schools and teachers as "in the business of saving children"—from their families, from drugs and violence, from themselves—but that individual teachers are mostly unable to live up to the job. Thus the rare good teacher is seen as a saint who must figure out who can be saved before it's too late. The savior's approach includes firmly establishing discipline then delivering the curriculum. But as Ayers points out, "real learning requires assertion, not obedience, action not passivity"; it is deeply human, intimate, intellectual, ambiguous, and unpredictable work.[40] Compounding this image of teacher as savior is the fact that it is usually white teachers saving kids of color. As Robert Lowe points out, films such as *Dangerous Minds* "appear to offer White teachers models to emulate that might advance the project of racial justice." Lowe contends, however, that in fact the films justify white supremacy.[41]

A teacher is a conductor.

"We can visualize an orchestra conductor who approaches the orchestra stand; all members of the orchestra have their eyes fixed on the conductor." The members of the orchestra are the students. Teachers who are conductors take responsibility for assuring that the students achieve excellence; they lead their students toward it. But as is often the case in performances of orchestras, "so powerful can the personality of the conductor be that the audience and musical critics describe the quality of the performance in terms of the conductor's performance, even though the conductor did not play a single note."[42]

A teacher is a gardener.

Scheffler contends that "there is an obvious analogy between the growing child and the growing plant," specifically in the sense that "in both cases the developing organism goes through phases that are relatively independent of the efforts of gardener or teacher." Scheffler argues that this metaphor constructs the teacher's role as one of studying and then indirectly helping the development of the child rather than shaping him "into some preconceived form." Growth and development "may be helped or hindered by [the teacher's] efforts."[43] But growth and development is the focus, and it is based on "an inner growth principle"—the notion that something simple grows into something complex "through various preordained stages."[44] A prospective teacher in an education course explains how this metaphor works for her. She writes an extended story within which she describes students as a "mixed bag of seeds" that the teacher "has to find a way to nurture." She "wants the best for the seeds" that she plants; to be the best teacher she can be, she learns "how to learn from the seedlings"; and "watching the stems, the leaves, and the blossoms dance in the breeze, the gardener too began to dance."[45]

A teacher is a dentist.

The teacher who crafted this metaphor to describe her work explains that "the dentist tells you what you have to do to have good teeth, but essentially, you have to do it." This teacher explains that some days in her classroom "it is as hard as pulling teeth" and that sometimes students come in and "if they didn't brush their teeth last night" not only can you not get near them because they have bad breath, but "you have this faint feeling as if they failed you in some way, or you failed because you did not impress upon them the importance of doing it."[46] Perhaps because the teacher herself formulated and explained this metaphor, one can vividly see the way that it works within its own terms. There seems to be a measure of humor as well in this teacher's explanation, and as Efron and Joseph point out, this metaphor is one of struggle, of compassion, of failure and perseverance.[47] The deeply complicated sense that teacher and student can fail one another in education represents a recognition of one of the most powerful aspects of education: that education is—or should be—a reciprocal dynamic, a co-constructed endeavor.[48]

Metaphors for Teaching

Teaching is persuasion.

Arguing in 2001 for the metaphor of teaching as persuasion, Murphy dismisses the pejorative meanings of persuasion—"influencing," "convincing," "manipulating," "tempting"—to assert that "at its simplest" persuasion can be understood "as evoking a change in one's understanding or judgment relative to a particular idea or premise."[49] Teaching as persuasion is premised on the notion of scaffolded instruction: "a joint venture in which students and teacher share responsibility for learning and refining strategies." Murphy argues that persuasion "rejects the idea that there can be a simple transmission of knowledge from teacher to student, or [sic] the assumption that all students will accept whatever information is introduced into the learning environment fully or in part."[50] I suggest, though, that persuasion is a fundamentally conservative metaphor of transmission and maintenance of the status quo. As Hynd writes, "Educators are concerned that students use . . . knowledge to gain influential positions in society (knowledge is power) in order to contribute to citizenship, safety, and productivity."[51] This statement is true of conservative educators, but liberal or radical educators are more interested in self actualization, challenging the status quo, and developing thinking skills, which Hynd goes on to acknowledge aren't so well suited to this metaphor. Underlying this metaphor is the implication that students don't have the capacity, or can't be trusted, to actually prove/discover/come to understand things themselves. Thus while it might make very good sense to think critically about how and why teachers try to persuade students, to argue that persuasion should be the guiding metaphor for teaching seems to undermine what Murphy and others who write about the metaphor argue for as a collaboration between teacher and students.

Teaching is improvisational dance.

Writing in 2000, Heaton argued that teaching itself is fundamentally improvisational, and she used the metaphor of improvisational dance to describe a mathematics classroom full of improvisation moving toward meaning. To discuss this metaphor she draws on the language of "preparation, improvisation, and contemplation." Describing her experience, Heaton writes: "I found myself *in* teaching in ways I had not experienced before. For a moment I felt what it was like to improvise, to be responsive, beyond the first few moves, to students' understanding and the mathematics I was trying to teach." This metaphor focuses on "the interdependent relationship among the participants" in the dance. It involves making different decisions at different points about who is going to lead and who is going to follow. Heaton opposes this metaphor to traditional textbook math teaching, which she sees as closer to traditional, rote dance. She discusses a sharing of leadership and control, and she describes creation through action and response. Implicitly important in this metaphor is expecting the unexpected and letting the learning emerge through the process of collaborative improvisation.[52]

Notes

Chapter 1. Living Translation

Note to epigraph: John Crowley, *The Translator* (New York: HarperCollins, 1995), 182, 163.

1. *Patenkind* translates into "godchild" in English, but this translation does not capture the nature of the relationship between godparent and godchildren in German culture. The relationship between *Patentante* (godaunt) and *Patenkinder* can be much closer than the typical godparent/godchild relationship in the United States; a *Patentante* can be like a third parent, as has been the case for me.

2. Throughout this chapter I refer now and then to Lisa and Moritz and our experiences of traveling or playing together. Much of the time I spent was also with Lisa and Moritz's parents, but my focus is on the unique relationship I had with the children and on the relationship between the kinds of learning in which they were engaged and the kind in which I was engaged.

3. John Dewey, *Democracy and Education: An Introduction to the Philosophy of Education* (New York: Macmillan, 1916).

4. The Goethe Institute is a network of 144 institutes in 78 countries that provide information on the culture, language, and other general aspects of Germany. At sixteen of these institutes one can attend language courses and sit exams. See http://www.goethe.de/enindex.htm for more information.

5. Beate Mambynek, Mona Kleine, and Ronald Thoden, *Stadtführer Göttingen* (Göttingen: Verlag Die Werkstatt, 1999).

6. All translations of excerpts from German texts or statements that follow the German in parentheses are my own.

7. See Jonathan Culler, "Identity, Identification, and the Subject," in *Literary Theory: A Very Short Introduction* (New York: Oxford University Press, 2000), 104–15.

8. Culler, "Identity," 113.

9. Psychologists call this self a subject—the "knower" that aggregates and integrates the experiences that the self has. William James made the original distinction between the self as subject and the self as object, designating "I" (self as subject) as the knower and "Me" (self as object) as "an empirical aggregate of things objectively known about the self." Susan Harter, "Historical Roots of

Contemporary Issues Involving Self-Concept," in *Handbook of Self-Concept: Developmental, Social, and Clinical Considerations,* ed. Bruce A. Bracken (New York: John Wiley, 1996), 1–37.

10. Daphna Oyserman and Hazel Rose Markus, "Possible Selves, Motivation, and Delinquency" (unpublished manuscript, University of Michigan, 1987), cited in Harter, "Historical Roots," 9.

11. Harter, "Historical Roots," 3.

12. Dorinne Kondo, *Crafting Selves: Power, Gender, and Discourses of Identity in a Japanese Workplace* (Chicago: University of Chicago Press, 1990), 33, 48.

13. Katherine Nelson, "Languages and the Self: From the 'Experiencing I' to the 'Continuing Me,'" in *The Self in Time: Developmental Perspectives,* ed. Chris Moore and Karen Lemmon (Mahwah, N.J.: Lawrence Erlbaum Associates, 2001), 15.

14. Alice Kaplan, *French Lessons* (Chicago: University of Chicago Press, 1993), 47.

15. Maxine Greene, "Uncoupling from the Ordinary," in *Variations on a Blue Guitar: The Lincoln Institute Lectures on Aesthetic Education* (New York: Teachers College Press, 2001), 67.

16. Kaplan, *French Lessons,* 55.

17. Dewey, *Democracy,* 326.

18. Sherod Santos, "A la Recherche de la Poésie Perdue (Poetry and Translation)," *The American Poetry Review* 29, no. 3 (2000): 14.

19. Azade Seyhan, *Writing Outside the Nation* (Princeton, N.J.: Princeton University Press, 2001), 108.

20. Emine Sevgi Özdamar, *Mutterzunge* (Berlin: Rotbuch, 1990), 24, quoted in Seyhan, *Writing,* 120.

21. Dewey, *Democracy.*

22. Ronald L. Martinez, "Life as a Foreign Language Student: What *Else* is There?" *Culture Shock* 5, no. 1 (Newsletter in the Department of French and Italian, University of Minnesota, October 2000): 1.

23. Kaplan, *French Lessons,* 54.

24. Verena Stefan, "Here's Your Change 'N Enjoy the Show," in *Language Crossings: Negotiating the Self in a Multicultural World,* ed. Karen Ogulnick (New York: Teachers College Press, 2000), 23.

25. Karen Ogulnick, "Introduction," in *Language Crossings,* 1.

26. Richard Rodriguez, "The Achievement of Desire," in *Rereading America: Cultural Contexts for Critical Thinking and Writing,* ed. Gary Colombo et al. (Boston: Bedford Books of St. Martin's Press, 1992), 543, 544.

27. Eva Hoffman, *Lost in Translation: A Life in Language* (New York: Penguin Books, 1989), 269, 274.

28. Arthur Schopenhauer, "On Language and Words," trans. Peter Mollenhauer, in *Theories of Translation: An Anthology of Essays from Drydan to Derrida,* ed. Rainer Schulte and John Biguenet (Chicago: University of Chicago Press, [1800] 1992), 33.

29. David Constantine, "Gedanken des Kommandanten" (lecture, Literarisches Zentrum Göttingen, Göttingen, Germany, October 13, 2001).

30. Branislaw Malinowski, *The Language of Magic and Gardening* (Bloomington: Indiana University Press, 1965), 11.

31. Constantine, "Gedanken."

32. Ibid.

33. David Constantine, "Finding the Words: Translation and Survival of the Human," *The Times Literary Supplement* (May 21, 1999), 14.

34. For discussions of these points, see the following: Eugene Nida, "Principles of Correspondence" in *The Translation Studies Reader,* ed. Lawrence Venuti (London: Routledge, 2000), 126; Constantine, "Gedanken"; Constantine, "Finding," 15.

35. Schopenhauer, "On Language," 33; Nida, "Principles," 126–33.

36. Dewey, *Democracy*.

37. Bertolt Brecht, *Brecht on Theatre: The Development of an Aesthetic*, ed. and trans. John Willet (New York: Hill and Wang, 1964).

38. Mark Twain, *Die schreckliche deutsche Sprache [The Awful German Language]* (n.p., n.d.), 10.

39. Paulo Freire, *Pedagogy of the Oppressed* (New York: Continuum, 1990), 81.

40. Dewey, *Democracy*.

41. See George Steiner, *After Babel: Aspects of Language and Translation*, 3rd ed. (Oxford: Oxford University Press, 1998), particularly chapter 1, "Understanding as Translation."

42. Michael M. J. Fischer, "Ethnicity and the Postmodern Arts of Memory," in *Writing Culture: The Politics and Poetics of Ethnography*, ed. James Clifford and George E. Marcus (Berkeley: University of California Press, 1986), 232–33, quoted in Seyhan, *Writing*, 67.

43. Jerome S. Allender, *Teacher Self: The Practice of Humanistic Education* (Lanham, Md.: Rowman & Littlefield, 2001), 46.

44. Lev Vygotsky, *Thought and Language*, ed. Alex Kozulin (Cambridge, Mass.: MIT Press, 1986); Lev Vygotsky, *Mind in Society: The Development of Higher Psychological Processes*, ed. Michael Cole et al. (Cambridge, Mass.: Harvard University Press, 1978).

45. J. O'Connor and J. Seymour, *Introducing NLP* (n.p., 1990).

46. John Dewey, "My Pedagogic Creed," in *John Dewey on Education*, ed. Reginald D. Archambault (Chicago: University of Chicago Press, 1964), 436.

47. Eleanor Duckworth, "The Virtues of Not Knowing," in *"The Having of Wonderful Ideas" and Other Essays on Teaching and Learning* (New York: Teachers College Press, 1987), 65.

48. Peter McLaren, *Life in Schools: An Introduction to Critical Pedagogy in the Foundations of Education* (New York: Longman, 1998), 186.

49. Ira Shor, *Empowering Education: Critical Teaching for Social Change* (Chicago: University of Chicago Press, 1992), 16.

50. Carolyn Heilbrun, *Writing a Woman's Life* (New York: Ballantine Books, 1988), 18.

51. T. S. Eliot, "The Dry Salvages," in *Collected Poems 1909–1962* (London: Faber and Faber, 1983), 208.

52. Victor Turner, "Social Dramas and Stories about Them," in *On Narrative*, ed. W. J. T. Mitchell (Chicago: University of Chicago Press, 1981), 159.

53. Maxine Greene, "In Search of Metaphor" (paper presentation, Annual Meeting of the American Educational Research Association), New Orleans, April 2000.

54. Mary Soliday, "Translating Self and Difference through Literacy Narratives," *College English* 56, no. 5 (1994): 511.

55. Robert A. Nisbet, quoted in Victor Turner, *Dramas, Fields, and Metaphors*, ed. Victor Turner (Ithaca, N.Y.: Cornell University Press, 1974), 25.

56. In the terms of metaphor used by literary scholars, these students fused various "separated realms of experience" to formulate "some similarity antecedently existing," to express "significant and surprising truths," or to provide "new perspectives." These points are quoted from and can be further explored in the following: Turner, *Dramas*, 25; Max Black, *Models and Metaphors: Studies in Language and Philosophy* (Ithaca, N.Y.: Cornell University Press, 1962), 37; Israel Scheffler, *In Praise of the Cognitive Emotions and Other Essays in the Philosophy of Education* (New York: Routledge, 1991), 45; Turner, *Dramas*, 31; Black, *Models*, 37.

57. Mary Louise Pratt, "Arts of the Contact Zone," in *Ways of Reading: An Anthology for Writers*, 5th ed., ed. David Bartholomae and Anthony Petrosky (Boston: St. Martin's, 1999), 584.

58. Anna Sfard, "On Two Metaphors for Learning and the Dangers of Choosing Just One," *Educational Researcher* 27, no. 2 (March 1998): 4–13.

59. Susan Bassnett and Harish Trivedi, "Introduction: Of Colonies, Cannibals, and Vernaculars," in *Post-Colonial Translation: Theory and Practice*, edited by Susan Bassnett and Harish Trivedi (London: Routledge, 1999), 2.

60. Constantine, "Finding," 15.

61. Constantine, "Gedanken."

62. Bassnett and Trividi, "Introduction," 3.

63. Stefan, "Here's Your Change," 29.

64. Françoise Lionnet, *Autobiographical Voices: Race, Gender, and Self-Portraiture* (Ithaca, N.Y.: Cornell University Press, 1989), 18, quoted in Seyhan, Writing, 67.

65. Jörg Modeß, personal communication, December 2001.

66. Donald Schön, "Generative Metaphor: A Perspective on Problem-Setting in Social Policy," in *Metaphor and Thought*, ed. Andrew Ortony (Ithaca, N.Y.: Cornell University Press, 1979), 259, 277.

67. Carol Cohn, "'Clean Bombs' and Clean Language," *in Women, Militarism, and War: Essays in History, Politics, and Social Theory*, ed. Jean Bethke Elshtain and Sheila Tobias (Lanham, Md.: Rowman & Littlefield, 1990), 50.

Chapter 2. A Metaphor for Change in Learning and Teaching

Note to epigraph: George Lakoff and Mark Johnson, *Metaphors We Live By* (Chicago: University of Chicago Press, 1980), 22.

1. Jerome Bruner, *The Process of Education* (Cambridge, Mass.: Harvard University Press, 1977), ix.

2. Verena Stefan, "To Make a Prairie: On Immigration, Broken Language, and the Fabric of the Imagination" (lecture, Bryn Mawr College German Department, Bryn Mawr, Pa., February 18, 2002). See Karen Ogulnick, ed., *Language Crossings*, for essays on living between languages and cultures written by Stefan and others.

3. *erfahren: Das Verb mhd ervarn, ahd. irfaran bedeutet ursprünglich "reisen," durchfahren, durchziehen; erreichen, wurde aber schon früh im heutigen Sinne gebraucht als "erforschen, kennenlernen, durchmachen"* [hear, know, experience: The verb from Middle High German—*ervarn*—Old High German—*irfahren*—originally meant "to travel," go through, pull through; reach (a destination), but was already used early on in the contemporary sense as "to explore (examine, investigate, inquire, search), to get to know, to go through (pass through, endure)"] (*Duden. Vol. 7. Das Herkunftswörterbuch: Etymologie der deutschen Sprache*, 2nd. ed., Günther Drosdowski. Mannheim; Vienna; Zürich, 1989).

4. *Webster's New International Dictionary*, 2nd ed. (unabridged) (Springfield, Mass.: G. & C. Merriam Company, 1951), s.v. "Translation." In an interesting combination of these concepts, the word "tralatition" means metaphor, and the word "tralalitious" means handed down or passed on or transmitted from hand to hand or mouth to mouth or generation to generation.

5. Constantine, "Finding," 15. See also Dewey, *Democracy*.

6. Maxine Greene, "Defining Aesthetic Education," in *Variations on a Blue Guitar:*

The Lincoln Center Institute Lectures on Aesthetic Education (New York: Teachers College Press, 2001), 5.

7. Paul de Man, "The Epistemology of Metaphor," in *On Metaphor*, ed. Sheldon Sacks (Chicago: University of Chicago Press, 1979), 15. Also interesting about the word "übersetzen" is that it can be a word with a separable or an inseparable prefix. When it has a separable prefix, it means to move from one place to another with a ferry over a river: *Mit der Fähre setze ich über* (I take the ferry across). When it has an inseparable prefix, it means to translate: *Ich übersetze das Gedicht* (I translate the poem).

8. All definitions drawn from *Webster's New International Dictionary*, 2nd ed.

9. Stephen C. Pepper, *World Hypotheses* (Berkeley: University of California Press, 1942), 38–39. See also Ortony, ed., *Metaphor and Thought* and James W. Fernandez, "The Performance of Ritual Metaphors," in *The Social Use of Metaphor: Essays on the Anthropology of Rhetoric*, ed. J. David Sapir and J. Christopher Crocker (Philadelphia: University of Pennsylvania Press, 1977) for a discussion organic and mechanical metaphors.

10. James W. Fernandez, "Persuasions and Performances: Of the Beast in Every Body . . . And the Metaphors of Everyman," in *Myth, Symbol, and Culture*, ed. Clifford Geertz (New York: W. W. Norton, 1971), 57. See also Willard Van Orman, *Word and Object* (Cambridge, Mass.: MIT Press, 1963), 83ff.

11. See Fernandez, "Persuasions and Performances," 57, where he asserts that the study of metaphors involves the study of "the movement they make in semantic space." See also Clifford Geertz, "Deep Play: Notes on the Balinese Cockfight," in *Myth, Symbol, and Culture*, 26, where Geertz writes: "any expressive form works (when it works) by disarranging semantic contexts in such a way that properties conventionally ascribed to certain things are unconventionally ascribed to other things, which are then seen actually to possess them." See also J. David Sapir, "The Anatomy of Metaphor," in *The Social Use of Metaphor*.

12. See Black, *Models*, 39; I. A. Richards, *The Philosophy of Rhetoric* (London: Oxford University Press, 1965); Schön, "Generative Metaphor," 254, where he writes that metaphor refers both to "a perspective or frame—a way of looking at things—and to a certain kind of process—a process by which new perspectives on the world come into existence" and 276–77, where he writes that the cognitive work of understanding a metaphor "involves the participants in attending to new features and relations of the phenomenon, and in renaming, regrouping, and reordering those features and relations."

13. Sapir, "The Anatomy of Metaphor," 3.

14. Maxine Greene, "Multiple Visions: Aesthetic Moments and Experiences," in *Variations on a Blue Guitar: The Lincoln Center Institute Lectures on Aesthetic Education* (New York: Teachers College Press, 2001), 12.

15. Black, *Models*, 37.

16. Scheffler, *In Praise of the Cognitive Emotions*, 45; see also Mary Oliver, *A Poetry Handbook* (San Diego, Calif.: Harcourt, Brace, 1994), and Andrew Ortony, "Metaphor: A Multidisciplinary Problem," in *Metaphor and Thought*, 5.

17. Turner, *Dramas*, 31; Black, *Models*, 37. See also Hugh G. Petrie, "Metaphor and Learning," in *Metaphor and Thought*, 438–61.

18. Greene, "Defining Aesthetic Education," 5.

19. Fernandez, "The Performance of Ritual Metaphors," 102. See also E. W. Van Steenburgh, "Metaphor," *The Journal of Philosophy* 62 (1965), 687–88.

20. Nathan Dickmeyer, "Metaphor, Model, and Theory in Education Research," *Teachers College Record* 91, no. 2 (winter 1989), 151.

21. T. S. Eliot, "Tradition and the Individual Talent," in *Selected Prose of T.S. Eliot*, ed. Frank Kermode (New York: Harcourt, Brace, Jovanovich, 1975). In this essay, Eliot elaborates on the need to dislocate language into meaning.

22. Black, "More about Metaphor," 21. See also Aristotle, *Poetics*.

23. Black, *Models*, 41. See also Ortony, "Metaphor: A Multidisciplinary Problem," 6.

24. See Schön, "Generative Metaphor," 259, and also 281, where he refers in an endnote to Wittgenstein's notions of seeing as, its relation to thinking as and to literal seeing, and its relevance to an understanding of description.

25. Schön, "Generative Metaphor," 259, 268.

26. Maxine Greene, "Imagination and Aesthetic Literacy," in *Landscapes of Learning* (New York: Teachers College Press, 1978), 186.

27. Jorge Luis Borges, "The Metaphor," in *This Craft of Verse*, ed. Calin-Andrei Mihailescu (Cambridge, Mass.: Harvard University Press, 2000), 23.

28. Greene, "In Search of Metaphor"; Borges, "The Metaphor."

29. Turner, "Social Dramas," 159.

30. Turner, *Dramas*, 25.

31. Kaplan, *French Lessons*, 155.

32. Turner, *Dramas*, 25.

33. Philip Ellis Wheelwright, *Metaphor and Reality* (Bloomington: Indiana University Press, 1962), quoted in Roland Bartel, *Metaphors and Symbols: Forays into Language* (Urbana, Ill.: National Council of Teachers of English, 1983), 55. Wheelwright asks as well: What is the "psychic depth at which the things of this world, whether actual or fancied, are transmuted by the cool heat of the imagination"?

34. Dickmeyer, "Metaphor, Model, and Theory," 152.

35. Bartel, *Metaphors and Symbols*, 55.

36. Winifred Nowottny, *The Language Poets Use* (London: Athlone Press, 1962), quoted in Bartel, *Metaphors and Symbols*, 55.

37. Scheffler, *In Praise*, 46.

38. Lakoff and Johnson, *Metaphors We Live By*, 11.

39. Ibid., 4.

40. Laurel Richardson, *Fields of Play: Constructing an Academic Life* (New Brunswick, N.J.: Rutgers University Press, 1997), 45.

41. Gareth Morgan, *Images of Organization* (Beverly Hills, Calif.: Sage Publications, 1986), 12. See Dickmeyer, "Metaphor, Model, and Theory," for a discussion of how this property of metaphors can affect education research.

42. Morgan, *Images*, 13.

43. Sfard, "On Two Metaphors," 5.

44. Greene, "In Search."

45. Robert V. Bullough, Jr. and Andrew Gitlin, *Becoming a Student of Teaching: Methodologies for Exploring Self and School Context* (New York: Garland Publishing, 2001), 49.

46. Nowottny, *The Language Poets Use*, 89.

47. Kevin Chambers, "Mixed Metaphors and Mexican Students," unpublished manuscript, 1994, quoted in Rodney S. Earle, "Teacher Imagery and Metaphors: Windows to Teaching and Learning," *Educational Technology* (July/August 1995): 55.

48. Gary D. Fenstermacher and Jonas F. Soltis, *Approaches to Teaching*, 2nd ed. (New York: Teachers College Press, 1992), 4.

49. Earle, "Teacher Imagery," 53.

50. Sue Johnson, "Images: A Way of Understanding the Practical Knowledge of

Student Teachers" (*Teaching and Teacher Education* 8, no. 2 [April 1992]), quoted in Earle, "Teacher Imagery," 53.

51. Dickmeyer, "Metaphor, Model, and Theory," 152.

52. Sfard, "On Two Metaphors," 5.

53. I am grateful to my colleagues Maria Cristina Quintero and Graciela Michelotti for discussions of this point.

54. All definitions of translation referenced here are drawn from *Webster's New International Dictionary*, 2nd ed.

55. See Steiner, *After Babel: Aspects of Language and Translation*, 3rd ed. (Oxford: Oxford University Press, 1998), particularly chapter 1, "Understanding as Translation."

56. Ibid., 49.

57. Bullough and Gitlin, *Becoming a Student of Teaching*, xiii. Bullough and Gitlin critique this notion of student.

58. This process is analogous to the translation of literary texts in this way: Because "the art of translation will always have to cope with the reality of untranslatability from one language to another" and because "[t]he total impact of a translation may be reasonably close to the original, but there can be no identity in detail," translators seek "the equivalence, the effect, and not a replica of method or letters themselves." A successful translation emphasizes "the total workings of a text, not just the words," because translation is more than transliteration; it is the "re-articulation of a complex human experience." These quotations as well as elaborations on these points can be found in the following texts: Hugo Friedrich, "On the Art of Translation," in *Theories of Translation: An Anthology of Essays from Dryden to Derrida*, ed. Rainer Schulte and John Biguenet (Chicago: University of Chicago Press, 1992), 11; Nida, "Principles," 126; Constantine, "Gedanken"; Constantine, "Finding," 15. See also Steiner, *After Babel*.

59. Steiner, *After Babel*, 7.

60. Marjorie Agosín, "A Writer's Thoughts on Translation and Always Living in Translation," *MultiCultural Review* (September 2000): 57.

61. Walter Benjamin, "The Task of the Translator," in *The Translation Studies Reader*, ed. Lawrence J. Venuti (London: Routledge, 2000), 20.

62. John Locke was the first to propose a notion of personal identity and self-hood based on consciousness; it is the "self" that accepts as our own mental and physical acts performed now and in the past. Hazlitt added the question of how we form a notion of the changing self that extends into the future. He argues that, while our relationship to our past and present selves depends on causal relations of sensation and memory, our relationship to our future selves depends on imagination. For a discussion of this point, see John Barresi, "Extending Self-Consciousness into the Future," in *The Self in Time*, 141–42.

63. Jonathan F. Zaff and Elizabeth C. Hair, "Positive Development of the Self: Self-Concept, Self-Esteem, and Identity," in *Well-Being: Positive Development across the Life Course*, ed. Marc H. Bornstein, Lucy Davidson, Corey L. M. Keyes, and Kristin A. Moore (Mahwah, N.J.: Lawrence Erlbaum Associates, 2003), 236.

64. Susan Harter and Ann Monsour, "Developmental Analysis of Conflict Caused by Opposing Self-Attributes in the Adolescent Self-Portrait," *Developmental Psychology* 28, no. 2 (March 1992): 251–60.

65. Robyn Fivush, "Owning Experience: Developing Subjective Perspective in Autobiographical Narratives," in *The Self in Time*, 51. See also Chris Moore and Karen Lemmon, "The Nature and Utility of the Temporally Extended Self," in *The Self in Time*.

66. Nelson, "Languages and the Self," 30.

67. Moore, "Nature and Utility," 1–2.

68. Ibid., 2, 4, 5.

69. James A. Holstein and Jaber F. Gubrium, *The Self We Live By: Narrative Identity in a Postmodern World* (New York: Oxford University Press, 2000), 13.

70. Constantine, "Gedanken."

71. Santos, "A la Recherche," 13.

72. A. S. Byatt, *The Biographer's Tale* (New York: Alfred A. Knopf, 2000), 167.

73. Friedrich, "On the Art of Translation," 12.

74. Donald Robinson, *What is Translation? Centrifugal Theories, Critical Interventions* (Kent, Oh.: Kent State University Press, 1997), 83.

75. This is Santos's interpretation of Donoghue's argument in Santos, "A la Recherche," 14.

76. For two important discussions of power dynamics in translation, see Myriam Diaz-Diocaretz, *Translating Poetic Discourse: Questions on Feminist Strategies in Adrienne Rich* (Amsterdam: John Benjamins, 1985), and Suzanne Jill Levine, *The Subversive Scribe: Translating Latin American Fiction* (Saint Paul, Mn.: Graywolf Press, 1991).

77. Jiri Levy, "Translation as a Decision Process," in *The Translation Studies Reader,* 148.

78. Elizabeth Ellsworth, *Teaching Positions: Differences, Pedagogy and the Power of Address* (New York: Teachers College Press, 1997), 58–59.

79. Hoffman, *Lost,* 175.

80. Hoffman, *Lost,* 211.

81. Stefan, "Here's Your Change," 23. See also Schopenhauer, "On Language and Words," 34.

82. Kondo, *Crafting Selves,* 10.

83. Ibid., 33, 48.

84. Hoffman, *Lost,* 269, 274.

85. William A. Proefriedt, "The Immigrant or 'Outsider' Experience as Metaphor for Becoming an Educated Person in the Modern World: Mary Antin, Richard Wright and Eva Hoffman," *MELUS: The Journal of the Society for the Study of the Multi-Ethnic Literature of the United States* 16, no. 2 (1990): 87–88.

86. Fernandez, "Persuasions and Performances," 57.

87. Turner, *Dramas,* 159.

88. Sfard, "On Two Metaphors," 8.

89. Another version of this survey and analysis was published as Alison Cook-Sather, "Movements of Mind: *The Matrix,* Metaphors, and Re-Imagining Education," *Teachers College Record* 105, no. 6 (August 2003): 946–77.

90. Philip Ellis Wheelwright, *Metaphor & Reality* (Bloomington: Indiana University Press, 1962).

91. Raymond Callahan, *Education and the Cult of Efficiency: A Study of the Social Forces That Have Shaped the Administration of the Public Schools* (Chicago: University of Chicago Press, 1962).

92. Joel Spring, *The Sorting Machine: National Educational Policy Since 1945* (New York: McKay, 1976).

93. Robert V. Bullough, Jr., *The Forgotten Dream of American Education* (Ames: Iowa State University Press, 1988). See also Philip C. Schlechty, *Schools for the 21st Century: Leadership Imperatives for Educational Reform* (San Francisco: Jossey-Bass, 1991).

94. Schlechty, *Schools,* 21.

95. Ibid., 21

96. Stanley K. Schultz, *The Culture Factory: Boston Public Schools, 1789–1860* (New York: Oxford University Press, 1973), 131.

97. Schlechty, *Schools,* 42, 21.

98. Stanley J. Zehm, "Deciding to Teach: Implications of a Self-Development Perspective," in *The Role of Self in Teacher Development,* ed. Richard P. Lipka and Thomas M. Brinthaupt (New York: State University of New York Press, 1999), 43.

99. William F. Pinar, "The Reconceptualization of Curriculum Studies," in *The Curriculum Studies Reader,* ed. Stephen J. Thornton and David J. Flinders (New York: Routledge, 1997), 205.

100. Vito Perrone, *Lessons for New Teachers* (Boston: McGrawHill, 2000), 30.

101. Alfie Kohn, *The Case Against Standardized Testing: Raising the Scores, Ruining the Schools* (Portsmouth, N.H.: Heinemann, 2000).

102. Schlechty, *Schools,* 23.

103. All references in this paragraph are from Sara Efron and Pamela Bolotin Joseph, "Reflections in a Mirror: Metaphors of Teachers in Teaching," in *Images of Schoolteachers in America,* 2nd ed., ed. Pamela M. Joseph and Gail E. Burnaford (Mahwah, N.J.: Lawrence Erlbaum Associates, 2001), 78.

104. Fenstermacher, *Approaches,* 16.

105. Schlechty, *Schools,* 23.

106. Fenstermacher, *Approaches,* 16.

107. Joseph Mayor Rice, *The Public School System of the United States* (New York: Century Company, 1893), 31.

108. Efron and Joseph, "Reflections," 78.

109. Fenstermacher, *Approaches,* 16.

110. Efron and Joseph, "Reflections," 79.

111. John Dewey, *Experience and Education* (New York: Touchstone, 1938), 49.

112. Discussion among high-school students as part of Teaching and Learning Together (see Chapter 5), September 25, 2002.

113. Denise Clark Pope, *"Doing School": How We Are Creating a Generation of Stressed Out, Materialistic, and Miseducated Students* (New Haven, Conn.: Yale University Press, 2001).

114. Schlechty, *Schools,* 25.

115. Cotton Mather, quoted in Clinton Allison, *Present and Past: Essays for Teachers in the History of Education* (New York: Peter Lang, 1995), 9.

116. Robinson, quoted in Allison, *Present and Past,* 9.

117. Allison, *Present and Past,* See also Joel Spring, *The American School, 1642–1993* (New York: McGraw Hill, 1994).

118. Schön, "Generative Metaphor."

119. Joel Spring, *American Education: An Introduction to Social and Political Aspects* (New York: Longman, 1978), 3.

120. Schlechty, *Schools,* 26.

121. David Hawkins, "I, Thou, and It," in *The Informed Vision: Essays on Learning and Human Nature* (New York: Agathon Press), 53.

122. Mildred Z. Solomon, ed., *The Diagnostic Teacher: Constructing New Approaches to Professional Development* (New York: Teachers College Press, 1999), xvi.

123. Ibid., xvi–xvii.

124. Mildred A. Solomon and Catherine Cobb Morocco, "The Diagnostic Teacher," in *The Diagnostic Teacher,* 231.

125. Hawkins, "I, Thou, and It," 53, 54.

126. Fenstermacher, *Approaches,* 4.

127. Ibid., 33.

128. Joseph Fischer and Anne Kiefer, "Constructing and Discovering Images of Your Teaching," in *Images of Schoolteachers in America*, 108.

129. Fischer, "Constructing," 108.

130. Schlechty, *Schools*, 26.

131. Ibid., 27.

132. Ray McDermott and Herve Varenne, "Culture *as* Disability," *Anthropology & Education Quarterly* 26, no. 3 (1995): 324–48.

133. Alison Cook-Sather, "Authorizing Students' Perspectives: Toward Trust, Dialogue, and Change in Education," *Educational Researcher* 31, no. 4 (May 2002), 3–14.

134. H. Dickson Corbett and Bruce Wilson, "Make a Difference with, Not for, Students: A Plea for Researchers and Reformers," *Educational Researcher* 24, no. 5 (1995): 12–17.

135. Greene, "Defining Aesthetic Education," 65.

136. The following are references for the predecessors and proponents of constructivist education as described in this paragraph: Jean-Jacques Rousseau, "Emile," in *The Emile of Jean-Jacques Rousseau: Selections*, ed. W. Boyd (New York: Teachers College Press [1762] 1965); John Frederick Herbart, *Outlines of Educational Doctrine*, trans. A. F. Lenge (New York: Macmillan, 1901); Dewey, *Democracy*; Bruner, *The Process of Education*, xi; Duckworth, *The Having of Wonderful Ideas*.

137. This metaphor surfaces not only in the United States but also in China. See Lynne Paine, "Teacher Education in Search of a Metaphor: Defining the Relationship between Teachers, Teaching, and the State in China," in *The Political Dimensions in Teacher Education: Comparative Perspectives on Policy Formation, Socialization, and Society*, ed. Mark Ginsburg and Beverly Lindsay (London: The Falmer Press, 1995).

138. Scheffler, *In Praise*, 46, 47.

139. Turner, *Dramas*, 31.

140. Allender, *Teacher Self*, 23, 117, 118, 123.

141. Arthur G. Powell, Eleanor Farrar, and David K. Cohen, *The Shopping Mall High School: Winners and Losers in the Educational Marketplace* (Boston: Houghton Mifflin, 1985), 8, 8, 9, 8, 118, 22, 172, 1.

142. Ibid., 46, 24, 9.

143. Freire, *Pedagogy of the Oppressed*, 58.

144. Sfard, "On Two Metaphors," 5, 5, 5, 8.

145. Karen S. Evans, "Fifth-Grade Students' Perceptions of How They Experience Literature Discussion Groups," *Reading Research Quarterly*, 37, no. 1 (January–March 2002): 49.

146. Michael Fielding, "Students as Radical Agents of Change," *Journal of Educational Change* 2, no. 3 (July 2001): 123.

147. Penny Oldfather et al., "The Nature and Outcomes of Students' Longitudinal Participatory Research on Literacy Motivations and Schooling," *Research in the Teaching of English* 34 (1999), 313.

148. For thorough treatments of these issues, see the following: Penny Oldfather, ed., "Learning from Student Voices," *Theory into Practice* 43 (1995a), 84–87; Jeffrey Shultz and Alison Cook-Sather, eds., *In Our Own Words: Students' Perspectives on School* (Lanham, Md.: Rowman & Littlefield, 2001); Lois Weis and Michelle Fine, eds., *Beyond Silenced Voices: Class, Race, and Gender in United States Schools* (Albany: State University of New York Press, 1993); Bruce L. Wilson and H. Dickson Corbett, *Listening to Urban Kids: School Reform and the Teachers They Want* (New York: State University of New York Press, 2001).

149. Nelson Goodman, *Language of Art*, 2nd ed. (Indianapolis, In.: Hackett, 1998), 241, quoted in Greene, "Uncoupling," 68.

150. Earle, "Teacher Imagery," 54.

151. Paine, "Teacher Education," 78, 94.

152. Petrie, "Metaphor and Learning," 441.

153. See earlier discussions of this metaphor in Alison Cook-Sather, "Translating Themselves: Becoming a Teacher through Text and Talk," in *Talking Shop: Authentic Conversation in Teacher Education and Professional Development*, ed. Christopher M. Clark (New York: Teachers College Press, 2001), and "Between Student and Teacher: Teacher Education as Translation," *Teaching Education* 12, no. 2 (2001): 177–90.

Chapter 3. Translating Compositions and Selves

Parts of this chapter rely on work that I discussed in "Education as Translation: Students Transforming Notions of Narrative and Self," *College Composition and Communication* 55, no. 1 (September 2003), 91–114. Copyright 2003 by the National Council of Teachers of English. Reprinted with permission.

Note to epigraph: Santos, "A la Recherche," 9.

1. These definitions taken from the *Webster's New International Dictionary*, 2nd ed.

2. Zaff, "Positive Development," 236.

3. Moore and Lemmon, "The Nature and Utility," 2.

4. Markus, "The Self in Thought," 64.

5. These definitions taken from the *Webster's New International Dictionary*, 2nd ed.

6. The students whose experiences I analyze in this chapter were enrolled in "Finding the Bias" in 1998, 1999, or 2000.

7. The first iteration of this course was taught by Joseph Kramer, Elliott Shore, and me. The second iteration was taught by Katherine Rowe, Elliott Shore, and me. And the third was taught by Karen Tidmarsh, Elliott Shore, and me. For another discussion of this course, see Alison Cook-Sather, Katherine Rowe, and Elliott Shore, "Finding the Biases in a Community of Scholars," *Liberal Education*, winter 2002, 48–53.

8. Linda Brodkey, "Writing on the Bias," *College English* 56 (1994), 527–47.

9. Jamaica Kincaid, *The Autobiography of My Mother* (New York: Farrar, Straus, Giroux, 1996).

10. Olivia Lahs-Gonzales, ed., *Defining Eye: Women Photographers of the 20th Century*, Selections from the Helen Kornblum collection (St. Louis, Mo.: Saint Louis Art Museum, 1997).

11. Mary Louise Pratt, "Arts of the Contact Zone," in *Ways of Reading: An Anthology for Writers*, 5th ed., ed. David Bartholomae and Anthony Petrosky (Boston: St. Martin's, 1999), 584. Skorczewski, "'Everybody Has Their Own Ideas,'" 223.

12. Paulo Freire, *Pedagogy of Freedom: Ethics, Democracy, and Civil Courage* (Lanham, Md.: Rowman & Littlefield, 1998), 67.

13. Markus, "Self in Thought," 64.

14. Janis Forman, ed., *What Do I Know: Reading, Writing, and Teaching the Essay* (Portsmouth, N.H.: Heinemann-Boynton/Cook, 1996), 5.

15. All student names are pseudonyms.

16. Melissa Holt, final portfolio for the course "Finding the Bias," Bryn Mawr College, 2000.

17. Brodkey, "Writing," 546.

18. Adrienne Rich, "Blood, Bread, and Poetry: The Location of the Poet," in *Arts of the Possible: Essays and Conversations* (New York: W. W. Norton, 1983/2001), 49.

19. Forman, *What Do I Know*, 5.

20. Skorczewski, "'Everybody Has Their Own Ideas,'" 231.

21. Comfort, "Becoming a Writerly Self," 542.

22. Constantine, "Finding."

23. Jeannette Winterson, *Oranges Are Not the Only Fruit* (New York: The Atlantic Monthly Press, 1985); Maxine Hong Kingston, "Silence," in *Rereading America: Cultural Contexts for Critical Thinking and Writing*, ed. Gary Colombo et al. (Boston: Bedford Books of St. Martin's Press, 1992), 583–87; Rodriguez, "The Achievement of Desire"; Mike Rose, "I Just Wanna Be Average" 11–37 and "Entering the Conversation," 39–65 in *Lives on the Boundary* (New York: Free Press, 1989); Jane Tompkins, "Talking in Class" 62–65 and "Higher Education," 66–84 in *A Life in School: What the Teacher Learned* (Reading, Mass.: Addison-Wesley, 1996).

24. Paul John Eakin, *Fictions in Autobiography: Studies in the Act of Self-Invention* (Princeton, N.J.: Princeton University Press, 1985), 9.

25. Sana Abida, final portfolio for the course "Finding the Bias," Bryn Mawr College, 2000.

26. Raushan Rakhmetullin, final portfolio for the course "Finding the Bias," Bryn Mawr College, 1999.

27. Elizabeth Bonner, final portfolio for the course "Finding the Bias," Bryn Mawr College, 1999.

28. Brodkey, "Writing," 546.

29. Dawn Jankov, final portfolio for the course "Finding the Bias," Bryn Mawr College, 1999.

30. Her discussion also echoes psychologists' debate about the nature of self: Susan Harter explains that William James emphasized the self as unique while symbolic interactionist scholars asserted that the self is primarily a social construction "crafted through linguistic exchanges with others." "Historical Roots," 3.

31. Jankov, final portfolio, 1999.

32. Soliday, "Translating Self," 511–12.

33. Serena Matthews, final portfolio for the course "Finding the Bias," Bryn Mawr College, 1999.

34. Jean McMann, final portfolio for the course "Finding the Bias," Bryn Mawr College, 1998.

35. Marianna Jolie, final portfolio for the course "Finding the Bias," Bryn Mawr College, 1998.

36. Mindy Sutton, final portfolio for the course "Finding the Bias," Bryn Mawr College, 1998.

37. Melissa Welch-Ross, "Personalizing the Temporally Extended Self: Evaluative Self-Awareness and the Development of Autobiographical Memory," in *The Self in Time*, 97.

38. Clifford Geertz, "Thick Description: Toward an Interpretative Theory of Culture," in *The Interpretation of Cultures* (New York: Basic Books, 1973).

39. Winterson, *Oranges*, 93.

40. Moore and Lemmon, "The Nature and Utility," 5.

41. Comfort, "Becoming a Writerly Self," 549.

42. Rakhmetullin, final portfolio, 1999.

43. Seyhan, *Writing*, 71.

44. Comfort, "Becoming a Writerly Self," 552.

45. Madelaine Grumet, "Voice: The Search for a Feminist Rhetoric for Educational Studies," *Cambridge Journal of Education* 20, no. 3 (1990): 281–82.

46. Katherine Stevenson, final portfolio for the course "Finding the Bias," Bryn Mawr College, 2000.

47. Holt, final portfolio, 2000.

48. Rebecca Jansen, final portfolio for the course "Finding the Bias," Bryn Mawr College, 2000.

49. Santos, "A la Recherche," 13.

50. Linda Evanson, final portfolio for the course "Finding the Bias," Bryn Mawr College, 2000.

51. Elizabeth Bonner, final portfolio for the course "Finding the Bias," Bryn Mawr College, 1999.

52. Byatt, *Biographer's Tale*, 167.

53. Agosín, "A Writer's Thoughts," 57.

54. Brenda Gillman, final portfolio for the course "Finding the Bias," Bryn Mawr College, 1998.

55. W. Benjamin, "The Task of the Translator," 20.

56. Andrew E. Benjamin, *Translation and the Nature of Philosophy: A New Theory of Words* (London: Routledge, 1989); see also Steiner, *After Babel*, 47, 49.

57. Abida, final portfolio, 2000.

58. Santos, "A la Recherche," 13.

59. Robinson, *What Is Translation?* 155, 83.

60. See Constantine, "Finding," and Branislow Malinowsi, *The Language of Magic and Gardening* (Bloomington: Indiana University Press, [1965] 2000).

61. Constantine, "Finding," 15.

62. Agosín, "A Writer's Thoughts," 57.

63. W. Benjamin, "The Task of the Translator," 20.

64. Abida, final portfolio, 2000.

65. Levy, "Translation as Decision Process," 148.

66. Jansen, final portfolio, 2000.

67. Prema Nabin, final portfolio for the course "Finding the Bias," Bryn Mawr College, 1999.

68. Steiner, *After Babel*, 315.

69. Stevenson, final portfolio, 2000.

70. Ortega y Gasset, "Misery and Splendor," 49.

71. Gentzler, "Foreword" in *What Is Translation?* xi.

72. June Novak, final portfolio for the course "Finding the Bias," Bryn Mawr College, 2000.

73. Holt, final portfolio, 2000.

74. Ibid.

75. Jansen, final portfolio, 2000.

76. Robinson, *What Is Translation?* 25.

77. Santos, "A la Recherche," 11.

78. Katharina Reiss, "Type, Kind and Individuality of Text: Decision Making in Translation," in *The Translation Studies Reader*, 160.

79. Lahs-Gonzales, *Defining Eye*, 136.

80. John Berger, *Ways of Seeing* (London: BBC, Penguin Books, 1973), 45–47.

81. Lahs-Gonzales, *Defining Eye*, 86.

82. Abida, final portfolio, 2000.

83. Lahs-Gonzales, *Defining Eye*, 64.

84. Holt, final portfolio, 2000.

85. Novak, final portfolio, 2000.

86. Lucy R. Lippard, "Brought to Light," in *Defining Eye*, 131.

87. Maxine Greene, "Imagination and Transformation," in *Variations*, 65.

88. Mawusi Jones, final portfolio for the course "Finding the Bias," Bryn Mawr College, 2000.

89. Abida, final portfolio, 2000.

90. Hoffman, *Lost*, 274.

91. Robinson, *What Is Translation?* 83.

92. Adrienne Rich, "Diving into the Wreck," in *Diving into the Wreck* (New York: W. W. Norton, 1973), 24.

93. Each student has "a sense of a continuing self that extends over time but that also changes over time and that is different in significant ways from others' selves." Nelson, "Languages and the Self," 15.

94. Santos, "A la Recherche," 10.

95. Kondo, *Crafting Selves*, 8.

96. McMann, final portfolio, 1998.

97. Penny Miller, final portfolio for the course "Finding the Bias," Bryn Mawr College, 1999.

98. Ellen Barton, final portfolio for the course "Finding the Bias," Bryn Mawr College, 1998.

99. Hope Kaiser, final portfolio for the course "Finding the Bias," Bryn Mawr College, 1998.

100. See Sfard, "On Two Metaphors," for a discussion of this metaphor.

101. See Cook-Sather, "Between Student and Teacher."

102. Gregory Rabassa, "No Two Snowflakes Are Alike: Translation as Metaphor," in *The Craft of Translation*, 7.

103. Holt, final portfolio, 2000.

104. Stevenson, final portfolio, 2000.

105. Freire, *Pedagogy of Freedom*, 58.

106. Nida, "Principles," 126.

Chapter 4. Translating Within and Against Institutional Structures

1. Variously called information technologists, instructional technologists, computarians, or cybarians, these newcomers to higher education have been transported from the technical into the educational realm and have been members of educational communities for only the last ten or twenty years at the most. In the present discussion I use the term instructional technologist to refer to people whose primary background is in computers and computing and who have joined college communities to serve in a support capacity to faculty. There is great variation in what constitutes the instructional technologist's role and set of responsibilities. Depending on the institution and its faculty members, the instructional technologist, like the librarian, can function as a resource person the faculty members consult (usually in a rather last-minute fashion) for what would be considered primarily technical support, or she can function as a collaborator or partner in designing and facilitating a course.

2. The workshop was offered to a group of social scientists in the summer of 2000, to a group of humanists in 2001, and to a group of natural scientists in 2002.

3. Nida, "Principles."

4. Constantine, "Gedanken."

5. Malinowski, *Language.*

6. This workshop was co-designed and co-facilitated by Elliott Shore, Chief Information Officer and Professor of History at Bryn Mawr College; Susan Perry, then College Librarian, Director of Library Information and Technology Services at Mount Holyoke College and now with the Mellon Foundation; Sandra Lawrence, Professor of Education and Chair of the Psychology and Education Department at Mount Holyoke College; and me. We also had the invaluable assistance and participation of four student interns, Diana Applegate, Aliya Curmally, Maria Hristova, and Nancy Strippel, and an anthropologist, Jonathan Church, who documented the workshop.

7. See Alison Cook-Sather, "Unrolling Roles in Techno-Pedagogy: Toward Collaboration in Traditional College Settings," in *Innovative Higher Education* 26, 2 (winter 2001), 121–39, for a discussion of some of the challenges that face members of the higher education community when they strive to engage in ongoing education.

8. All the quotations that I include in this chapter are drawn from audio-recorded conversations among participants, texts written by participants in one of these three workshops, or from follow-up conversations or interviews. I include no personal or place-names, dates, or other identifying markers to preserve the confidentiality of participants.

9. Participating colleges were dictated by the terms of the grant. Almost all were liberal arts colleges on the East Coast.

10. Turner, "Social Dramas," 159.

11. Ibid., 161.

12. A. W. Tony Bates, *Managing Technological Change: Strategies for College and University Leaders* (San Francisco: Jossey-Bass, 2000).

13. James J. O'Donnell, "The Digital Challenge," *Wilson Quarterly* 20 (1996): 49.

14. Ibid.

15. James Levin, Sandra R. Levin, and Gregory Waddoups, "Multiplicity in Learning and Teaching: A Framework for Developing Innovative Online Education," *Journal of Research on Computing in Education* 32 (1999): 256.

16. Nida, "Principles."

17. Constantine, "Gedanken."

18. Malinowski, *Language.*

19. Constantine, "Gedanken."

20. Constantine, "Finding," 15.

21. Seyhan, *Writing,* 108.

22. For discussions of these points see Mary Johnson, Barb Linnenbrink, and Lorena Mitchell, "'I Spy' in the Library," *Colorado Libraries* 25, no. 3 (fall 1999): 34–36.

23. Lisa Delpit, "The Silenced Dialogue: Power and Pedagogy in Educating Other People's Children," *Harvard Educational Review* 58, no. 3 (August 1988): 298.

24. Oldfather, "Learning from Student Voices," 87.

25. Steiner, *After Babel,* 312.

Chapter 5. Translating Between Student and Teacher

Another version of this discussion was published as "Between Student and Teacher: Teacher Education as Translation," *Teaching Education* 12, no. 2 (2001): 177–90. [At their request, I include the publisher's Web site: http://www.tandf.co.uk/journals.]

Note to epigraph: Hoffman, *Lost*, 211.

1. Bullough and Gitlin, *Becoming a Student*, xiii.
2. Dennis J. Sumara and Rebecca Luce-Kapler, "(Un)becoming a Teacher: Negotiating Identities While Learning to Teach," *Canadian Journal of Education* 21, no. 1 (1996): 65–83.
3. Allender, *Teacher Self*, 17.
4. Deborah Britzman, *Practice Makes Practice: A Critical Study of Learning How to Teach* (New York: SUNY Press, 1991), 10.
5. Hoffman, *Lost*, 274.
6. Britzman, *Practice*, 13.
7. The design and three years of support of this project were provided by a grant from the Arthur Vining Davis Foundations. Bryn Mawr and Haverford Colleges now support the project without outside funding. From 1995 to 1998, I co-facilitated this project with Ondrea Reisinger, then an English teacher at a suburban public high school in Springfield, Pennsylvania. Since then I have co-facilitated this project with Jean McWilliams, Assistant Principal at a suburban public high school in Ardmore, Pennsylvania. For further discussions of the project, see Cook-Sather, "Between Student and Teacher," and Cook-Sather, "Translating Themselves."
8. See Cook-Sather, "Authorizing."
9. See Alison Cook-Sather, "Re(in)forming the Conversations: Power, Position, Student Voice in Teacher Education," *Radical Teacher* 64 (2002): 21–28.
10. Discussions of making assumptions about students can be found in the following: Alison Cook-Sather and Ondrea Reisinger, "Seeing the Students Behind the Stereotypes: The Perspectives of Three Preservice Teachers," *The Teacher Educator* 37, no. 3 (2001), 91–99; Bullough and Gitlin, *Becoming a Student*; Rhona S. Weinstein, S. M. Madison, and Margaret R. Kuklinski, "Raising Expectations in Schooling: Obstacles and Opportunities for Change," *American Educational Research Journal* 32, no. 1 (1995): 121–59; and Jerry E. Brophy and Thomas L. Good, *Teacher-Student Relationships: Causes and Consequences* (New York: Holt, Rinehart and Winston, 1974).
11. Britzman, *Practice*, 3.
12. Bullough and Gitlin, *Becoming a Student*, 23.
13. bell hooks, *Teaching to Transgress: Education as the Practice of Freedom* (New York: Routledge, 1994), 35.
14. For extensive discussions of this issue, see the following: Alison Cook-Sather and Jeffrey Shultz, "Starting Where the Learner Is: Listening to Students," in *In Our Own Words*, 1–17; John H. Ingram and Norman Weston, "Distant Voices, Shared Lives: Students Creating the Global Learning Community," *Educational Horizons* 75, no. 4 (summer 1997): 165–71; Corbett and Wilson, "Make a Difference"; Robert W. Connell, "Poverty and Education," in *Harvard Educational Review* 64, no. 2 (1994): 125–49; Sonia Nieto, "Lessons from Students on Creating a Chance to Dream," *Harvard Educational Review* 64, no. 4 (1994): 392–426; Frederick Erickson and Jeffrey Shultz, "Students' Experience of Curriculum," in *Handbook of Research on Curriculum*, ed. Philip W. Jackson (New York: Macmillan, 1992), 465–85; Patricia Phelan, Ann Locke Davidson, and Hahn Cao Yu, "Speaking Up: Students' Perspectives on School," *Phi Delta Kappan* 73 (1992): 695–704.
15. David Bartholomae, "Inventing the University," in *Perspectives on Literacy*, ed. Eugene R. Kintgen, Barry M. Kroll, and Mike Rose (Carbondale: Southern Illinois University Press, 1988), 273.
16. Soliday, "Translating," 511.

17. Lisa Grant, classroom discussion during the course "Curriculum and Pedagogy," Bryn Mawr College, 1997. All names of preservice teachers are pseudonyms. For high school students, I used first names only, sometimes real names and sometimes pseudonyms.

18. Mary McClean, dialogue analysis paper for the course "Curriculum and Pedagogy," Bryn Mawr College, 1997.

19. Steiner, *After Babel*, 312.

20. All quotations from Pia Rao, dialogue analysis paper for the course "Curriculum and Pedagogy," Bryn Mawr College, 1996.

21. Nicki Weaver, classroom discussion during the course "Curriculum and Pedagogy," Bryn Mawr College, September 30, 1998.

22. Ibid.

23. Bruner, *Process*, ix.

24. Linda Russell, classroom discussion during the course "Curriculum and Pedagogy," Bryn Mawr College, October 5, 1995.

25. Jessye Patterson, classroom discussion during the course "Curriculum and Pedagogy," Bryn Mawr College, September 17, 1996.

26. Grant, dialogue analysis paper for the course "Curriculum and Pedagogy," Bryn Mawr College, 1996.

27. Russell, classroom discussion, September 19, 1995.

28. Eileen Dormand, classroom discussion during the course "Curriculum and Pedagogy," Bryn Mawr College, September 19, 1995.

29. Ibid.

30. Cohn, "'Clean Bombs,'" 50.

31. W. Benjamin, "The Task of the Translator"; Santos, "A la Recherche"; Agosín, "A Writer's Thoughts"; Constantine, "Gedanken."

32. Grant, classroom discussion, 1996.

33. Nancy Chadwick, classroom discussion, 1996.

34. Barnett, classroom discussion, 1997.

35. Steiner, *After Babel*, 312.

36. All quotations drawn from a classroom discussion during the course "Curriculum and Pedagogy," Bryn Mawr College, October 7, 1997.

37. McClean, dialogue analysis, 1997.

38. Ibid.

39. Unless otherwise noted, all references to her exchange with her high school partner taken from Jessica Barnett, dialogue analysis paper for the course "Curriculum and Pedagogy," Bryn Mawr College, 1997.

40. Barnett, classroom discussion during the course "Curriculum and Pedagogy," Bryn Mawr College, 1997.

41. Steiner, *After Babel*, 312.

42. Constantine, "Finding," 15.

43. Michael Wilder, classroom discussion during the course "Curriculum and Pedagogy Seminar," Bryn Mawr College, 1997.

44. Unless otherwise noted, all references to his exchange with his high school partner taken from Michael Wilder, dialogue analysis paper for the course "Curriculum and Pedagogy," Bryn Mawr College, 1997.

45. Constantine, "Finding," 15.

46. Melanie Jones, dialogue analysis paper for the course "Curriculum and Pedagogy," Bryn Mawr College, 1997.

47. Unless otherwise noted, all references to his exchange with his high school partner taken from Jeffrey Livingston, dialogue analysis paper for the course "Curriculum and Pedagogy," Bryn Mawr College, 1997.

48. Classroom discussion during the course "Curriculum and Pedagogy," Bryn Mawr College, December 16, 1997.

49. Dormand, dialogue analysis paper for the course "Curriculum and Pedagogy," Bryn Mawr College, 1995.

50. Nicki Weaver, dialogue analysis paper for the course "Curriculum and Pedagogy," Bryn Mawr College, 1998.

51. Turner, "Social Dramas," 159, 161.

52. Greene, "In Search of Metaphor."

53. Nancy Chadwick, dialogue analysis paper for the course "Curriculum and Pedagogy," Bryn Mawr College, 1996.

54. Sharita Watkins, dialogue analysis paper for the course "Curriculum and Pedagogy," Bryn Mawr College 1996.

55. Lynne Castle, dialogue analysis paper for the course "Curriculum and Pedagogy," Bryn Mawr College, 1995.

56. Richard Rorty, *Philosophy and the Mirror of Nature* (Princeton, N.J.: Princeton University Press, 1979).

57. Castle, dialogue analysis, 1995.

58. Kondo, *Crafting Selves*, 10.

59. Unless otherwise noted, all references to her exchange with her high school partner taken from Tina Spinelli, dialogue analysis paper for the course "Curriculum and Pedagogy," Bryn Mawr College, 1996.

60. Agosín, "A Writer's Thoughts," 57.

61. W. Benjamin, "The Task of the Translator," 20.

62. Santos, "A la Recherche," 14.

63. Unless otherwise noted, all quotations taken from a classroom discussion among the preservice teachers and the high school students during the course "Curriculum and Pedagogy," Bryn Mawr College, December 16, 1997.

64. "Learners Teaching and Teachers Learning: A Collaborative Project Between High School Students and Preservice Teachers" (presentation at the Meeting of the Pennsylvania Association of Colleges and Teacher Educators, November 10, 1995).

65. Julie Arribas, dialogue analysis paper for the course "Curriculum and Pedagogy," Bryn Mawr College, 1997.

66. Barnett, dialogue analysis, 1997.

67. Arribas, dialogue analysis, 1997.

68. Bullough and Gitlin, *Becoming a Student*, 8.

69. McLean, "Becoming a Teacher," in *The Role of Self*, 58.

70. Deborah Britzman, *Practice Makes Practice: A Critical Study of Learning to Teach* (Albany: State Univeristy of New York Press), 6.

71. McLean, "Becoming a Teacher," 55.

72. Constantine, "Finding," 15.

73. George Herbert Palmer, *The Ideal Teacher* (Boston: Houghton Mifflin, 1908/1910), 29.

74. Freire, *Pedagogy of Freedom*, 58.

75. Gregory Rabassa, "No Two Snowflakes Are Alike: Translation as Metaphor," in *The Craft of Translation*, 7.

Chapter 6. "Desiring the Exhilarations of Changes"

Notes to epigraphs: Jacques Derrida, *Writing and Difference* (Chicago: University of Chicago Press, 1978), 102; Abdelkebir Khatibi, *Love in Two Languages*

(Minneapolis: University of Minnesota Press, 1990), 28; Ellsworth, *Teaching Positions*, 44.

1. Constantine, "Finding," 15. See also Dewey, *Democracy*.
2. Wallace Stevens, "The Motive for Metaphor," *The Palm at the End of the Mind: Selected Poems and a Play*, ed. Holly Stevens (New York: Vintage Books, 1972), 240.
3. Fernandez, "Persuasions," 57.
4. Britzman, *Practice*, 13.
5. Greene, "In Search of Metaphor."
6. Soliday, "Translating Self," 511.
7. Turner, *Dramas*, 25, 35, 37.
8. Scheffler, *In Praise*, 45.
9. J. Christopher Crocker, "The Social Functions of Rhetorical Forms," in *The Social Use of Metaphor*, 34. See also Kenneth Burke, *A Grammar of Motives* (New York: Prentice-Hall, 1945).
10. All definitions of translation referenced here are drawn from *Webster's New International Dictionary*, 2nd ed.
11. Khatibi, *Love*, 44.
12. Wendy Lesser, *Nothing Remains the Same: Rereading and Remembering* (Boston: Houghton Mifflin, 2002), 8. See also Mary Karr, *Cherry* (New York: Penguin, 2000), 276.
13. Malinowski, *Language*, 11.
14. Constantine, "Gedanken."
15. Constantine, "Finding," 15.
16. Nida, "Principles," 126.
17. W. Benjamin, "The Task of the Translator," 20.
18. Santos, "A la Recherche," 14.
19. Sfard, "On Two Metaphors," 8.
20. Ibid., 6.
21. Constantine, "Finding," 14.
22. Steiner, *After Babel*, 312.
23. Holt, final portfolio, 2000.
24. Jansen, final portfolio, 2000.
25. *Webster's New International Dictionary*, 2nd ed.
26. Heilbrun, *Writing*, 18.
27. Cohn, "'Clean Bombs,'" 50.
28. Steiner, *After Babel*, 315.
29. Jansen, final portfolio, 2000.
30. Freire, *Pedagogy of the Oppressed*, 81.
31. Pratt, "Arts," 584.
32. McMann, final portfolio, 1998.
33. Miller, final portfolio, 1999.
34. Kaiser, final portfolio, 1998.
35. Cook-Sather, "Unrolling Roles," 134.
36. Castle, dialogue analysis, 1995.
37. Watkins, dialogue analysis, 1996.
38. Sfard, "On Two Metaphors," 6.
39. For a discussion of self-authoring, see Robert Keegan, *In Over Our Heads: The Mental Demands of Modern Life* (Cambridge, Mass.: Harvard University Press, 1994).
40. Joan M. Ferraro, "Reflective Practice and Professional Development" (*ERIC Clearinghouse on Teaching and Teacher Education*, Washington, D.C., 2000).
41. Carol Rodgers, "Defining Reflection: Another Look at John Dewey and

Reflective Thinking," *Teachers College Record* 4, no. 4 (2002): 842–66; Carol Rodgers, "Seeing Student Learning: Teacher Change and the Role of Reflection," *Harvard Educational Review* 72, no. 2 (2002): 230–53; Amy Burnstein Colton and Georgea M. Sparks-Langer, "A Conceptual Framework to Guide the Development of Teacher Reflection and Decision Making," *Journal of Teacher Education* 44, no. 1 (January–February 1990), 45–54; Anna Richert, "Teaching Teachers to Reflect: A Consideration of Programme Structure," *Journal of Curriculum Studies* 22, no. 6 (1990): 509–27; Gwen L. Rudney and Andrea Guillaume, "Reflective Teaching for Student Teachers," *The Teacher Educator* 25, no. 3 (1990): 13–20; Kenneth M. Zeichner and Daniel P. Liston, "Teaching Student Teachers to Reflect," *Harvard Educational Review* 57, no. 1 (1987): 23–48.

42. Alan J. Reiman and Lois Thies-Sprinthall, *Mentoring and Supervision for Teacher Development* (New York: Longman-Addison, 1998), 262.

43. Freire, *Pedagogy of the Oppressed.*

44. Freema Elbaz, "Teachers' Knowledge of Teaching: Strategies for Reflection," *Educating Teachers: Changing the Nature of Pedagogical Knowledge,* ed. John Smyth (Philadelphia: Farmer Press, 1987), 45.

45. Zehm, "Deciding to Teach"; see also Stanley J. Zehm and Jeffrey A. Kottler, *On Being a Teacher: The Human Dimension,* 2nd ed. (Thousand Oaks, Calif.: Corwin Press, 2000).

46. Robert J. Yinger, "Learning the Language of Practice," *Curriculum Inquiry* 17, 299–318, cited in McLean, "Becoming a Teacher," 68.

47. Rodgers, "Seeing."

48. Lesnick, "Mirror," 34.

49. Greene, "Notes," 22.

50. Hawkins, "I, Thou, and It," 48.

51. Cook-Sather, "Authorizing"; Colsant, "'Hey, Man'"; Hawkins, "I, Thou, and It"; Oldfather, *Research;* Sanon et al., "Cutting Class"; and Shultz and Cook-Sather, *In Our Own Words.*

52. Sharon Welch, *A Feminist Ethic of Risk* (Minneapolis, Minn.: Fortress Press, 1990), 20.

53. Freire, *Pedagogy of Freedom,* 58.

54. Palmer, *The Ideal Teacher,* 29.

55. Watkins, dialogue analysis, 1996.

56. Rabassa, "No Two Snowflakes," 7, 12.

57. Donald Davidson, "What Metaphors Mean," in *On Metaphor,* ed. Sheldon Sacks (Chicago: University of Chicago Press, 1979), 44–45.

58. Robert A. Nisbet, *Social Change and History: Aspects of the Western Theory of Development* (London: Oxford University Press, 1969), 6.

59. Borges, "Metaphor," 41.

60. Turner, *Dramas,* 13–14.

61. Martinez, "Life," 2.

62. Earle, "Teacher Imagery," 54.

63. Constantine, "Finding."

64. Quoted in Earle, "Teacher Imagery," 58.

65. Earle, "Teacher Imagery," 58.

66. Greene, "Imagination," 65.

67. Ibid.

68. Wayne Booth, "Metaphor as Rhetoric: The Problem of Evaluation," in *On Metaphor,* ed. Sheldon Sacks (Chicago: University of Chicago Press, 1978), 62.

69. Ellsworth, *Teaching Positions,* 195.

70. Freire, *Pedagogy of Freedom,* 89.

71. Greene, "Notes," 7.
72. Stevens, "Motive," 240.
73. See note 3 in Chapter 2.
74. Greene, "In Search of Metaphor."
75. Constantine, "Gedanken."
76. Ellsworth, *Teaching Positions*, 145.

Appendix. A Sampling of Educational Metaphors

1. Anthony Patrick Carnevale and Susan Carol Stone, *The American Mosaic: An In-Depth Report on the Future of Diversity at Work* (New York: McGraw-Hill, 1995), 14.
2. Patricia A. L. Ehrensal, Robert L. Crawford, Joseph A. Castellucci, and Gregory Allen, "The American Melting Pot versus the Chinese Hot Pot," in *Ethical Leadership and Decision Making in Education: Applying Theoretical Perspectives to Complex Dilemmas*, ed. Joan Polimer Shapiro and Jaqueline A. Stefkovich (Mahwah, N.J.: Lawrence Erlbaum Associates, 2001), 65.
3. Ehrensal, Crawford, Castellucci, and Allen, "American Melting Pot," 65.
4. Carnevale and Stone, *The American Mosaic*, 14–15.
5. Andrew T. Kopan, "Melting Pot; Myth or Reality?" in *Cultural Pluralism*, ed. Edgar G. Epps (Berkeley, Calif.: McCutchan, 1974); Milton J. Gold and Harry N. Rivlin, *Teachers for Multicultural Education* (Office of Education [DHEW], Washington, D.C., 1975); Mark Krug, "The Melting of the Ethnics: Education of the Immigrants, 1880–1914," in *Perspectives in American Education* (Bloomington, Ind.: Phi Delta Kappa Educational Foundation, 1976); Miriam Wasserman, "Demystifying the Schools," *Education Exploration Center Journal* 3 (October–November 1973), 4–6.
6. Rod Janzen, "Melting Pot or Mosaic?" *Educational Leadership* 51, no. 8 (May 1994): 9–11.
7. Arthur Eugene Bestor, *Educational Wastelands: The Retreat from Learning in Our Public Schools* (Urbana: University of Illinois Press, 1953).
8. E. D. Hirsch, Joseph Kett, and James Trefil, *Cultural Literacy: What Every American Needs to Know* (Boston: Houghton Mifflin, 1987).
9. Allan Bloom, *The Closing of the American Mind: How Education Has Failed Democracy and Impoverished the Souls of Today's Students* (New York: Simon and Schuster, 1987).
10. Powell, Fararr, and Cohen, *Shopping Mall High School*, 8, 8, 8, 11, 8, 22, 17, 2, 1.
11. Rousseau, "Emile"; Herbart, *Outlines*.
12. Dewey, *Democracy*, 2.
13. Bruner, *Process*, xi.
14. Duckworth, "Virtues."
15. Freire, *Pedagogy of the Oppressed*, 58.
16. Sfard, "On Two Metaphors," 5, 8.
17. Ibid., 6.
18. Joseph, "The Ideal Teacher," 139.
19. I. N. McFee, *The Teacher, the School, and the Community* (New York: American Book, 1918), cited in Joseph, "The Ideal Teacher," 139.
20. A. Snyder and T. Alexander, "Teaching as a Profession: Guidance Suggestions for Students," *Teachers College Bulletin* 23, no. 1, 65 quoted in Joseph, "The Ideal Teacher," 139.

21. Carol Rodgers, "Defining Reflection: Another Look at John Dewey and Reflective Thinking," *Teachers College Record* 4, no. 4 (2002): 842–66; Carol Rodgers, "Seeing Student Learning: Teacher Change and the Role of Reflection, *Harvard Educational Review* 72, no. 2 (2002): 230–53; Amy Bernstein Colton and Georgea M. Sparks-Langer, "A Conceptual Framework to Guide the Development of Teacher Reflection and Decision Making," *Journal of Teacher Education* 44, no. 1 (January-February 1990): 45–54; Anna Richert, "Teaching Teachers to Reflect: A Consideration of Programme Structure," *Journal of Curriculum Studies* 22, 6 (1990): 509–27; Gwen L. Rudney and Andrea Guillaume, "Reflective Teaching for Student Teachers," *The Teacher Educator* 25, no. 3 (1990): 13–20; Kenneth M. Zeichner and Daniel P. Liston, "Teaching Student Teachers to Reflect," *Harvard Educational Review* 57, no. 1 (1987): 23–48.

22. Alan J. Reiman and Lois Thies-Sprinthall, *Mentoring and Supervision for Teacher Development* (New York: Longman-Addison Wesley Longman,1998), 262.

23. Freire, *Pedagogy of the Oppressed*.

24. Freema Elbaz, "Teachers' Knowledge of Teaching: Strategies for Reflection," in *Educating Teachers: Changing the Nature of Pedagogical Knowledge*, ed. John Smyth (Philadelphia: Farmer Press, 1987), 45.

25. Zehm, "Deciding to Teach"; see also Stanley J. Zehm and Jeffrey A. Kottler, *On Being a Teacher: The Human Dimension*, 2nd ed. (Thousand Oaks, Calif.: Corwin Press, 2000).

26. Robert J. Yinger, "Learning the Language of Practice," *Curriculum Inquiry* 17, 299–318, cited in Vianne S. McLean, "Becoming a Teacher," 68.

27. Lucy Calkins, *The Art of Teaching Writing* (Portsmouth, N.H.: Heinemann, 1994).

28. Gail E. Burnaford and David Hobson, "Responding to Reform: Images for Teaching in the New Millennium," in *Images of Schoolteachers*, 235. For discussions of teacher research, see Marilyn Cochran-Smith and Susan L. Lytle. *INSIDE/OUTSIDE: Teacher Research and Knowledge* (New York: Teachers College Press, 1993); James Berlin, "The Teacher as Researcher: Democracy, Dialogue, and Power," in *The Writing Teacher as Researcher: Essays in the Theory and Practice of Class-Based Research*, ed. Donald A. Daiker and Max Morenberg (Portsmouth, N.H.: Boynton/Cook Publishers, 1990); Nancy Martin, "On the Move: Teacher-Researchers," in *Reclaiming the Classroom: Teacher Research as an Agency for Change*, ed. Dixie Goswami and Peter R. Stillman (Portsmouth, N.H.: Boynton/Cook Publishers, 1987).

29. Scheffler, *In Praise*, 47, 48.

30. Dewey, *Art as Experience*, 6.

31. Burnaford, "Responding to Reform," 232.

32. Nate L. Gage, *The Scientific Basis for the Art of Teaching* (New York: Teachers College Press, 1987), 15.

33. Burnaford, "Responding to Reform," 233.

34. Allender, *Teacher Self*, 125.

35. Robert Henri, *The Art Spirit* (Boulder, Colo.: Westview Press, 1923), 15.

36. Ibid., 44.

37. Ibid., 55.

38. Gloria Ladson-Billings, *The Dreamkeepers: Successful Teachers of African American Children* (San Francisco: Jossey-Bass, 1994), 23, 24, 25.

39. Allender, *Teacher Self*, 5.

40. William Ayers, "A Teacher Ain't Nothin' but a Hero: Teachers and Teaching in Film," in *Images of Schoolteachers*, 201, 202, 209.

41. Robert Lowe, "Teachers as Saviors, Teachers Who Care," in *Images of Schoolteachers,* 212.

42. Ladson-Billings, *Dreamkeepers,* 23.

43. Scheffler, *In Praise,* 46. 47.

44. Turner, *Dramas,* 31.

45. Allender, *Teacher Self,* 123, 117, 118, 123.

46. Efron, "Reflections," 75.

47. Ibid.

48. A. S. Palinscar, "The Role of Dialogue in Providing Scaffolded Instruction," *Educational Psychologist* 21 [Special Issue], ed. J. Levin and M. Pressley (1986), 73; see also Arthur Applebee and Judith Langer, "Instructional Scaffolding: Reading and Writing as Natural Language Activities," *Language Arts* 60 (1983): 168–75.

49. Karen Murphy, "Teaching as Persuasion," *Theory into Practice* 40, no. 4 (2001), 224.

50. Murphy, "Teaching as Persuasion," 224.

51. Cyndie Hynd, "Persuasion and Its Role in Meeting Educational Goals," *Theory into Practice* 40, no. 4 (Autumn 2001), 273.

52. Ruth M. Heaton, *Teaching Mathematics to the New Standards: Relearning the Dance* (New York: Teachers College Press, 2000), 60, 68, 90.

Bibliography

Agosín, Marjorie. "A Writer's Thoughts on Translation and Always Living in Translation." *MultiCultural Review*, September 2000: 56–59.

Allender, Jerome S. *Teacher Self: The Practice of Humanistic Education.* Lanham, Md.: Rowman & Littlefield, 2001.

Allison, Clinton B. *Present and Past: Essays for Teachers in the History of Education.* New York: Peter Lang, 1995.

Applebee, Arthur, and Judith Langer. "Instructional Scaffolding: Reading and Writing as Natural Language Activities." *Language Arts* 60 (1983): 168–75.

Aristotle. *Poetics* 21 (1457).

Ayers, William. "A Teacher Ain't Nothin' But a Hero: Teachers and Teaching in Film." In *Images of Schoolteachers in America*, edited by Pamela Bolotin Joseph and Gail E. Burnaford, 201–9. Mahwah, N.J.: Lawrence Erlbaum Associates, 2001.

Barresi, John. "Extending Self-Consciousness into the Future." In *The Self in Time: Developmental Perspectives*, edited by Chris Moore and Karen Lemmon, 141–61. Mahwah, N.J.: Lawrence Erlbaum Associates, 2001.

Bartel, Roland. *Metaphors and Symbols: Forays into Language.* Urbana, Ill.: National Council of Teachers of English, 1983.

Bartholomae, David. "Inventing the University." In *Perspectives on Literacy*, edited by Eugene R. Kintgen, Barry M. Kroll, and Mike Rose, 273–85. Carbondale: Southern Illinois University Press, 1988.

Bassnett, Susan, and Harish Trivedi. "Introduction: Of Colonies, Cannibals, and Vernaculars." *Post-Colonial Translation: Theory and Practice*, edited by Susan Bassnett and Harish Trivedi, 1–18. London: Routledge, 1999.

Bates, A. W. Tony. *Managing Technological Change: Strategies for College and University Leaders.* San Francisco, Calif.: Jossey-Bass, 2000.

Benjamin, Andrew E. *Translation and the Nature of Philosophy: A New Theory of Words.* London: Routledge, 1989.

Benjamin, Walter. "The Task of the Translator." In *The Translation Studies Reader*, edited by Lawrence J. Venuti, 15–25. London: Routledge, 2000.

Berger, John. *Ways of Seeing.* London: BBC and Penguin Books, 1972.

Berlin, James A. "The Teacher as Researcher: Democracy, Dialogue, and Power." In *The Writing Teacher as Researcher: Essays in the Theory and Practice of Class-Based Research*, edited by Donald A. Daiker and Max Morenberg, 3–14. Portsmouth, N.H.: Boynton/Cook Publishers, 1990.

Bestor, Arthur Eugene. *Educational Wastelands: The Retreat from Learning in Our Public Schools.* Urbana: University of Illinois Press, 1953.

Biguenet, John, and Rainer Schulte, eds. *The Craft of Translation.* Chicago: University of Chicago Press, 1989.

Black, Max. "More About Metaphors." In *Metaphor and Thought,* edited by Andrew Ortony, 19–43. Cambridge: Cambridge University Press, 1979.

———. *Models and Metaphors: Studies in Language and Philosophy.* Ithaca, N.Y.: Cornell University Press, 1962a.

Bloom, Allan. *The Closing of the American Mind: How Education Has Failed Democracy and Impoverished the Souls of Today's Students.* New York: Simon and Schuster, 1987.

Booth, Wayne. "Metaphor as Rhetoric: The Problem of Evaluation." In *On Metaphor,* edited by Sheldon Sacks, 29–48. Chicago: University of Chicago Press, 1978.

Borges, Jorge Luis. "The Metaphor." In *This Craft of Verse,* edited by Calin-Andrei Mihailescu, 21–41. Cambridge, Mass.: Harvard University Press, 2000.

Brecht, Bertolt. *Brecht on Theatre: The Development of an Aesthetic.* Edited and translated by John Willet. New York: Hill and Wang, 1964.

Britzman, Deborah. *Practice Makes Practice: A Critical Study of Learning to Teach.* New York: State University of New York Press, 1991.

Brodkey, Linda. "Writing on the Bias." *College English* 56 (1994): 527–47.

Brophy, Jerry E., and Thomas L. Good. *Teacher-Student Relationships: Causes and Consequences.* New York: Holt, Rinehart and Winston, 1974.

Bruner, Jerome. *The Process of Education.* Cambridge, Mass.: Harvard University Press, 1977.

Bullough, Robert V., Jr., *The Forgotten Dream of American Education.* Ames: Iowa State University Press, 1988.

Bullough, Robert V., Jr., and Andrew Gitlin. *Becoming a Student of Teaching: Methodologies for Exploring Self and School Context.* New York: Garland, 2001.

Burke, Kenneth. *A Grammar of Motives.* New York: Prentice-Hall, 1945.

Burnaford, Gail E., and David Hobson. "Responding to Reform: Images for Teaching in the New Millennium." In *Images of Schoolteachers in America,* 2nd ed., edited by Pamela B. Joseph and Gail E., Burnaford, 229–44. Mahwah, N.J.: Lawrence Erlbaum Associates, 2001.

Byatt, A. S. *The Biographer's Tale.* New York: Alfred A. Knopf, 2000.

Calkins, Lucy. *The Art of Teaching Writing.* Portsmouth, N.H.: Heinemann, 1994.

Callahan, Raymond E. *Education and the Cult of Efficiency: A Study of the Social Forces that Have Shaped the Administration of the Public Schools.* Chicago: University of Chicago Press, 1962.

Carnevale, Anthony Patrick, and Susan Carol Stone. *The American Mosaic: An In-Depth Report on the Future of Diversity at Work.* New York: McGraw-Hill, 1995.

Cochran-Smith, Marilyn, and Susan L. Lytle. *INSIDE/OUTSIDE: Teacher Research and Knowledge.* New York: Teachers College Press, 1993.

Cohn, Carol. "'Clean Bombs' and Clean Language." In *Women, Militarism, and War: Essays in History, Politics, and Social Theory,* edited by Jean Bethke Elshtain and Sheila Tobias, 33–55. Savage, Md.: Rowman & Littlefield, 1990.

Colsant, Lee C., Jr. "'Hey, Man, Why Do We Gotta Take This . . . ?' Learning to Listen to Students." In *Reasons for Learning: Expanding the Conversation on Student-Teacher Collaboration,* edited by John G. Nicholls and Theresa A. Thorkildsen, 62–89. New York: Teachers College Press, 1995.

Colton, Amy Bernstein, and Georgea M. Sparks-Langer. "A Conceptual Framework to Guide the Development of Teacher Reflection and Decision Making." *Journal of Teacher Education* 44, no. 1 (January–February 1990): 45–54.

Comfort, Juanita Rodgers. "Becoming a Writerly Self: College Writers Engaging Black Feminist Essays." *College Composition and Communication* 51 (2000): 540–59.

Connell, R. W. "Poverty and Education." *Harvard Educational Review* 64 (1994): 125–49.

Constantine, David. "Gedanken des Kommandanten." Lecture, Literarisches Zentrum, Göttingen, Germany, October 13, 2001.

———. "Finding the Words: Translation and Survival of the Human." *Times Literary Supplement* (May 21, 1999): 14–15.

Cook-Sather, Alison. "Education as Translation: Students Transforming Notions of Narrative and Self." *College Composition and Communication* 55, no. 1 (September 2003), 91–114.

———. "Re(in)forming the Conversations: Student Position, Power, and Voice in Teacher Education." *Radical Teacher* 64 (2002): 21–28.

———. "Authorizing Student Perspectives: Toward Trust, Dialogue, and Change in Education." *Educational Researcher* 31, no. 4 (May 2002): 3–14.

———. "Unrolling Roles in Techno-Pedagogy: Toward Collaboration in Traditional College Settings." *Innovative Higher Education* 26, no. 2 (winter 2001): 121–39.

———. "Translating Themselves: Becoming a Teacher Through Text and Talk." In *Talking Shop: Authentic Conversation and Teacher Learning*, edited by Christopher M. Clark, 16–39. New York: Teachers College Press, 2001.

———. "Between Student and Teacher: Teacher Education as Translation." *Teaching Education* 12, no. 2 (2001): 177–90.

Cook-Sather, Alison, Katherine Rowe, and Elliott Shore. "Finding the Biases in a Community of Scholars." *Liberal Education*, winter 2002: 48–53.

Cook-Sather, Alison, and Ondrea Reisinger. "Seeing the Students Behind the Stereotypes: The Perspectives of Three Pre-Service Teachers." *Teacher Educator* 37, no. 2 (autumn 2001): 91–99.

Cook-Sather, Alison, and Jeffrey Shultz. "Starting Where the Learner Is: Listening to Students." In *In Our Own Words: Students' Perspectives on School*, edited by Jeffrey Shultz and Alison Cook-Sather, 1–17. Lanham, Md.: Rowman & Littlefield, 2001.

Cooley, Charles Norton. *Human Nature and the Social Order*. New York: Scribner's, 1922.

Corbett, H. Dickson, and Bruce Wilson. "Make a Difference with, Not for, Students: A Plea for Researchers and Reformers." *Educational Researcher* 24, no. 5 (1995): 12–17.

Crocker, J. Christopher. "The Social Functions of Rhetorical Forms." In *The Social Use of Metaphor: Essays on the Anthropology of Rhetoric*, edited by J. David Sapir and J. Christopher Crocker, 33–66. Philadelphia: University of Pennsylvania Press, 1977.

Crowley, John. *The Translator*. New York: HarperCollins, 1995.

Culler, Jonathan. "Identity, Identification, and the Subject." In *Literary Theory: A Very Short Introduction*, 104–15. New York: Oxford University Press, 2000.

Davidson, Donald. "What Metaphors Mean." In *On Metaphor*, edited by Sheldon Sacks, 29–48. Chicago: University of Chicago Press, 1979.

Delpit, Lisa. "The Silenced Dialogue: Power and Pedagogy in Educating Other People's Children." *Harvard Educational Review* 58, no. 3 (August 1988): 280–98.

de Man, Paul. "The Epistemology of Metaphor." In *On Metaphor*, edited by Sheldon Sacks, 11–28. Chicago: University of Chicago Press, 1979.

Derrida, Jacques. *Writing and Difference*. Translated by Alan Bass. Chicago: University of Chicago Press, 1978.

Dewey, John. *Democracy and Education.* New York: Macmillan, 1916.

———. *Art as Experience.* New York: Minton, Balch & Company, 1934.

———. *Experience and Education.* New York: Touchstone, 1938.

———. "My Pedagogic Creed." In *John Dewey on Education,* edited by Reginald D. Archambault, 427–39. Chicago: University of Chicago Press, 1964.

Díaz-Diocaretz, Myriam. *Translating Poetic Discourse: Questions on Feminist Strategies in Adrienne Rich.* Amsterdam: John Benjamins, 1985.

Dickmeyer, Nathan. "Metaphor, Model, and Theory in Education Research." *Teachers College Record* 91, no. 2 (winter 1989): 151–60.

Duckworth, Eleanor. "The Virtues of Not Knowing." In *"The Having of Wonderful Ideas" and Other Essays on Teaching and Learning,* 64–69. New York: Teachers College Press, 1987.

Eakin, Paul John. *Fictions in Autobiography: Studies in the Act of Self-Invention.* Princeton, N.J.: Princeton University Press, 1985.

Earle, Rodney S. "Teacher Imagery and Metaphors: Windows to Teaching and Learning." *Educational Technology,* July–August 1995: 52–59.

Efron, Sara, and Pamela Bolotin Joseph. "Reflections in a Mirror: Metaphors of Teachers in Teaching." In *Images of Schoolteachers in America,* 2nd ed., edited by Pamela M. Joseph and Gail E. Burnaford, 75–92. Mahwah, N.J.: Lawrence Erlbaum Associates, 2001.

Ehrensal, Patricia A. L., Robert L. Crawford, Joseph A. Castellucci, and Gregory Allen. "The American Melting Pot Versus the Chinese Hot Pot." In *Ethical Leadership and Decision Making in Education: Applying Theoretical Perspectives to Complex Dilemmas,* edited by Joan Polimer Shapiro and Jaqueline A. Stefkovich, 65–75. Mahwah, N.J.: Lawrence Erlbaum Associates, 2001.

Elbaz, Freema. "Teachers' Knowledge of Teaching: Strategies for Reflection." In *Educating Teachers: Changing the Nature of Pedagogical Knowledge,* edited by John Smyth, 45–53. Philadelphia: Farmer Press, 1987.

Eliot, T. S. "Tradition and the Individual Talent." In *Selected Prose of T. S. Eliot.* Edited by Frank Kermode, 37–44. New York: Harcourt, Brace, Jovanovich, 1975.

———. "The Dry Salvages." *T. S. Eliot, Collected Poems, 1909–1962.* London: Faber and Faber, 1983.

Ellsworth, Elizabeth. *Teaching Positions: Differences, Pedagogy, and the Power of Address.* New York: Teachers College Press, 1997.

Erickson, Frederick, and Jeffrey Shultz. "Students' Experience of Curriculum." In *Handbook of Research on Curriculum,* edited by Philip W. Jackson, 465–85. New York: Macmillan, 1992.

Evans, Karen S. "Fifth-Grade Students' Perceptions of How They Experience Literature Discussion Groups." *Reading Research Quarterly* 37, no. 1 (January–March 2002): 46–49.

Fenstermacher, Gary D., and Jonas F. Soltis. *Approaches to Teaching.* New York: Teachers College Press, 1992.

Fernandez, James W. "The Performance of Ritual Metaphors." In *The Social Use of Metaphor: Essays on the Anthropology of Rhetoric,* edited by J. David Sapir and J. Christopher Crocker, 100–131. Philadelphia: University of Pennsylvania Press, 1977.

———. "Persuasions and Performances: Of the Beast in Every Body . . . and the Metaphors of Everyman." In *Myth, Symbol, and Culture,* edited by Clifford Geertz, 39–60. New York: W. W. Norton, 1971.

Ferraro, Joan M. "Reflective Practice and Professional Development." *ERIC Clearinghouse on Teaching and Teacher Education,* Washington, D.C., 2000.

Fielding, Michael. "Students as Radical Agents of Change." *Journal of Educational Change* 2, no. 3 (June 2001): 123–41.

Fischer, Joseph, and Anne Kiefer. "Construction and Discovering Images of Your Teaching." In *Images of Schoolteachers in America*, 2nd ed., edited by Pamela B. Joseph and Gail E. Burnaford, 93–114. Mahwah, N.J.: Lawrence Erlbaum Associates, 2001.

Fischer, Michael. "Ethnicity and the Postmodern Arts of Memory." In *Writing Culture: The Politics and Poetics of Ethnography*, edited by James Clifford and George E. Marcus, 194–233. Berkeley: University of California Press, 1986.

Fivush, Robyn. "Owning Experience: Developing Subjective Perspective in Autobiographical Narratives." In *The Self in Time: Developmental Perspectives*, edited by Chris Moore and Karen Lemmon, 35–52. Mahwah, N.J.: Lawrence Erlbaum Associates, 2001.

Forman, Janis, ed. *What Do I Know: Reading, Writing, and Teaching the Essay*. Portsmouth, N.H.: Heinemann-Boynton/Cook, 1996.

Forster, E. M. *Howards End*. New York: A. A. Knopf, [1921] 1943.

Foshay, Arthur Wellesley. *The Curriculum: Purpose, Substance, and Practice*. New York: Teachers College Press, 2000.

Friedrich, Hugo. "On the Art of Translation." Translated by Rainer Schulte and John Biguenet. In *Theories of Translation: An Anthology of Essays from Drydan to Derrida*, edited by Rainer Schulte and John Biguenet, 11–16. Chicago: University of Chicago Press, [1965] 1992.

Freire, Paulo. *Pedagogy of Freedom: Ethics, Democracy, and Civil Courage*. Translated by Patrick Clarke. Lanham, Md.: Rowman & Littlefield, 1998.

———. *Pedagogy of the Oppressed*. Translated by Myra Bergman Ramos. New York: Continuum, 1990.

Fueyo, Vivian, and Mark A. Koorland. "Teacher as Researcher: A Synonym for Professionalism." *Journal of Teacher Education* 48, no. 5 (1997): 336–344.

Gage, Nathan L. *The Scientific Basis for the Art of Teaching*. New York: Teachers College Press, 1987.

Geertz, Clifford. "Thick Description: Toward an Interpretative Theory of Culture." In *The Interpretation of Cultures*. New York: Basic Books, 1973.

———. "Deep Play: Notes on the Balinese Cockfight." In *Myth, Symbol, and Culture*, edited by Clifford Geertz, 1–37. New York: W. W. Norton, 1971.

Gentzler, Edward. "Foreword." In Douglas Robinson, *What Is Translation? Centrifugal Theories, Critical Interventions*, ix–xvii. Kent, Oh.: Kent State University Press, 1997.

Gold, Milton J., and Harry N. Rivlin. *Teachers for Multicultural Education*. Office of Education [DHEW], Washington, D.C., 1975.

Goodman, Nelson. *Language of Art*, 2nd ed. Indianapolis, In.: Hackett, 1988.

Greene, Maxine. "Defining Aesthetic Education." In *Variations on a Blue Guitar: The Lincoln Center Institute Lectures on Aesthetic Education*, 5–6. New York: Teachers College Press, 2001.

———. "Imagination and Aesthetic Literacy." In *Landscapes of Learning*. New York: Teachers College Press, 1978.

———. "Uncoupling from the Ordinary." In *Variations on a Blue Guitar: The Lincoln Center Institute Lectures on Aesthetic Education*, 67–72. New York: Teachers College Press, 2001.

———. "Imagination and Transformation." In *Variations on a Blue Guitar: The Lincoln Center Institute Lectures on Aesthetic Education*, 65–66. New York: Teachers College Press, 2001.

————. "Multiple Visions: Aesthetic Moments and Experiences." In *Variations on a Blue Guitar: The Lincoln Center Institute Lectures on Aesthetic Education*, 11–15. New York: Teachers College Press, 2001.

————. "In Search of Metaphor." Talk presented at the Annual Meeting of the American Educational Research Association. New Orleans, April 2000.

————. *Landscapes of Learning*. New York: Teachers College Press, 1978.

Grumet, Madeleine. "Voice: The Search for a Feminist Rhetoric for Educational Studies." *Cambridge Journal of Education* 20, no. 3 (1990): 277–82.

Harter, Susan. "Historical Roots of Contemporary Issues Involving Self-Concept." In *Handbook of Self-Concept: Developmental, Social, and Clinical Considerations*, edited by Bruce A. Bracken, 1–37. New York: John Wiley, 1996.

Harter, Susan, and Ann Monsour. "Developmental Analysis of Conflict Caused by Opposing Self-Attributes in the Adolescent Self-Portrait." *Developmental Psychology* 28, no. 2 (March 1992): 251–60.

Hawkins, David. "I, Thou, and It." In *The Informed Vision: Essays on Learning and Human Nature*, 48–62. New York: Agathon Press, 1974.

Heaton, Ruth M. *Teaching Mathematics to the New Standards: Relearning the Dance*. New York: Teachers College Press, 2000.

Heilbrun, Carolyn. *Writing a Woman's Life*. New York: Ballantine Books, 1988.

Heller-Ross, Holly. "Librarian and Faculty Partnerships for Distance Education." *MC Journal: The Journal of Academic Media Librarianship* 4 (summer 1996): 57–68.

Henri, Robert. *The Art Spirit*. Boulder, Colo.: Westview Press, 1923.

Herbart, Johann Friedrich. *Outlines of Educational Doctrine*. Translated by A. F. Lenge. New York: Macmillan, 1901.

Hirsch, E. D., Joseph Kett, and James Trefil. *Cultural Literacy: What Every American Needs to Know*. Boston: Houghton Mifflin, 1987.

Hoffman, Eva. *Lost in Translation: A Life in a New Language*. New York: Penguin Books, 1989.

Holstein, James A., and Jaber F. Gubrium. *The Self We Live By: Narrative Identity in a Postmodern World*. New York: Oxford University Press, 2000.

hooks, bell. *Teaching to Transgress: Education as the Practice of Freedom*. New York: Routledge, 1994.

Hynd, Cyndie. "Persuasion and Its Role in Meeting Educational Goals." *Theory into Practice* 40, no. 4 (autumn 2001): 270–77.

Ingram, John H., and Norman Weston. "Distant Voices, Shared Lives: Students Creating the Global Learning Community." *Educational Horizons* 75, no. 4 (summer 1997): 165–171.

Janzen, Rod. "Melting Pot or Mosaic?" *Educational Leadership* 51, no. 8 (May 1994), 9–11.

Johnson, Mary, Barb Linnenbrink, and Lorena Mitchell. "'I Spy' in the Library." *Colorado Libraries* 25, no. 3 (fall 1999): 34–36.

Johnston, Sue. "Images: A Way of Understanding the Practical Knowledge of Student Teachers." *Teaching and Teacher Education* 8, no. 2 (April 1992): 123–136.

Joseph, Pamela Bolotin. "The Ideal Teacher: Images in Early 20th Century Teacher Education Textbooks." In *Images of Schoolteachers in America*, 2nd ed., edited by Pamela B. Joseph and Gail E. Burnaford, 135–59. Mahwah, N.J.: Lawrence Erlbaum Associates, 2001.

Joseph, Pamela Bolotin, and Gail E. Burnaford, eds. *Images of Schoolteachers in America*, 2nd ed. Mahwah, N.J.: Lawrence Erlbaum Associates, 2001.

Kaplan, Alice. *French Lessons*. Chicago: University of Chicago Press, 1993.

Karr, Mary. *Cherry*. New York: Penguin, 2000.

Keegan, Robert. *In over Our Heads: The Mental Demands of Modern Life.* Cambridge, Mass.: Harvard University Press, 1994.

Khatibi, Abdelkebir. *Love in Two Languages.* Minneapolis: University of Minnesota Press, 1990.

Kincaid, Jamaica. *The Autobiography of My Mother.* New York: Farrar, Straus & Giroux, 1996.

Kingston, Maxine Hong. "Silence." In *Rereading America: Cultural Contexts for Critical Thinking and Writing,* edited by Gary Colombo, Robert Cullan, and Bonnie Lisle, 583–87. Boston: Bedford Books of St. Martin's Press, 1992.

Kohn, Alfie. *The Case Against Standardized Testing: Raising the Scores, Ruining the Schools.* Portsmouth, N.H.: Heinemann, 2000.

Kondo, Dorinne. *Crafting Selves: Power, Gender, and Discourses of Identity in a Japanese Workplace.* Chicago: University of Chicago Press, 1990.

Kopan, Andrew T. "Melting Pot; Myth or Reality?" In *Cultural Pluralism,* edited by Edgar G. Epps, 37–55. Berkeley, Calif.: McCutchan, 1974.

Krug, Mark. *The Melting of the Ethnics: Education of the Immigrants, 1880–1914.* Perspectives in American Education. Bloomington, In.: Phi Delta Kappa Educational Foundation, 1976.

Ladson-Billings, Gloria. *The Dreamkeepers: Successful Teachers of African American Children.* San Francisco, Calif.: Jossey-Bass, 1994.

Lahs-Gonzales, Olivia, ed. *Defining Eye: Women Photographers of the 20th Century.* Selections from the Helen Kornblum collection. St. Louis, Mo.: Saint Louis Art Museum, 1997.

Lakoff, George, and Mark Johnson. *Metaphors We Live By.* Chicago: University of Chicago Press, 1980.

Langer, Susanne K. *Philosophy in a New Key.* Cambridge, Mass.: Harvard University Press, 1942.

Lesnick, Alice. "The Mirror in Motion: Redefining Reflective Practice in an Undergraduate Field Work Seminar." *Reflective Practice* 5, no. 3 (Feb. 2005): 33–47.

Lesser, Wendy. *Nothing Remains the Same: Rereading and Remembering.* Boston: Houghton Mifflin, 2002.

Levin, James S., Sandra R. Levin, and Gregory Waddoups. "Multiplicity in Learning and Teaching: A Framework for Developing Innovative Online Education." *Journal of Research on Computing in Education* 32, no. 2 (winter 1999): 256–69.

Levine, Suzanne Jill. *The Subversive Scribe: Translating Latin American Fiction.* St. Paul, Minn.: Gray Wolf, 1991.

Levy, Jiri. "Translation as a Decision Process." In *The Translation Studies Reader,* edited by Lawrence J. Venuti, 148–59. London: Routledge, [1967] 2000.

Lionnet, Françoise. *Autobiographical Voices: Race, Gender, and Self-Portraiture.* Ithaca, N.Y.: Cornell University Press, 1989.

Lippard, Lucy R. "Brought to Light." In *Defining Eye: Women Photographers of the 20th Century,* edited by Olivia Lahs-Gonzales. Selections from the Helen Kornblum collection. St. Louis, Mo.: Saint Louis Art Museum, 1997.

Lowe, Robert. "Teachers as Saviors, Those Who Care." In *Images of Schoolteachers in America,* edited by Pamela Bolotin Joseph and Gail E. Burnaford, 211–25. Mahwah, N.J.: Lawrence Erlbaum Associates, 2001.

Malinowski, Branislow. *The Language of Magic and Gardening.* Bloomington: Indiana University Press, [1965] 2000.

Mambynek, Beate, Mona Kleine, and Ronald Thoden. *Stadtführer Göttingen.* Göttingen: Verlag Die Werkstatt, 1999.

Markus, Hazel Rose. "The Self in Thought and Memory." In *The Self in Social Psychology*, edited by Daniel M. Wegner and Robyn R. Vallacher. New York: Oxford University Press, 1980.

Martin, Nancy. "On the Move: Teacher-Researchers." In *Reclaiming the Classroom: Teacher Research As an Agency for Change*, edited by Dixie Goswami and Peter R. Stillman, 20–28. Portsmouth, N.H.: Boynton/Cook Publishers, 1987.

Martinez, Ronald L. "Life as a Foreign Language Student: What *Else* is There?" *Culture Shock*, 5, no. 1, newsletter of the Department of French and Italian, University of Minnesota (October 2000): 1–2.

McDermott, Ray, and Herve Varenne. "Culture As Disability." *Anthropology & Education Quarterly* 26, no. 3 (September 1995): 324–48.

McLaren, Peter. *Life in Schools: An Introduction to Critical Pedagogy in the Foundations of Education*. New York: Longman, 1998.

McLean, S. Vianne. "Becoming a Teacher: The Person in the Process." In *The Role of Self in Teacher Development*, edited by Richard P. Lipka and Thomas M. Brinthaupt, 55–91. Albany: SUNY Press, 1999.

McFee, I. N. *The Teacher, the School, and the Community*. New York: American Book, 1918.

Mead, George Herbart. "The Genesis of the Self and Social Control." *International Journal of Ethics* 35 (1925): 251–73.

Moore, Chris, and Karen Lemmon. "The Nature and Utility of the Temporally Extended Self." In *The Self in Time: Developmental Perspectives*, edited by Chris Moore and Karen Lemmon, 1–13. Mahwah, N.J.: Lawrence Erlbaum Associates, 2001.

Moore, Chris, and Karen Lemmon, eds. *The Self in Time: Developmental Perspectives*. Mahwah, N.J.: Lawrence Erlbaum Associates, 2001.

Morgan, Gareth. *Images of Organization*. Beverly Hills, Calif.: Sage, 1986.

Murphy, Karen, ed. "Teaching as Persuasion." *Theory into Practice* 40, no. 4 (2001): 224–27.

Nelson, Katherine. "Languages and the Self: From the 'Experiencing I' to the 'Continuing Me.'" In *The Self in Time: Developmental Perspectives*, edited by Chris Moore and Karen Lemmon, 15–33. Mahwah, N.J.: Lawrence Erlbaum Associates, 2001.

Nida, Eugene. "Principles of Correspondence." In *The Translation Studies Reader*, edited by Lawrence J. Venuti, 126–40. London: Routledge, [1964] 2000.

Nieto, Sonia. "Lessons from Students on Creating a Chance to Dream." *Harvard Educational Review* 64 (1994): 392–426.

Nisbet, Robert A. *Social Change and History: Aspects of the Western Theory of Development*. London: Oxford University Press, 1969.

Nowottny, Winifred. *The Language Poets Use*. London: Athlone Press, 1962.

O'Connor, J. and J. Seymour. *Introducing NLP*. n.p., 1990.

O'Donnell, James J. "The Digital Challenge." *The Wilson Quarterly* 20 (1996): 48–49.

Ogulnick, Karen, ed. *Language Crossings: Negotiating the Self in a Multicultural World*. New York: Teachers College Press, 2000.

Oldfather, Penny. "Songs 'Come Back Most to Them': Students' Experiences as Researchers." *Theory into Practice* 43 (1995b): 131–37.

Oldfather, Penny, ed. "Learning from Student Voices." *Theory into Practice* 43 (1995), 84–87.

Oldfather, Penny, Sally Thomas, Lizz Eckert, Florencia Garcia, Nicki Grannis, John Kilgore, Any Newman-Gonchar, Brian Peterson, Paul Rodriguez, and Marcel Tjioe. "The Nature and Outcomes of Students' Longitudinal Participatory

Research on Literacy Motivations and Schooling." *Research in the Teaching of English* 34 (1999): 281–320.

Oliver, Mary. *A Poetry Handbook.* San Diego: Harcourt, Brace, 1994.

Ortega y Gasset, Jose. "The Misery and the Splendor of Translation." In *The Translation Studies Reader,* edited by Lawrence J. Venuti, 49–64. London: Routledge, [1937] 2000.

Ortony, Andrew. "Metaphor: A Multidisciplinary Problem." In *Metaphor and Thought,* edited by Andrew Ortony, 1–16. Ithaca, N.Y.: Cornell University Press, 1979.

Ortony, Andrew, ed. *Metaphor and Thought.* Ithaca, N.Y.: Cornell University Press, 1979.

Oyserman, Daphna and Hazel Rose Markus. "Possible Selves, Motivation, and Delinquency." Unpublished manuscript, University of Michigan, 1987.

Özdamar, Emine Sevgi. *Mutterzunge.* Berlin: Rotbuch, 1990.

Paine, Lynn. "Teacher Education in Search of a Metaphor: Defining the Relationship between Teachers, Teaching and the State in China." In *The Political Dimension in Teacher Education: Comparative Perspectives on Policy Formation, Socialization and Society,* edited by Mark B. Ginsburg and Beverly Lindsay, 76–98. London: Falmer Press, 1995.

Palinscar, A. S. "The Role of Dialogue in Providing Scaffolded Instruction." *Educational Psychologist* 21 [Special Issue] edited by J. Levin and M. Pressley (1986): 73–98.

Palmer, George Herbert. *The Ideal Teacher.* Boston: Houghton Mifflin, 1908/1910.

Pepper, Stephen C. *World Hypotheses.* Berkeley: University of California Press, 1942.

Perrone, Vito. *Lessons for New Teachers.* Boston: McGraw-Hill, 2000.

Petrie, Hugh G. "Metaphor and Learning." In *Metaphor and Thought,* edited by Andrew Ortony, 438–61. Ithaca, N.Y.: Cornell University Press, 1970.

Phelan, Patricia, Ann Locke Davidson, and Hahn Cao Yu. "Speaking Up: Students' Perspectives on School." *Phi Delta Kappan* 73 (1992): 695–704.

Pinar, William. "The Reconceptualization of Curriculum Studies." In *The Curriculum Studies Reader,* edited by Stephen J. Thornton and David J. Flinders, 121–129. New York: Routledge, 1997.

Pope, Denise Clark. *"Doing School": How We Are Creating a Generation of Stressed Out, Materialistic, and Miseducated Students.* New Haven, Conn.: Yale University Press, 2001.

Powell, Arthur G., Eleanor Farrar, and David K. Cohen. *The Shopping Mall High School: Winners and Losers in the Educational Marketplace.* Boston: Houghton Mifflin, 1985.

Pratt, Mary Louise. "Arts of the Contact Zone." In *Ways of Reading: An Anthology for Writers,* 5th ed. edited by David Bartholomae and Anthony Petrosky, 581–600. Boston: St. Martin's, 1999.

Proefriedt, William A. "The Immigrant or 'Outsider' Experience as Metaphor for Becoming an Educated Person in the Modern World: Mary Antin, Richard Wright and Eva Hoffman." In *MELUS: The Journal of the Society for the Study of the Multi-Ethnic Literature of the United States* 16, no. 2 (1990): 77–89.

Quine, Willard Van Orman. *Word and Object.* Cambridge, Mass.: MIT Press, 1963.

Rabassa, Gregory. "No Two Snowflakes Are Alike: Translation as Metaphor." In *The Craft of Translation,* edited by J. Biguenet and R. Schulte, 1–12. Chicago: University of Chicago Press, 1989.

Reiman, Alan J., and Lois Thies-Sprinthall. *Mentoring and Supervision for Teacher Development.* New York: Longman, 1998.

Reiss, Katharina. "Type, Kind and Individuality of Text: Decision Making in Translation." In *The Translation Studies Reader*, edited by Lawrence J. Venuti, 160–71. London: Routledge, [1971] 2000.

Rice, Joseph Mayer. *The Public School System of the United States*. New York: The Century Company, 1893a.

Rich, Adrienne. "Blood, Bread, and Poetry: The Location of the Poet." In *Arts of the Possible: Essays and Conversations*, 41–61. New York: W. W. Norton, [1983] 2001.

———. "Diving into the Wreck." In *Diving into the Wreck*. New York: W. W. Norton, 1973.

Richards, Ivor Armstrong. *The Philosophy of Rhetoric*. London: Oxford University Press, 1965.

Richardson, Laurel. *Fields of Play: Constructing an Academic Life*. New Brunswick, N.J.: Rutgers University Press, 1997.

Richert, Anna. "Teaching Teachers to Reflect: A Consideration of Programme Structure." *Journal of Curriculum Studies* 22, no. 6 (1990): 509–27.

Robinson, Douglas. *What Is Translation? Centrifugal Theories, Critical Interventions*. Kent, Oh.: Kent State University Press, 1997.

Rodgers, Carol. "Defining Reflection: Another Look at John Dewey and Reflective Thinking." *Teachers College Record* 4, no. 4 (2002): 842–66.

———. "Seeing Student Learning: Teacher Change and the Role of Reflection." *Harvard Educational Review* 72, no. 2 (2002): 230–53.

Rodriguez, Richard. "The Achievement of Desire." In *Rereading America: Cultural Contexts for Critical Thinking and Writing*, edited by Gary Colombo, Robert Cullan, and Bonnie Lisle. 541–53. Boston: Bedford Books of St. Martin's Press, 1992.

Rorty, Richard. *Philosophy and the Mirror of Nature*. Princeton, N.J.: Princeton University Press, 1979.

Rose, Mike. *Lives on the Boundary*. New York: Free Press, 1989.

Rousseau, Jean-Jacques. "Emile." In *The Emile of Jean Jacques Rousseau: Selections*, edited by W. Boyd. New York: Teachers College Press, [1762] 1965.

Rudney, Gwen L., and Andrea Guillaume. "Reflective Teaching for Student Teachers." *Teacher Educator* 25, no. 3 (1990): 13–20.

Sanon, Fredo, Maurice Baxter, Lydia Fortune, and Susan Opotow. "Cutting Class: Perspectives of Urban High School Students." In *In Our Own Words: Students' Perspectives on School*, edited by Jeffrey Shultz and Alison Cook-Sather, 73–91. Lanham, Md.: Rowman & Littlefield, 2001.

Santos, Sherod. "A la Recherche de la Poésie Perdue (Poetry and Translation)." *American Poetry Review* 29, no. 3 (2000): 9–14.

Sapir, J. David. "The Anatomy of Metaphor." In *The Social Use of Metaphor: Essays on the Anthropology of Rhetoric*, edited by J. David Sapir and J. Christopher Crocker, 3–16. Philadelphia: University of Pennsylvania Press, 1977.

Sapir, J. David, and J. Christopher Crocker, eds. *The Social Use of Metaphor: Essays on the Anthropology of Rhetoric*. Philadelphia: University of Pennsylvania Press, 1977.

Scheffler, Israel. *In Praise of the Cognitive Emotions and Other Essays in the Philosophy of Education*. New York: Routledge, 1991.

Schlechty, Phillip C. *Schools for the 21st Century: Leadership Imperatives for Educational Reform*. San Francisco: Jossey-Bass, 1991.

Schopenhauer, Arthur. "On Language and Words." Translated by Peter Mollenhauer. In *Theories of Translation: An Anthology of Essays from Drydan to Derrida*, edited by Rainer Schulte and John Biguenet, 32–35. Chicago: University of Chicago Press, [1800] 1992.

Schön, Donald A. *The Reflective Practitioner: How Professionals Think in Action.* New York: Basic Books, 1983.

———. "Generative Metaphor: A Perspective on Problem-Setting in Social Policy." In *Metaphor and Thought,* edited by Andrew Ortony, 254–83. Ithaca, N.Y.: Cornell University Press, 1979.

Schulte, Rainer, and John Biguenet, eds. *Theories of Translation: An Anthology of Essays from Dryden to Derrida.* Chicago: University of Chicago Press, 1992.

Schultz, Stanley K. *The Culture Factory: Boston Public Schools, 1789–1860.* New York: Oxford University Press, 1973.

Seyhan, Azade. *Writing Outside the Nation.* Princeton, N.J.: Princeton University Press, 2001.

Sfard, Anna. "On Two Metaphors for Learning and the Dangers of Choosing Just One." *Educational Researcher* 27, no. 2 (March 1998): 4–13.

Shapiro, Joan Poliner, and Jacqueline A. Stefkovich. *Ethical Leadership and Decision Making in Education: Applying Theoretical Perspectives to Complex Dilemmas.* Mahwah, N.J.: Lawrence Erlbaum Associates, 2001.

Shor, Ira. *Empowering Education: Critical Teaching for Social Change.* Chicago: University of Chicago Press, 1992.

Shultz, Jeffrey, and Alison Cook-Sather, eds. *In Our Own Words: Students' Perspectives on School.* Lanham, Md.: Rowman & Littlefield, 2001.

Skorczewski, Dawn. "'Everybody Has Their Own Ideas': Responding to Cliché in Student Writing." *College Composition and Communication* 52, no. 2 (2000): 220–239.

Snyder, A., and T. Alexander. "Teaching as a Profession: Guidance Suggestions for Students." *Teachers College Bulletin,* 23, no. 1, 1–69.

Soliday, Mary. "Translating Self and Difference Through Literacy Narratives." *College English* 56, no. 5 (September 1994): 511–26.

Solomon, Mildred, ed. *The Diagnostic Teacher: Constructing New Approaches to Professional Development.* New York: Teachers College Press, 1999.

Solomon, Mildred, and Catherine Cobb Morocco. "The Diagnostic Teacher." In *The Diagnostic Teacher: Constructing New Approaches to Professional Development,* edited by Mildred Solomon, 231–46. New York: Teachers College Press, 1999.

Spring, Joel. *American Education: An Introduction to Social and Political Aspects.* New York: Longman, 1978.

———. *The Sorting Machine: National Educational Policy Since 1945.* New York: McKay, 1976.

———. *The American School, 1642–1993.* New York: McGraw-Hill, 1994.

Stefan, Verena. "To Make a Prairie: On Immigration, Broken Language, and the Fabric of the Imagination." Lecture, Bryn Mawr College, February 18, 2002.

———. "Here's Your Change 'N Enjoy the Show." In *Language Crossings: Negotiating the Self in a Multi-Cultural World,* edited by Karen L. Ogulnick, 21–29. New York: Teachers College Press, 2000.

Steiner, George. *After Babel: Aspects of Language and Translation,* 3rd ed. London: Oxford University Press, 1998.

Stevens, Wallace. "The Motive for Metaphor." In *The Palm at the End of the Mind: Selected Poems and a Play,* edited by Holly Stevens. New York: Vintage Books, 1972.

Sumara, Dennis J., and Rebecca Luce-Kapler. "(Un)becoming a Teacher: Negotiating Identities While Learning to Teach." *Canadian Journal of Education* 21, no. 1 (1996): 65–83.

Tompkins, Jane. *A Life in School: What the Teacher Learned.* Reading, Mass.: Addison-Wesley, 1996.

Turner, Victor. "Social Dramas and Stories About Them." In *On Narrative*, edited by W. J. T. Mitchell, 137–64. Chicago: University of Chicago Press, 1981.

———. "Preface." In *Dramas, Fields, and Metaphors: Symbolic Action in Human Society*, edited by Victor Turner, 13–19. Ithaca, N.Y.: Cornell University Press, 1974.

Turner, Victor, ed. *Dramas, Fields, and Metaphors: Symbolic Action in Human Society*. Ithaca, N.Y.: Cornell University Press, 1974.

Twain, Mark. *Die schrekliche deutsche Sprache* [The Awful German Language]. n.p., n.d.

Van Orman, Willard. *Word and Object*. Cambridge, Mass.: MIT Press, 1963.

Van Steenburgh, E. W. "Metaphor." *Journal of Philosophy* 62 (1965): 687–88.

Venuti, Lawrence, ed. *The Translation Studies Reader*. London: Routledge, 2000.

Vygotsky, Lev. *Thought and Language*. Translated by Alex Kozulin. Cambridge, Mass.: MIT Press, 1986.

———. *Mind in Society: The Development of Higher Psychological Processes*. Edited by Michael Cole et al. Cambridge, Mass.: Harvard University Press, 1978.

Wasserman, Miriam. "Demystifying the Schools." *Education Exploration Center Journal* 3 (October/November 1973), 4–6.

Webster's New International Dictionary, 2nd Edition (unabridged). Springfield, Mass.: G. & C. Merriam Company, 1951.

Wegner, Daniel M., and Robin R. Vallacher, eds. *The Self in Social Psychology*. New York: Oxford University Press, 1980.

Weis, Lois, and Michelle Fine, eds. *Beyond Silenced Voices: Class, Race, and Gender in United States Schools*. Albany: State University of New York Press, 1993.

Welch-Ross, Melissa. "Personalizing the Temporally Extended Self: Evaluative Self-Awareness and the Development of Autobiographical Memory." In *The Self in Time: Developmental Perspectives*, edited by Chris Moore and Karen Lemmon, 97–120. Mahwah, N.J.: Lawrence Erlbaum Associates, 2001.

Weinstein, Rhona S., S. M. Madison, and Margaret R. Kuklinski. "Raising Expectations in Schooling: Obstacles and Opportunities for Change." *American Educational Research Journal* 32, no. 1 (1995): 121–159.

Wheelwright, Philip Ellis. *Metaphor and Reality*. Bloomington: Indiana University Press, 1962.

Wilson, Bruce L., and H. Dickson Corbett. *Listening to Urban Kids: School Reform and the Teachers They Want*. New York: State University of New York Press, 2001.

Winterson, Jeanette. *Oranges Are Not the Only Fruit*. New York: Atlantic Monthly Press, 1985.

Yinger, Robert J. "Learning the Language of Practice." *Curriculum Inquiry* 17, 299–318.

Zaff, Jonathan F., and Elizabeth C. Hair. "Positive Development of the Self: Self-Concept, Self-Esteem, and Identity." In *Well-Being: Positive Development Across the Life Course*, edited by Marc H. Bornstein, Lucy Davidson, Corey L. M. Keyes, and Kristin A. Moore, 235–51. Mahwah, N.J.: Lawrence Erlbaum Associates, 2003.

Zehm, Stanley J. "Deciding to Teach: Implications of a Self-Development Perspective." In *The Role of Self in Teacher Development*, edited by Richard P. Lipka and Thomas M. Brinthaupt, 36–52. New York: State University of New York Press, 1999.

Zehm, Stanley J., and Jeffrey A. Kottler, *On Being a Teacher: The Human Dimension*, 2nd ed. Thousand Oaks, Calif.: Corwin Press, 2000.

Zeichner, Kenneth M., and Daniel P. Liston. "Teaching Student Teachers to Reflect." *Harvard Educational Review* 57, no. 1 (1987): 23–48.

Index

Acknowledgments

Many people made both the years of preparation for writing this book and the actual writing of it not only possible but also truly enjoyable.

First, I want to thank those with whom I have worked over the past ten years at Bryn Mawr College, particularly all the students from whom I learned as much as I taught: participants in my College Seminar course, in the Talking Toward Techno-Pedagogy workshops, and in my Curriculum and Pedagogy seminar. You are too numerous to name here, but you know who you are and I am deeply thankful to you for your passions and insights, for your openness and your willingness to take risks, for the ways you deeply and lastingly educated yourselves. I wish to thank as well my colleagues in the Bryn Mawr/Haverford Education Program for creating a challenging, inspiring, and enjoyable work environment for students and colleagues alike and for protecting my time when I was on leave: Shirley Brown, Jody Cohen, Alice Lesnick, and Robyn Newkumet. Thanks also Jody, Alice, and Robyn for responding in supportive and constructive ways to drafts of chapters of this book. Special thanks go to Jody and Alice, who read multiple drafts of every chapter, offered insightful and supportive critiques, and helped me to keep open so many spaces of imagination.

I am grateful as well to my many colleagues, friends, and students who read numerous drafts of parts or all of this book and commented in caring and constructive ways: Jon Church, David Constantine, Paul Grobstein, Sally Henrikson, Ron Martinez, Jean McWilliams, Tracey Posluszny, Ondrea Reisinger, Carol Rodgers, Azade Seyhan, Janet Theophano, and Martha Wintner. My admiration and gratitude go as well to Nancy Strippel, whose readings of my own and others' scholarly texts are woven throughout the pages of this book, to Aliya Curmally and Trecia Pottinger for their careful reading and editing, to Katrina Magdol for her editorial assistance, and to Andrew Patterson for his bibliographic expertise, and to Berry Chamness for his proofreading.

Having the opportunity to take up once more the formal role of student enriched me as a teacher and deepened the analysis I offer in this book. Therefore, I wish to thank those who were central to the experience: my three teachers at the Goethe-Institut in Göttingen, Germany, Andreas Hübner, Jörg Modeß, and Annette Paulsen. I am especially grateful to Jörg for working with me through so many drafts of parts of the book, for securing for me a grant for my studies through the Goethe-Institut Director, Herr Klieme, and for continuing to be such a good teacher. I wish also to thank Imke Meyer for her generosity in letting me participate in her advanced German course at Bryn Mawr College, which helped me to bridge my experiences in Göttingen and my life at home as well as to continue my process of education.

In both the educational and the personal realms of life I am grateful to Lisa Shore, Moritz Shore, and Maria Sturm for so beautifully embodying the translation process and helping me with mine, and to Maria for her reading of the book manuscript and her helpful suggestions. To Elliott Shore my deepest gratitude for reading every word of this book almost as many times as I did and for always pushing me further both on this project and throughout the years over which we have worked together. Thanks also to my editor, Peter A. Agree, and to Ellie Goldberg, Acquisitions Assistant, Erica Ginsburg, Associate Managing Editor, and Noreen O'Connor-Abel, Project Editor, at University of Pennsylvania Press, for being so responsive and supportive. And my final thanks go to my husband, Scott Cook-Sather, who understood both the literal and the metaphorical translation that work on this book required and unflaggingly supported me in both.

Support for writing this book came in part from the Rosalyn A. Schwartz Teaching Award I received from Bryn Mawr College in May 2001.